Shakespeare's histories and counter-histories

Manchester University Press

Shakespeare's histories and counter-histories

edited by
Dermot Cavanagh,
Stuart Hampton-Reeves
and Stephen Longstaffe

Manchester University Press

Manchester and New York
distributed exclusively in the USA by Palgrave

Published by Manchester University Press
Oxford Road, Manchester M13 9NR, UK
and Room 400, 175 Fifth Avenue, New York, NY 10010, USA
www.manchesteruniversitypress.co.uk

Distributed exclusively in the USA by
Palgrave, 175 Fifth Avenue, New York,
NY 10010, USA

Distributed exclusively in Canada by
UBC Press, University of British Columbia, 2029 West Mall,
Vancouver, BC, Canada V6T 1Z2

British Library Cataloguing-in-Publication Data
A catalogue record for this book is available from the British Library

Library of Congress Cataloging-in-Publication Data applied for

ISBN   0 7190 7074 0 *hardback*
EAN   978 0 7190 7075 9

First published 2006

15 14 13 12 11 10 09 08 07 06   10 9 8 7 6 5 4 3 2 1

Typeset in Adobe Sabon
by Servis Filmsetting Ltd, Manchester
Printed in Great Britain
by Bell & Bain Ltd, Glasgow

Contents

Notes on contributors   vii

1 Staring at Clio: artists, histories and counter-histories   1
   Stuart Hampton-Reeves

I Memory and mourning

2 *Richard II* and the performance of grief   15
   John J. Joughin
3 History, mourning and memory in *Henry V*   32
   Dermot Cavanagh
4 There is a history in all men's lives: reinventing
   history in *2 Henry IV*   49
   Alison Thorne
5 Good sometimes Queen: *Richard II*, Mary Stuart and the
   poetics of queenship   67
   Alison Findlay

II Counter-histories

6 Strange truths: the Stanleys of Derby on the
   English Renaissance stage   85
   Lisa Hopkins
7 A sea of troubles: the thought of the outside in
   Shakespeare's histories   101
   Richard Wilson
8 The commons will revolt: *Woodstock* after the Peasants' Revolt   135
   Stephen Longstaffe
9 National history to foreign calamity: *A Mirror for
   Magistrates* and early English tragedy   152
   Jessica Winston

III Identity and performance

10 **Warlike women: 'reproofe to these degenerate
    effeminate dayes?**   169
    Carol Banks
11 **Of tygers' hearts and players' hides**   182
    Carol Chillington Rutter
12 **Mapping Shakespeare's Britain**   198
    Peter Holland

    Afterword – *Mots d'escalier:* Clio, Eurydice, Orpheus   219
    Graham Holderness

Index   241

Notes on contributors

Carol Banks is Associate Lecturer in English at the University of Central Lancashire. She has published several articles on Shakespeare's plays addressing issues of gender, textuality, imagery and the visual arts.

Dermot Cavanagh is Lecturer in English at the University of Edinburgh and the author of *Language and Politics in the Sixteenth-Century History Play* (2003).

Alison Findlay is Professor of Renaissance Drama at Lancaster University. She is author of *Illegitimate Power: Bastards in Renaissance Drama* (1994) and *A Feminist Perspective on Renaissance Drama* (1999). She has just completed *Playing Spaces in Early Women's Drama*, to be published by Cambridge University Press, and is currently working on *Women in Shakespeare* for Continuum Press.

Stuart Hampton-Reeves is Principal Lecturer in English and Drama at the University of Central Lancashire. His publications include *Shakespeare in Performance: The Henry VI Plays*, co-written with Carol Chillington Rutter. He is the performance editor for the journal *Shakespeare*.

Graham Holderness is Professor of English at the University of Hertfordshire and author or editor of numerous studies in early modern and modern literature and drama, most recently *Textual Shakespeare: Writing and the Word* (2003). He is also a creative writer whose novel *The Prince of Denmark* was published in 2002 and whose poetry collection *Craeft* (2002) was awarded a Poetry Book Society recommendation.

Peter Holland is McMeel Family Professor in Shakespeare Studies in the Department of Film, Television and Theatre at the University of Notre

Dame. He is Editor of *Shakespeare Survey* and General Editor (with Stanley Wells) of the *Oxford Shakespeare Topics* series for Oxford University Press and of the *Redefining British Theatre History* series for Palgrave Macmillan. He is currently editing *Coriolanus* for the *Arden Shakespeare* 3rd Series.

Lisa Hopkins is Professor of English at Sheffield Hallam University. Her most recent publications are *Beginning Shakespeare* (2005) and *Shakespeare on the Edge* (2005). She is currently editing *The Broken Heart* and *The Fancies, Chaste and Noble* for the Oxford Complete John Ford.

John J. Joughin is Professor of English at the University of Central Lancashire. He is the editor of several books on Shakespeare, including *Shakespeare and National Culture* and *Philosophical Shakespeares* and edits the journal *Shakespeare*.

Stephen Longstaffe is a lecturer in English and Drama at St Martin's College Lancaster and has published widely on the English history play in journals such as *Shakespeare Quarterly* and *Year's Work in English Studies*. He is the editor of *A Critical Edition of the Life and Death of Jack Straw* (2002).

Carol Chillington Rutter, Professor of English at the University of Warwick, is the author of *Clamorous Voices: Shakespeare's Women Today* (1988) and *Enter the Body: Women and Representation on Shakespeare's Stage* (2001). General editor of the Shakespeare in Performance Series for Manchester University Press, she is co-author of *Shakespeare in Performance: The* Henry VI *plays*, has edited *Documents of the Rose Playhouse* (1984) for the Revels Plays Companion Library and has written the Introduction to the Penguin *Macbeth* (2005). Her current project is *Shakespeare and Child's Play*.

Alison Thorne is Senior Lecturer in English at the University of Strathclyde. She is the author of *Vision and Rhetoric in Shakespeare* (Palgrave, 2000), editor of *Shakespeare's Romances* (2002) for the New Casebook series and co-editor of a forthcoming collection on *Renaissance Rhetoric, Gender and Politics* (2006). She is currently writing a monograph on female supplication in early modern drama and culture.

Richard Wilson is Professor of English Literature at the University of Cardiff and the 2006 International Shakespeare's Globe Fellow. His publications include *Will Power: Essays on Shakespearean authority* (revised edition, 2007), *Secret Shakespeare: Studies in theatre, religion and resistance* (2004), and *King of Shadows: Shakespeare in French theory* (2006). He is currently completing a new collection of essays, *Free Will: Essays on Shakespearean autonomy*.

Jessica Winston is Assistant Professor of English at Idaho State University, where she is completing a book on the literary culture of the mid-Tudor Inns of Court. Her essays on this topic appear in *Studies in Philology*, *Early Theatre* and *Renaissance Quarterly*.

Staring at Clio: artists, histories and counter-histories

In the Renaissance, the archetype for history was the classical muse Clio, a much-painted figure in an era when the 'history painting' was one of the predominant genres in European visual art. Clio was usually depicted as a young woman holding a book (often Herodotus' histories) and a trumpet.[1] The book signified the written record of the past, and with her trumpet Clio was meant to tell the stories of the past to the present. This double perspective of archive and representation defined Clio who was, after all, the daughter of Jupiter (and so a voice of authority) and of Mnemosyne, the goddess of memory and from whom we derive the word *mnemonic*. Clio gave voice and life to the dead. However, although Clio was often called 'the proclaimer', portraits of her rarely (if ever) showed her doing so. Rather, she was depicted holding book and trumpet but using neither – caught, as it were, in a moment of idle reflection. Clio is coolly leaning on a huge book of Thucydices, her trumpet lying next to it, in Jacques de Stella's 1640 painting *Minerva with the Muses*. In Eustache le Sueur's *Clio, Euterpe and Thalia* (c. 1655) she stares vacantly, leaning on her book, an unused trumpet in one hand, her breast casually exposed. In Hendrick van Balen's *The Banquet of the Gods* (c. 1615), Clio does play her trumpet, but as part of a Bacchanalian dance, her robe slipping to expose her back and buttocks. These latter images call attention to an unexpected sensuality about the representation of history: history is seductive, alluring, tempting. Whether in the bored gaze of Le Sueur and De Stella's paintings or in Van Balen's depiction of history as an ecstatic dance, Clio is an ambivalent figure for history.

The twentieth-century poet Joseph Brodsky was fascinated with the look of vagueness often to be seen on Clio's face in her representations and wondered if this was because 'so many eyes have stared at her with uncertainty'.[1] In Le Sueur's painting, the exposed breast highlights the voyeuristic nature of being a writer or spectator of history; in Van Balen's painting, we see Clio apparently forgetting herself in the act of proclaiming history. The historian is caught between 'two voids', the past and the future, but the past at least offers the possibility of control over the 'personal terror' of death. Brodsky observed that 'those to whom we owe the very notion of history . . . are dead', that 'the closer one gets to one's future, i.e. to the graveyard, the better one sees the past' (114–15).

The struggle between the artist and Clio is the subject of perhaps the most famous – and the most modern – depiction of Clio: Vermeer's *The Allegory of Painting* (c. 1665; sometimes known as *The Artist's Studio*). In this beautiful but troubling painting (which is reproduced on our cover), Clio stands at the back, curiously marginal and central at the same time. She has all the right paraphernalia: the laurel wreath, the trumpet and the book. Yet her eyes are cast down, she faces neither forwards nor backwards but inwards. Vermeer suggests another way of representing history by introducing this displaced gaze, this counter-history of history. The painting has usually been interpreted as Vermeer's homage to the *grande genre* of Renaissance art, the history painting. As defined by André Félibien in his preface to *Conférences de l'Académie Royale de Peinture et de Sculpture* (1669), this genre emphasised the heroic and didactic in history: stories from the past were moral lessons from the present and the individual was frequently ennobled, even mythologised, through the act of representation. There may even be a virtual history underlying the painting, for above Clio's face is a map of the newly united Netherlands: the near-blank canvas with which it rhymes perhaps suggesting a history yet to be enacted and so still beyond the heroic representation which it must one day fulfil. Francis-Noel Thomas suggests a strikingly different interpretation; he argues that Vermeer's subject is the *absurdity* of the history painting genre.[2] In this reading, the curiously attired painter is being lampooned for his pompous attempt to turn an ordinary peasant girl into a goddess. Real history, perhaps, lies in the model herself and is hinted at by Vermeer's careful emphasis, through light and shadow, on her face. Between her head and the map lies the vanishing point, so the eye is naturally drawn to them rather than to the painter. The true power of the scene is completely missed by the painter, whose studio we seem to be creeping into, drawing back the curtain like a curtain drawn on a stage.[3] In this complex, multilayered double work, this painting of a painter painting, Vermeer not only articulates a manifesto for his own art (which of course was fascinated with the poetry of the mundane and the ordinary) but seizes a dominant European tradition of representation and pulls it on to a wholly different course.

Brodsky wrote only about Clio's visual representations; but as a poet himself he might also have reflected on her equally ambivalent representation in writing. In Renaissance poetry, Clio is equally coy and just as demanding. Poets depicted her celebrating the achievements of the past, but many also showed her lamenting the deficiencies of the present. Conventionally, Clio was invoked to celebrate glory, as in Anthony Nixon's 'Hymen's Holiday' (1613), a straightforward poetic appeal to the muse to go to the wedding of James I's daughter Elizabeth and 'in her prayse, tune your heroicke Songs' (l. 10) and then 'proclaime' the wedding 'with golden Trumpe and Pen' (l. 19). Nixon plagiarised George Peele, who had in the previous century made exactly the same kind of elevated address to Queen Elizabeth in 'Anglorum Feriae (England's Holidays)' (1595), in which the poet asks Clio to 'proclaim with golden trump and pen' Elizabeth's 'happy days' (ll. 20–1).[4] However, Peele's poem is more in keeping with the ecstatic reverie of history in Van Balen's painting than Nixon's later imitation for Princess Elizabeth's wedding. To 'proclaim the day of England's happiness' (i.e. Elizabeth's birthday) the poet asks the nymphs to 'lead England's lovely shepherds in a dance', as the verse itself dances through increasingly wild commemorations of 'The day of joy, the day of jollity!' However, by the end of the sixteenth century it was common to present Clio as a tragic figure. In Richard Johnson's 'Musarum Plangores' (1591), Clio laments that her 'ancient bookes of graven monuments' are 'claspt forever up with dusty leaves' because in the margins 'lyes my discontents' (ll. 127–8). She continues to say that with this death, 'Fate and Death of honour me bereaves' (l. 130) and pledges to embalm the body with 'Muses breath' and 'daunce about his Toombe' (l. 139). Johnson casts Clio not as proclaimer but as mourner, a theme which is foreshadowed by Matthew Grove's poet-voice in 'Pelops and Hippodamia' (1587), where the poet calls on Clio to help him because 'Ther was not since the world began / a wight that felt such greefe / As how I feele' (ll. 471–3). The elegaic voice is again used for Clio's soliloquy in Thomas Rogers' 'Celestial Elegies' (1598), which begins 'Great princes actes I use to royalise' (l. 1) but ends 'yet my heart in pittie takes remorse' (l. 13).

Clio is an elegist in Edmund Spenser's 'Teares of the Muses' (1591). The present faces historical oblivion because it offers nothing worth singing about. Through history 'men to God thereby are nighest raised' (l. 90) – that is, history elevates human action, but in the present people 'do only strive themselves to raise' and in place of deeds worthy of history they offer only 'pompous pride, and foolish vanitie' (ll. 91–2). Finding nothing in their 'bad doings' or 'base slothfulness', nothing 'worthy to be writ, or told' (ll. 99–100), Clio fears that history itself is at risk:

> So shall succeeding ages have no light
> Of things forepast, nor moniments of time
> And all that in this world is worthie hight
> Shall die in darknesse, and lie hid in slime:
> Therefore I mourne with deep harts sorrowing,
> Because I nothing noble have to sing.
>
>   (103–108)[5]

Clio mourns not the dead but the living. Indeed, the dead are celebrated in song and, through being elevated to deities, have a certain kind of immortality. It is the present, as Spenser writes it, that faces oblivion – the absence of being that Brodsky writes about. Formulated thus, Clio's face is not ambivalent about death in the past but in the present: it is only through Clio, through history, that death can be mitigated.

A similar language is used by Thomas Nashe when, in *Pierce Penniless* (1592), he defends the theatre's cultural importance by citing its ability to bring history to life, to be in effect the 'proclaimer'. Nashe recalls seeing a play (likely to have been Shakespeare's *1 Henry VI*) in which the great English soldier John Talbot was reincarnated by a 'great tragedian' in a London playhouse and audiences wept as they watched him bleeding (the full passage can be read on page 17). Nashe describes history as 'our forefathers' valiant acts' which have been 'long buried in rusty brass and worm-eaten books' – a line which may directly recall Richard Johnson's 'ancient bookes of graven monuments . . . claspt forever up with dusty leaves' (Johnson's poem was published a year earlier). Both images depict the history book as a grave within which the dead are buried or 'claspt forever up'. However, instead of Clio, it is the 'great tragedian' who gives new life to Talbot. Clio gives new life to the dead through song; theatre revives the dead through performance. In language similar to that of Peele's euphoric Clio, Nashe insists that it would have 'joyed brave Talbot' to be so reincarnated, his story made immortal through theatrical repetition. However, Nashe also introduces a striking reference to mourning. For what would have 'joyed' Talbot most of all was to know that 'his bones' would be 'new embalmed with the tears of ten thousand spectators' who wept not at Talbot's death but at the lack of equivalent heroic virtue in the present – or, as Nashe puts it cuttingly, 'these degenerate effeminate days'. For Nashe at least, history was bound up with a sense of loss, of absence; it is not for nothing that in his description audiences become, in effect, new mourners. But they do not mourn the past; like Spenser's Clio, they mourn the present and its destined historical oblivion.

One Renaissance dramatist and poet who never made reference to Clio was William Shakespeare – which is ironic, because no other writer of the period spent as much time adapting the history chronicles and no writer before or since has been as closely identified with the representation of English history and, more recently, of British and Irish history as well. Shakespeare could easily *be* Clio: his monument in Stratford-upon-Avon shows him Clio-like, staring vacantly at the multitudes who look at him 'with uncertainty', a page from a book in one hand (perhaps a leaf of a history chronicle?) and a quill (in place of a trumpet) in the other. However, Shakespeare did write a Clio: Cleopatra, whose name derives from the same

Greek root (*kleos*, meaning 'glory'), whose role as both a constant pro-claimer of Antony's glory and, finally, as Antony's mourner seems to be ghosted by the Clio trope. A similar pun is more obviously at work with Antony's servant Eros, whose name of course references not only the cherub but also the muse of lyric poetry, Erato. And it is to Eros that Antony complains that Cleopatra has 'false-played my glory' (4.15.19). After Antony dies, Cleopatra insists, like Spenser's Clio, that 'there is nothing left remark-able' on earth. However, Cleopatra is also self-conscious that *her* history will be written by poets, 'scald rhymers', who will 'ballad us out o'tune'. Her suicide will cheat 'the quick comedians' she boasts as she imagines 'some squeaking Cleopatra' who will 'boy my greatness' in the 'posture of a whore' (5.2.210–17). It may have 'joyed brave Talbot' to have his life and death per-formed onstage but not Cleopatra, who fears theatre's inability to capture her 'greatness'. Of course, it was a squeaking Cleopatra who first spoke these lines, a theatre audience which heard them. Cleopatra's refusal to play the game of history, her need to cheat those who would represent her, makes her a different kind of Clio from that of Spenser, of Richard Johnson. She is more like Vermeer's model, already resisting the artists who will make her the subject of their histories, writing her own counter-history to 'mock / The luck of Caesar' (5.2.280–1).[6]

The writing of history

This book is about official and unofficial versions of the past, histories and counter-histories, in Shakespeare's works and their subsequent appropri-ations. It builds on a long period in which those of us working in literary and theatre studies have developed an awareness of the extent to which conven-tional recreations of the past are mediated through the fictionalising struc-tures of narrative. In several influential books, Hayden White interrogated the implications of thinking of history as a kind of text and Michel de Certeau subjected historians to a psychoanalytical study.[7] Yet the now fami-liar postmodern maxim that history is a kind of text overlooks the peculiar power which the past can have on the imaginations of writers such as Shakespeare. Historians such as Michel Foucault and Pierre Nora have resisted the conventions of modern history by looking at folk stories, insti-tutional histories, funerals, commemorations and festivals, all of which suggest different ways in which Western societies remember and forget the dead.[8] More recently, Bryan Reynolds has reinvigorated the postmodern interest in history's multiplicity by exploring history's transversality. Reynolds reminds us, quoting Fredric Jameson, that 'history is *not* a text', it is 'fundamentally non-narrative and non-representational'. However, 'history is inaccessible to us except in textual form'.[9] Reynolds goes on to insist that, because the production of history is intertwined with the 'competing conductors of social power' which give it textuality, then 'there can never be just one history or a pure, correct history' (Reynolds, *Becoming Criminal*, 3–4).

Even in its rawest form, history emerges through a negotiation between memory, narrative and the leftover traces of the past in the archive. The paradox of history is that it can never be wholly recovered, that however rigorous the method is to ensure objectivity, historical knowledge is assembled through a selective process in which more is forgotten than remembered. One of the discoveries of the modern age is that, even when events are recorded on film, definitive accounts of that history remain elusive: if anything, film and photography have only stimulated the number of competing interpretations of 'what happened'. An aspect of this paradox is the disconnection between 'what happened' and 'what it felt like to be there'. The two are not the same and we know from our own experience that memory tends to be shaped more by sensation and emotion than the recollection of actual happenings. Yet the force of emotion in memory can lead to very powerful convictions about matters of fact. Take for example witness statements in the 2005 shooting of an innocent man by police on the London Underground. Initial versions of the events as related by impassioned spectators talking to news crews were later almost wholly discredited: their accounts said more about their own fear and anxiety than they did about what actually happened. One man described how he had seen the victim run on to the train looking terrified before being forced to the ground and shot five times. In fact, the man had boarded the train and was sat in his seat before the event happened: clearly, the witness, in trying to make sense of the confusion of events and sensations he had experienced, was telling a story shaped more by his emotional response than by a clear recollection of a sequence of events: his story to the news, accompanied with frantic gestures, was a self-dramatisation in which a more vivid account was given than actually happened. By fashioning himself as a storyteller, this witness tells us little about 'what happened', but perhaps he conveys the intensity of what it was like to be there. A dramatist or a film director might well prefer his version of events for just that reason. The real paradox of history, then, is that it needs the resources of narrative and theatre to give shape and emotional depth to 'what happened' even if, in doing so, those details are reworked. Sometimes, history needs a good editor.

In his earliest history plays, Shakespeare demonstrated his remarkable ability to make drama out of history in two scenes: one, in *1 Henry VI*, when the great English soldier John Talbot cradles the body of his only son, killed in a battle in which the elder Talbot had already received fatal wounds; and the other in *3 Henry VI* when Queen Margaret, in a memorably macabre image, smears Rutland's blood on his father's face. Shakespeare invented both incidents. The pathos of the Talbots' death is heightened because the younger Talbot is the only heir and so the only one who can continue the family name and fortune. Urging his son off the field, Talbot asks 'Shall all thy mother's hopes lie in one tomb?' But all her hopes did not reside in one tomb. The Talbot family were still around when Shakespeare wrote the play and were still the Earls of Shrewsbury. In the twenty-first Century, the Talbots (now the Chetwynd-Talbots) are *still* around and *still* the Earls of Shrewsbury. So as history the scene is nonsensical: but as counter-history the scene links Talbot's death with generational loss. The murder of Rutland in *3 Henry VI* is equally spurious. Shakespeare depicts Rutland as a child protected by his tutor and finally murdered by a psychopathic Clifford. In truth, Rutland died in battle: and at seventeen, he was hardly an innocent child. Yet in this play and in *Richard III*, the murder of Rutland is revisited as the main atrocity of the Wars of the Roses and one of the events which leads to Richard III's tyranny. The blood-smeared York's rebuke to Margaret was powerful enough to be quoted by Robert Greene in his bitter comments on Shakespeare in 1592. But this also did not happen: York and Margaret did not meet on the battlefield, Margaret did not kill him.

The different registers of truth possible in history and in drama were already familiar to the intellectual culture of the period. Shakespeare's near-contemporary Sir Philip Sidney defended poetry (including playwrights) in *The Defence of Poesy* (published posthumously in 1595) by arguing that 'other artists, and especially the historian, affirming many things, can, in the cloudy knowledge of mankind, hardly escape from many lies'.[10] By contrast, the poet (including dramatists)

> never maketh any circles about your imagination, to conjure you to believe for true what he writeth. He citeth not authorities of other histories, but even for his entry calleth the sweet Muses to inspire into him a good invention; in troth, not laboring to tell you what is or is not, but what should or should not be. (Sidney, 'Defence', 517)

Even this opposition between historians and poets is not stable for, though the historian is committed to recording the events of the past, 'their lips sound of things done', they invariably have 'some feeling of poetry', Sidney argues, when they put 'long orations' in 'the mouths of great kings and captains, which it is certain they never pronounced'. Historians 'borrow both fashion and . . . weight' from poets. Sidney even recognises that historiography probably has its roots in poetry: he cites 'the most barbarous and simple Indians' who have 'no writing' but record their 'ancestor's deeds' with 'areytos' (502–3), song and dance rituals through which tribal history was celebrated and communal identity affirmed.

Shakespeare sends up his own writing of history in *1 Henry IV* when Falstaff pretends that it was he and not Hal who killed the rebel Hotspur during the Battle of Shrewbsury. 'Why', says Hal, 'Percy I killed myself' (5.4.141); to which Falstaff insists that *he* fought with Hotspur for an hour after Hal left the field. Falstaff's counter-history is not challenged and so stands as a definitive account of the battle. Hal's climactic fight is never more than a private event between Hal and the audience, an unhistoricised conflict displaced by the fictionalising Falstaff who tells, as Lancaster puts it, 'the strangest tale that e'er I heard' (151). Of course, Falstaff is both a teller of stories and himself a pseudo-historical character and works through all of the Henriad as a destabilising force, a commentator and a liar, in some ways the opposite of the historian and yet the history play's most compelling historiographer. He says he is not a 'double man' (136) but he is, for 'false' Falstaff (whose name may even gesture to Shakespeare's own ancestry, his grandfather's surname was Shakestaff) embodies truth and fiction, a historical liar and a strange history. *1 Henry IV* has other counter-histories. When King Henry goes out on to the battlefield, he does so with numerous soldiers dressed in his clothes, each carrying with them a potential counter-history. 'Another king! They grow like Hydra's heads' complains one of the rebels; Henry reassures him that he is 'the King himself' and not one of the many 'shadows' already met on the battlefield (5.4.24–9). But who checks, who knows, if the Henry IV at the end of the play is the real one – or just one of the doubles?

Histories and counter-histories

We have organised this collection into three sections, each one focusing on a different aspect of Shakespeare's counter-histories. We begin with 'Memory and mourning' and end with 'Identity and performance'. The middle section collects together a series of counter-historical readings which highlight ways in which historicist criticism engages with alternative histories. Our contributors range across the spectrum of Shakespeare studies and include theorists, historicists and performance critics.

The first section, 'Memory and mourning', explores how the history plays construct counter-historical representations of the dead. In '*Richard II* and the performance of grief', John Joughin argues that the 'dislocutionary' threat of grief and the performance of the suffering body is a version of the kind of spectator/spectre relationship drawn in any ritualised encounter with the cult of the ancestor. Joughin relies heavily on a sense of the performative which, by invoking both spectator and spectre, displaces traditional conceptions of the history play. Joughin's work is echoed by Dermot Cavanagh (also one of the book's editors) who asks, in 'History, mourning and memory in *Henry V*', if we might think of *Henry V* not as a history play at all but as a *memory* play and, moreover, a play of memories which are not to be trusted. Cavanagh links memory closely to mourning, which he figures as a fusion of remembering and tragic awareness. Walter Benjamin's reflections on the German *Trauerspiel* gives Cavanagh a frame for rereading *Henry V*'s interweaving of memory, mourning and history. Memory is also a central concern of Alison Thorne who, in 'There is a history in all men's lives: reinventing history in 2 *Henry IV*', proposes that rumour and oral history in 2 *Henry IV* offer an alternative model of history. By giving more attention to the role of memory and oral history in the play, Thorne argues, we can arrive at a better understanding of the play's troubling inconclusiveness and its dynamic play between power and ordinary people. Mourning and memory are brought together in Alison Findlay's 'Good sometimes queen': *Richard II*, Mary Stuart and the poetics of queenship'. Findlay argues that Richard II's obsession with retelling his own tragedy can be interpreted as an allusion to Mary Stuart, whose own relatively recent martyrdom was equally preceded by Mary's Richard-like efforts to interpret her own story. Shakespeare, Findlay argues, brings to life the 'destructive and regenerative force' of martyrdom and so, in effect, endorses a tragic view of Catholic suffering.

'Counter-histories', the second part of the book, combines four historicist readings which explore counter-histories in the early modern period. Lisa Hopkins and Richard Wilson examine the relationship between Shakespeare's history plays and alternative dynastic histories. In 'Strange truths: the Stanleys of Derby on the English Renaissance stage', Hopkins argues that a set of English history plays articulate the historical perspective of the Stanley family, who included Lord Strange, Shakespeare's first theatrical patron. Hopkins considers the implications of this context for understanding the representation of the Stanley story in Shakespeare, Marlowe and Ford. Like Hopkins, Wilson reads *Richard III* within the frame of a Stanley counter-history, but he goes further in his chapter, 'A sea of troubles: the thought of the outside in Shakespeare's histories'. For where Hopkins is content to consider the Stanley rival claim in purely political terms, Wilson sees this as a nod not just to an alternative dynasty but to an alternative worldview driven by Catholic recusants. Catholic factions represented thoughts which may have been secretly held by many, an unspoken, illegal counter-history, which read the revolution of the past as a tragedy and looked for liberation in the future, in the counter-space of an invading army.

Our next two contributors, editor Stephen Longstaffe and Jessica Winston, look beyond Shakespeare's history plays to those of his contemporaries and, in Winston's case, his predecessors. In 'The commons will revolt: *Woodstock* after the Peasants' Revolt', Longstaffe turns his attention to one of the best non-Shakespearean plays, conventionally known as *Woodstock* but sometimes also called *1 Richard II*. Longstaffe begins by surveying plays,

among them 2 *Henry VI*, in which ordinary people are depicted as (and probably *by*) clowns. In *Woodstock*, this stereotype is turned on its head, for the
play depicts the ruling classes in this way and so, in effect, gives credence to
the murmuring commoners' grievances against the authorities. Longstaffe
both reminds us that the carnivalesque tends to assert the ruling order and
offers us a play which offers a different kind of subversion, where the carnivalesque clown is turned back on authority. In 'National history to foreign
calamity: *A Mirror for Magistrates* and early English tragedy', Winston also
writes about the depiction of authority in crisis in her illuminating chapter on
the relationship between English history and the Inns of court tragedies of the
1570s, among them *Gorboduc* and *Cambises*. This time, however, Winston's
starting point is that these plays were written by and for an educated audience and their purpose was not to subvert authority but rather to illustrate
through example the need to govern well. Shakespeare mocked this theatrical style in *1 Henry IV*, when Falstaff starts to ham up a performance: 'I must
speak in passion and I will do it in King Cambyses' vein' (2.5.390). The
smoking gun is *A Mirror for Magistrates*, a multi-authored poem cycle about
recent English history. Winston's authors were heavily influenced by the
poem's representation of history as a 'mirror' for present authorities but, by
invoking England's mythical past rather than the recent events of the Wars of
the Roses, these authors were able to make pointed interventions about issues
such as the succession crisis.

   The final section of the book, 'Identity and performance', consists of three
chapters which explore questions of history and identity, particularly as they
can be configured through performance. In 'Of tygers' hearts and players'
hides', Carol Chillington Rutter discusses female violence: that is to say,
women who are violent *and* violence done to women. Rutter traces the
various ways in which Shakespeare gives dramatic expression to extreme
female violence, perhaps so memorably that it earned him his first theatrical
notice from a seething Robert Greene. In conflating Shakespeare with
Margaret, Greene affirmed Margaret's theatrical potency, one which has
seen this character dominate recent productions. Margaret is not only a compelling character for modern audiences, she is also the one who breaks all
the rules and who continues to exceed expectations of the violence that
women do. Where Rutter, like Joughin and Findlay, turns most of her attention on the suffering body, Carol Banks considers empowered women and
their counter-histories. In her chapter, 'Warlike women: "reproofe to these
degenerate, effeminate dayes"?', Banks challenges the view that women
become progressively marginalised across the histories by arguing that
Shakespeare's warlike women enact a power onstage which forces us to
rethink official, patriarchal history. Even though the warriors of the first
tetralogy are replaced with domesticated women in the second, these figures

continue to exercise a particular power, if not through their actions then through their language. In *Henry V* in particular, the ghost of a warlike woman can be discerned haunting Katherine's exchanges with Henry.

In 'Mapping Shakespeare's Britain', Peter Holland reminds us of the potency of maps to record not just history but division as well. Focusing on Lear's division of the kingdoms, Holland argues that maps inherently record and enact division and that maps were a potent symbol to circulate in Jacobean culture. Looking first at other plays which map Britain, Holland sees in them a related but nevertheless different discourse about mapping. With Shakespeare, maps point to radical instabilities as Lear's mapped/unmapped world becomes open to all sorts of rewritings, invasions and so on. The indeterminacy of place in *Lear* is linked directly to a consciousness shaped by historical mappery. Modern performances continue to locate the map of Britain as a faultline that needs to be accounted for.

Finally, Graham Holderness's Afterword reflects on the book as a whole.

This collection is by no means an attempt to present a shared vision of how the history plays *should* be studied: on the contrary, we hope the reader will find a genuine diversity of views across the chapters and we encourage students to look carefully at the way in which our contributors approach similar questions differently, raising important debates not only about history and history plays but about how we approach such works historically, theoretically and through performance. The book began as a conference, 'Renaissance Histories', which was held at the University of Central Lancashire in 2002 and we are grateful to all who attended and presented papers for helping to generate the debate with which this collection engages.

Notes

1 Joseph Brodsky, 'Profile of Clio' in *Grief and Reason, Essays* (Harmondsworth: Penguin, 1995), 114–37.

2 See 'Image as Argument: Vermeer's "Artist in his Studio"' online at http://home.att.net/~francis-noel/thirdinternational.htm. I am also grateful to Carol Banks for useful discussions on this point.

3 Another history haunts this image, that of St Luke the Evangelist who, it was said, painted the Virgin Mary with her child soon after the birth of Christ. Because of this tradition, Luke became the patron saint of artists and many artists' guilds commissioned representations of the scene (Vermeer belonged to the Guild of St Luke in Delft). Vermeer invokes the classic relationship of the Virgin and Luke, of the artist trying to capture history.

4 See David H. Horne (ed.) *The Life and Minor Works of George Peele* (New Haven: Yale University Press, 1952).

5 See William A. Oram (ed.) *The Yale Edition of the Shorter Works of Edmund Spenser* (New Haven: Yale University Press, 1989).

6 The edition used here and throughout the volume is Stanley Wells and Gary Taylor (eds) *The Oxford Shakespeare: The Complete Works* (Oxford: Clarendon Press, 1986). Here and elsewhere, u/v and i/j are modernised.

7 Hayden White's most influential books are *Metahistory: The Historical Imagination* (Baltimore: Johns Hopkins University Press, 1973) and *Tropics of Discourse* (Baltimore: Johns Hopkins University Press, 1978). Michel de Certeau's major study of historiography is *The Writing of History*, trans. Tom Conley (New York: Columbia University Press, 1992).

8 See for example Foucault's *Discipline and Punish*, trans. Alan Sheridan (New York: Vintage, 1977). The best introduction to Nora's exemplary work is his article 'Between Memory and History: *Les Lieux de Mémoires*', *Representations*, 26 (1989), 7–25.

9 Bryan Reynolds, *Becoming Criminal: Transversal Performance and Cultural Dissidence in Early Modern England* (Baltimore: Johns Hopkins University Press, 2002), 3. He quotes from Fredric Jameson, *The Political Unconscious: Narrative as a Socially Symbolic Act* (Ithaca: Cornell University Press, 1981), 82.

10 'The Defence of Poesy' in Michael Payne and John Hunter (eds) *Renaissance Literature: An Anthology* (Oxford: Blackwells, 2003), 501–27.

I

Memory and mourning

Richard II and the performance of grief

The world of deep caring can be built once again out of grieving.[1]

The Shakespearean uncanny

In a recent account of *Shakespeare's Histories* Graham Holderness feels bound to remind us that his brand of materialist historiography is nothing more or less than a ghost hunt:

> I no longer seek the solid actuality of historical presence, but rather dwell on history's shadows and silences, those lost presences and potentialities that can by their absence disturb and disconcert the present . . . I find the ghost more interesting than the living being and the shadow more illuminating than the substance. My critical language, structured by such 'mighty opposites' as past and present, absence and presence, male and female, will also be found preoccupied by polarities such as nothing and something, language and silence, substance and shadow, image and reflection, womb and tomb.[2]

These days of course haunting and history are never that far removed, and Holderness's comments echo the pronounced tendency of historicist criticism to embrace the ontological uncertainties of what Jacques Derrida terms *hauntology*, wherein he enjoins us to anticipate a form of scholarship that dares to speak to the 'phantom', in order to become

> *a scholar of the future*, a scholar who, in the future and so as to conceive of the future, would dare to speak to the phantom. A scholar who would dare to admit that he knows how to speak *to* the phantom, even claiming that this not only neither contradicts nor limits his scholarship but will in truth have conditioned it, at the price of some still-inconceivable complication that may yet prove the other one, that is, the phantom, to be correct . . . to have the last word.[3]

In drawing an analogous distinction between spectrality and remembrance the new historicist Stephen Greenblatt famously compares his own profession as literature professor to that of the 'shaman', in so far as it entails a curious form of speaking with the dead:

> I began with the desire to speak with the dead . . . If I never believed that the dead could hear me, and if I knew that the dead could not speak, I was nonetheless certain that I could re-create a conversation with them. Even when I came to understand that in my most intense moments of straining to listen all I could hear was my own voice, even then I did not abandon my desire. It was true that I could hear only my own voice, but my voice was the voice of the dead, for the dead had contrived to leave textual traces of themselves, and those traces make themselves heard in the voices of the living . . . It is paradoxical, of course, to seek the living will of the dead in fictions, in places where there was no live bodily being to begin with. But those who love literature tend to find more intensity in simulations . . . Conventional in my tastes, I found the most satisfying intensity of all in Shakespeare.[4]

Speaking with Shakespeare constitutes a peculiar form of monolingualism in so far as speaking with Shakespeare is itself (Greenblatt suggests) merely to overhear oneself speak. As a result the critical act is curiously non-appropriative, for it is, as Derrida might say, 'conditioned by the spectral' – a form of possession that dispossesses – not the critic's own voice but the voice of the other whose ghostly intensity is, Greenblatt informs us, 'uncannily full of the will to be heard' (Greenblatt, *Shakespearean Negotiations*, 1). Recently Greenblatt goes further, in pondering whether Shakespeare's theatre might itself be construed as a 'cult of the dead', commenting that 'More than anyone of his age, Shakespeare grasped that there were powerful links between his art and the haunting of spirits'.[5] In fact, Greenblatt's work on *Hamlet in Purgatory* confirms that Shakespeare's theatre staged an elaborate 'ontological argument', an exercise in 'quasi-dying' where 'the dead appear to live again' and in the same process revive contemporary theological debates concerning the status of suffrage and repentance. In performance, the dislocationary potential of this phantom-like economy of remembrance is simultaneously disconcerting and regenerative, and, however unsettling it proves to be, the restoration of the past can result in a 'newly performed' openness to alterity, as well as producing a newly evaluative understanding of the spectator's role in conceding the limits of their own historical situation. In the process of resurrecting the dead, Shakespeare's theatre obviously has a direct role to play in reconstituting and rehabilitating the transformative interaction of culture and memory, and in this chapter I will interrogate the ethical and political implications of this hermeneutic encounter in relation to tragedy and history.

Speaking native English . . .

For Shakespeare's contemporary audience, witnessing the revival of ancient spirits and ancestors itself seems to constitute a crucial component of the aesthetic experience of playgoing. In *Pierce Penniless* for example, Thomas Nashe bases his justification of the 'virtue' of the theatre around a fairly detailed exegesis of the significance of the 'resurrection' of Talbot in Shakespeare's *1 Henry VI*:

> Nay, what if I prove plays to be no extreme, but a rare exercise of virtue? First, for the subject of them: for the most part it is borrowed out of our English Chronicles, wherein our forefathers' valiant acts, that have lain long buried in rusty brass and worm-eaten books, are revived and they themselves raised from the grave of oblivion and brought to plead their aged honours in open presence: than which, can be a sharper reproof to these degenerate, effeminate days of ours?
>
> How would it have joyed brave Talbot, the terror of the French, to think that after he had lain two hundred years in his tomb, he should triumph again on the stage and have his bones new embalmed with the tears of ten thousand spectators at least (at several times), who, in the tragedian that represents his person, imagine they behold him fresh bleeding!
>
> I will defend it against any cullion, or club-fisted usurer of them all, there is no immortality can be given a man on earth like unto plays.[6]

Nashe's comments serve to remind us that if Shakespeare's theatre does house a cult of the dead then it does so beyond the 'stale recuperative' mechanism of the historical archive. In its restaging of the past Nashe suggests that the history play is itself revived as a process of continual renewal, a re-enactment of a 'sacrificial ritual' – a 'plead[ing]' issued in 'open presence' on a daily basis (cf. Holderness, *The Histories*, 44–5). Again the cult of ancestors to which he directs us enables a ritualisation of suffering that sits at the intersection of tragedy and memory, and which in the process forges a complex affinity to the communal acts of remembering and myth-making that constitute an emergent sense of national culture. Indeed, one might say that Talbot's 'sacrifice' constitutes a historical site in which to reactivate a 'political' memory.

In Shakespeare's tragedies and histories the lyrical as well as the political legacy of suffering is certainly significant. In *Richard II* for example, determining moments of death stage numerous and indeterminate figures of and from which to choose 'otherness' – a form of testimony which incorporates an endlessly inventive 'oppositional historical consciousness' and which also constitutes its own form of counter-history (cf. Holderness, *The Histories*, 65). As such the 'poetry' as well as the performance of grief often conveys an autobiographical intensity which is at once uncommon and 'singular' and yet also somehow typical or exemplary. This poignant language of inconsolability which is at times almost reminiscent of the psalms in terms of its recitation of isolation and exile comes close to the experience of originary alienation characteristic of the 'native speaker' that Jacques Derrida provocatively terms monolingualism of the other – a testament to suffering uttered in a language which both precedes and exceeds the speaker:

> I am monolingual. My monolingualism dwells, and I call it my dwelling; it feels like one to me, and I remain in it and inhabit it. It inhabits me. The monolingualism in which I draw my very breath is, for me, my element. Not a natural element, not the transparency of the ether, but an absolute habitat. It is impassable, *indisputable*: I cannot challenge it except by testifying to its omnipresence in me. It would always have preceded me. It is me. For me, this monolingualism is me . . . I would not be myself outside it . . . This inexhaustible solipsism is myself before me. Lastingly [*A demeure*].
>
> Yet it will never be mine, this language, the only one I am destined to speak, as long as speech is possible for me in life and in death; you see, never will this language be mine. And truth to tell, it never was.
>
> You at once appreciate the source of my sufferings, the place of my passions, my desires, my prayers, the vocation of my hopes, since this language runs right through them all.[7]

In *Richard II* this lyrical excess of native language is not a matter of possession or dispossession in any straightforward sense, yet in so far as it is a language beyond temporal lease ('myself before me') it is certainly linked insistently to a more haunting sense of inheritance and testimony. This, at any rate, is what Gaunt seems to be driving at when he reminds Richard of the way in which his own native breath might prove inexhaustible in exceeding a monarch's power:

> KING RICHARD   Why, uncle, thou hast many years to live.
> JOHN OF GAUNT   But not a minute, King, that thou canst give.
> Shorten my days thou canst with sudden sorrow,
> And pluck nights from me, but not lend a morrow.
> Thou canst help time furrow me with age;
> But stop no wrinkle in his pilgrimage;
> Thy word is current with him for my death,
> But dead, thy kingdom cannot buy my breath.
>
> (1.3.218–25)

Beyond the sovereign authority of a king there is already an acknowledgement here that Gaunt's own legacy is already born into a sort of linguistic dispossession or exappropriation: 'thy kingdom cannot buy my breath'. And even while his own singular testimony fails to unstop Richard's ears, the Duke clearly understands the process by which one's native language already comes from an 'elsewhere' and that by a type of performative contradiction he is already in possession of a language that both is and is not, his.

In short, the death of sovereigns and princes constitute overdetermined chronotopes,[8] where in speaking of the past and prophesying the future we are continuously yoked together in untimely dislocation. In confirming this relation during *Richard II*, moments of leave-taking often then double as a space of invention, anticipating ulterior sites of resistance or new ways of being with the world. Gaunt returns to make the distinction clearer still in advance of his 'sceptred isle' speech:

> . . . they say the tongues of dying men
> Enforce attention, like deep harmony.
> Where words are scarce they are seldom spent in vain,
> For they breathe truth that breathe their words in pain.
> He that no more must say is listened more
> Than they whom youth and ease have taught to glose.
> More are men's ends marked then their lives before.
> The setting sun, and music at the close,
> As the last taste of sweets, is sweetest last,
> Writ in remembrance more than things long past.
> Though Richard my life's counsel would not hear,
> My death's sad tale may yet undeaf his ear.
> . . .
> Methinks I am a prophet new-inspired,
> And thus expiring, do foretell of him.
> His rash, fierce blaze of riot cannot last.
>
> (2.1.5–16; 31–3)

Beyond the close reading or smooth-talking 'glose' of the present it is as if the voices of the dead are already with us offering a prophetic anamnestic updating, 'Writ in remembrance more than things long past', so that again, as if by a type of paradoxical logic, 'less is more' as present scarcity and imminent demise will be fed by a type of superfluity, populated with the voices of the future living, hibernating within a past that will already some day be made present. These and other figures of and for death, language and national consciousness, are all-pervasive in *Richard II* as, in a variety of per-mutations, 'death' and 'breath' mark the most insistent rhyming couplet of the play. Moreover a sense of the impregnable insubstantiality of language also prevails – maybe it is a matter of native spirit or *Seelenstoff*? – and intriguingly it tends to resurface when the most material and time-bound matters of property are at stake. In this respect the theme of possession and dispossession is central to the play's topographical as well as its linguistic axes in terms which no doubt simultaneously attest, in terms of the play's representation of the body politic, both to the prepossession of feudalism and to the repossession and dislocation of a feudal world of which it is letting go.[9] As a consequence, the effect of speaking one's native tongue frequently enacts precisely a sense of the strange intimacy of which Derrida speaks – *I have only one language, yet it is not mine* – a surrender to the disconcerting awareness of being possessed or dispossessed by an other. Indeed, this sense of a gothic disorder of identity construed as history's last word occupies the very centre of the play, and most memorably of all perhaps in John of Gaunt's 'sceptred isle' speech which, whilst it has often been rehabilitated in order to idealise the past itself, prophesays nothing more or less than disinheritance, not least in so far as Gaunt himself of course already effectively speaks from a position of imminent dispossession (cf. 2.1.162–3). However often his last dying speech is invoked as an act of patriotism, the scene retains its place in the national psyche precisely because it purports to be a death scene, the powerful affectivity of which secures its place only in dislocation: the once tranquil garden England compared to a dystopic 'pelting farm', a run-down tenement 'leased out' and gone to seed (2.1.59–60).[10]

Gaunt views Richard's own tragedy as curiously akin to Lear's: 'possessed now to depose thyself' (2.1.108) and again of course the scene of suffering produced by Richard's actual deposition is also entwined in an analogous sense of linguistic exappropriation, not merely in the sense that his 'own breath' will release his sovereign oaths (4.1.200) but also in so far as he has cause to imagine that his own last breath might also serve as a political act of legacy, precisely in terms of a language which is insufficient to the present, but will live on in a future to come elsewhere:

> Think I am dead, and that even here thou tak'st,
> As from my death-bed, thy last living leave,
> In winter's tedious nights, sit by the fire
> With good old folks, and let them tell thee tales
> Of woeful ages long ago betid;
> And ere thou bid goodnight, to quit their griefs
> Tell thou the lamentable tale of me,
> And send the hearers weeping to their beds;
> Forwhy the senseless brands will sympathise
> The heavy accent of thy moving tongue,
> And in compassion weep the fire out;
> And some will mourn in ashes, some coal black,
> For the deposing of a rightful king.

$$(5.1.38–50)$$

Richard's claim is characteristically overblown, indeed, his sense of the way in which his language will 'move' the world, so that even the senseless brands (or logs) in the fire will sympathise, is directly reminiscent of the way in which, at an earlier juncture in the play, he attempts to change reality by conjuring the very earth and stones to help his cause (3.2.23–6); yet his evaluation of the poetic experience of language is actually far more precise and to the point: that in some sense this language is not his own and that the voice he uses must eventually cede to the tongue of another. In so far as Richard would willingly exchange death for a language in perpetuity, he does so in the knowledge that in death one no longer speaks the same language, invoking a sense of future advent or a 'coming to pass' – 'of an event that would no longer have the form or appearance of a *pas*: in sum, a coming without *pas*'.[11] In terms of the long march of history, 'Gaunt-like' Richard relies on the fact that, in dramatic terms at least, his testimony will live on even as he dies pronouncing it (cf. 2.1.59). His last breath will serve as his legacy, a tale to be retold in 'winter's tedious nights' sitting by the fire. Richard is confident that this, his mythology, will outlive him, as that which is insufficient to the present but which will in the future affect its audience in terms reminiscent of Nashe and send them 'weeping to their beds' (5.1.40, 45). If, as I am suggesting, the time and space of mourning are joined (explicitly in the case of Gaunt) with the state of the nation, then it is clearly because the suffering of sovereigns and princes constitutes the very 'borderline condition' which constitutes the nation and which thereby also opens up 'a certain play of difference' within the idealisation of national identity itself – in short, the performance of grief plays the troubling other to historicism. Indeed, for a monumental historicism committed to orderly succession, the danger of such figures of, and for, mourning is that they are sited simultaneously inside and outside the official archive where the sedimented memory of their sacrifice resides as an indeterminable countersignature for future national determination.[12] Here, 'for once', as Graham Holderness observes of Richard II, 'history is not written by the victors, but unforgettably formulated by the dispossessed, in a poignant poetry of defeat and inconsolable loss . . . the myth of the deposed king will live far longer than the practical achievements of his enemies' (Holderness, *The Histories*, 196).

The angel of history

In many respects, Richard constitutes the dramatic prototype for Hamlet and, unsurprisingly perhaps, critics are frequently attracted to Richard and Hamlet in a similar vein, often again in terms of plotting the grief-stricken inconsolability of each, a condition which Richard casts in terms roughly analogous to Hamlet, in so far as he tells us that the 'external manners' of his lament

Are merely shadows to the unseen grief
That swells with silence in the tortured soul
There [Richard assures us] lies the substance . . .

(4.1.287–9)

For his part, Hamlet's initial performance of grief already remains wilfully misunderstood by those who witness it, so that his uncle reprimands him for his 'obstinate condolement' (1.2.93). Curiously though, the attraction of these figures seems to lie in the fact that they manifest a form of nameless intimacy (particular yet common) so much so that, at one juncture, Richard desires the fate of the unknown soldier – often itself at times of emergency a powerful, if paradoxical, signifier of nationalism – offering to swap his kingdom 'for a little grave, / A little, little grave, an obscure grave' (3.3.152–3). Ironically, in historical terms at least, the question of Richard's actual burial place, which was never certain, has returned, even relatively recently, to haunt historians.[13] Yet even by the end of the play, like Old Hamlet, Richard is still in some sense without a tomb. Crucially, as Benedict Anderson reminds us, the question of national identity is less a case of forensic evidence and more a matter of what he terms 'ghostly national imaginings',[14] and in this respect, in what we might term the crypt of nationalism, we find nothing more or less than the sense of dispossession that lies at the heart of another tradition, 'the forgotten dead'. This spectre is raised insistently in *Richard II* as for Richard again, persistently, it is 'matter out of place' rather than an official narrative of monumental history that preoccupies him, often quite literally the recitation of a history from below, as Richard, like Hamlet (cf. *Hamlet* 1.2.71), spends his time with his eyes downcast seeking the past which has turned to dust:

> Let's talk of graves, of worms and epitaphs,
> Make dust our paper, and with rainy eyes
> Write sorrow on the bosom of the earth.
>
>   (3.2.141–3)

When they are cast as sacrificial victims then, characters like Richard and Hamlet remain haunting yet exemplary figures, each uncommon yet somehow typical in so far as each is cast in 'a supposedly singular situation by bearing witness to it in terms which go beyond it'.[15] As such, beyond the crude propagandising of nationalism Richard and Hamlet also articulate the exemplary in another register and in doing so they also arguably offer a more radical legacy for the future allegorisation of a political present. Rather like the unknown soldier, they serve to confirm that we cannot 'know' what they suffer, yet they do so in a language of generality which is in some sense transcendental and with which we can all identify. What goes for me, they seem to say, goes for everybody, it's enough to hear me, 'I am the universal sacrificial victim' (Derrida, *Monolingualism of the Other*, 19–20):

> . . . you have but mistook me all this while.
> I live with bread, like you; feel want,

Taste grief, need friends. Subjected thus,
How can you say to me, I am a king?

Richard II (3.2.170–3)

In short 'tis common, but then why seems it so particular with them? In the case of Hamlet, as Francis Barker remarks, it is almost as if history itself is hypostatised as individual grief. Hamlet is in some sense historical then because inconsolable and this again in turn points us to the problem of the political, as Hamlet's petition to justice (and indeed Richard's) remains in some sense unfulfillable – we can't 'set things right' . Grief introduces a disruptive continuum which will continue to haunt us partly because, as Freud reminds us, for human beings pain and memory are clearly linked, it is not so much that history makes us suffer, we suffer because we are historical. Yet having introduced this relation which hints at a being in common, Hamlet then still insists that this grief is particular only to him and thus simultaneously defies our comprehension (cf. 1.2.73–86):

. . . I have that within which passes show –
These but the trappings and suits of woe.

(85–6)

His father's death then like history manifests itself as an otherness which both attracts and defies our understanding, presenting us with unimaginable horrors to which we nevertheless share an affinity.

In speaking of history in these terms one is immediately drawn to Walter Benjamin's inconsolable 'angel of history'. Like Richard and Hamlet, the angel's gaze is directed downwards at the dust, this after all (as Benjamin reminds us) is one how one pictures the angel of history:

His face is turned toward the past . . . The angel would like to stay, awaken the dead, and make whole what has been smashed. But a storm is blowing from Paradise; it has got caught in his wings with such violence that the angel can no longer close them. This storm irresistibly propels him into the future to which his back is turned, while the pile of debris before him grows skyward.[16]

This storm (Benjamin adds) is 'what we call progress'. Again told from the point of view of the spectator, history is a matter of perspective: where monumental historicism perceives an orderly succession or 'a chain of events' the angel of history 'sees one single catastrophe which keeps piling wreckage upon wreckage and hurls it in front of his feet' – a disruptive continuum indeed. Interestingly, of course, Benjamin suggests here that history is an analogue of the sublime and part of the lure of the sublime of course is that it too can be construed as a category that simultaneously opens and limits manifesting a form of otherness which both attracts and defies our comprehension in presenting us with a form of history that both will and will not be recovered and, unsurprisingly of course, it follows that as a spectator of history the angel is left entranced and appalled in almost equal measure 'looking as though he is about to move away from something he is fixedly contemplating. His eyes are staring, his mouth is open, his wings are spread.'

It is clear, as Jacques Lacan remarks in speaking of St Teresa and others like her, 'that the essential testimony of the mystics is that they are experiencing [*jouissance*] but know nothing about it'.[17] The angel's vacant gaze and open mouth could be construed at one level as a moment of dumbfounded rapture. Yet as Homi Bhabha observes, 'If the testimony of rapture consists of a type of breach between experience and knowledge, then what account can it give of itself?' or, to put it another way: 'who speaks for rapture? Can it be witnessed or represented?' (See Bhabha, 'Aura and Agora', 8). It is as if the spectator experiences an untimely pause in both time and knowledge, a relation beyond relation in so far as it insinuates an 'absolutely asymmetrical relation with the wholly other'.[18] To return to the context of theatrical performance, I would want to argue that there is a link to be established here between Aristotle's doctrine of tragedy and the aesthetics of the sublime. There has been a tendency to psychologise tragedy, yet, if the 'tragic effect' condenses around the notion of the sublime it is in no small part because – as Philippe Lacoue-Labarthe reminds us – the tragic effect is a 'political effect':

> when Aristotle talks about a tragic effect, I think one would have to begin to analyse this as a *political* effect. 'Terror' and 'pity' are essentially political notions. They are absolutely not psychological. Pity refers to what the modern age, under the name of compassion thinks of, as the origin of the social bond (in Rousseau and Burke, for example): terror refers to the risk of the dissolution of the social bond and the pre-eminent place of that first social bond which is the relation with the other.[19]

The sublime then clearly comes close to the aesthetic register of indeterminate alterity we have traced so far, and certainly in so far as it touches on the risk of the political. Yet how then can we historicise and politicise this relation with that which is indeterminably other? In attempting to overcome the dissolution of the social bond that the image of the angel so clearly evokes as a mixture of terror and speechless compassion, can tragedy and history ever be reconciled? How are we to eventually come to terms with the forgotten dead if their history is fated only to be construed as the figure of and for inconsolable loss? Is it possible to construct a politics for this poetry of defeat or is it fated to remain, for all its poignancy, unreconciled and unreconcilable? Can the inconsolable be consoled? When will the angel of history close his wings and rest? How are we to embrace the nameless undead?

History from below, above and beyond . . .

In some sense of course these remain the key political questions that have haunted the work of materialist critics like Francis Barker and Graham Holderness.[20] It is evident now I think that much of the fascination of that work resided in tracing the erasure of corporeality and in witnessing the simultaneous emergence of a sense of otherness concerning our own being. Indeed one could go further and say that it is precisely because of the attraction of the body, and the manner in which our attempts to construe it, are exceeded that it too doubles as a site of the sublime. For, even as bourgeois history intrigues its disappearance, our body is also that which can never be laid to rest or closure. In short, it too constitutes a site that presents or expresses 'a forever non-appearing inside, interiority, outside' – so that, as Jay Bernstein reminds us: 'What cannot appear in itself, what cannot be made present (without the thought of its being simultaneously absent) is our autonomy',[21] or as Hamlet puts it: 'I have that within which passes show'.

One might even say that the ontological uncertainties of Richard's and Hamlet's 'hauntology' re-enact an exemplary horror tract, wherein those spectres that exceed embodiment paradoxically ensure the emergence of an equivocal 'self-consciousness'. In attempting to retell this story we are confronted with a subject 'tremulous' and alone from the point of its inception onwards: a 'self' hovering on the point of collapse as the unstable fiction that it 'actually is'. A self, unsure of its 'self', and equally unsure of its knowledge of the existence of others. Yet paradoxically of course, on this, the terrifying brink of the body's disappearance, new figures and forms of authenticity are simultaneously required to overcome and combat the condition of actually being individuated, or modern. And within the discourses that attempt to rationalise, justify and politicise the emergence of an autonomous self, every attempt is made to counteract the concomitant alienation and solitude that our possession of this dubious 'freedom' of individuality entails. This gives rise to what Jay Bernstein aptly labels the 'aporia of autonomy'.[22] So that, as a direct result of its positioning within the philosophical discourse of modernity, the 'self' which would do away with the body now also simultaneously strives to reincorporate that which is heteronomous to the self – the body, history, community – even as it (the self) continues to locate substantially new figures which acknowledge, in their very excess, the failure of these attempted acts of incorporation (see Bernstein, 'Autonomy and Solitude', 192–3). In turn, the failure to reassimilate that which is lost or beyond self-assimilation gives rise to the despairing mournful thought which was our first regret and our necessary accomplice in initially turning away from and doubting the body. And so, on it goes . . .

For his part, Richard returns compulsively to retrace this indeterminate boundary between self and other and self as other, as if in uncanny awareness

of the otherness of his own being. As such each claim for his identity too is
secured 'only in its non-appearing' or in its 'remaining in excess of whatever
form or configuration is given it' (Bernstein, 'Autonomy and Solitude', 175–6):

> I have been studying how I may compare
> This prison where I live unto the world;
> And for because the world is populous,
> And here is not a creature but myself,
> I cannot do it. Yet I'll hammer it out.
>
> . . .
>
>   Sometimes am I king;
> Then treasons make me wish myself a beggar,
> And so I am. Then crushing penury
> Persuades me I was better when a king;
> Then am I kinged again, and by and by
> Think I am unkinged by Bolingbroke,
> And straight am nothing. But whate'er I be,
> Not I, nor any man that but man is,
> With nothing shall be pleased, till he be eased
> With being nothing.

$$(5.5.1–5; 32–41)$$

As we have seen, in so far as figures of and for death and the experience of
demise litter the play they are consistently linked to Richard's problematic
relationship to language; wherein he contemplates the consequence of an
abyssal collapse – of 'becoming a nothing', which he can neither affirm or
deny, and which appears only 'in its non-appearing':

> Ay, no; no, ay; for I must nothing be;
> Therefore no, no, for I resign to thee.
> Now, mark me how I will undo myself.

$$(4.1.191–3)$$

Yet here again in the yoking of past and present the tension lies not so much
in what Richard once was, but in what he must become, as, in acknowledg-
ing the extent to which suffering secures testimonial exemplarity (where as
we've seen less is finally more), Richard nevertheless already finds it difficult
to embrace the obligation of his new-found singularity:

> . . . O, that I were as great
> As is my grief, or lesser than my name,
> Or that I could forget what I have been,
> Or not remember what I must be now!

$$(3.3.135–8)$$

The impossible relation of which Richard speaks only confirms and
relaunches endless new possibilities for his affinity to solitude and isolation

into being. As such, the soon to become former king experiences nothing more or less than a living interment; and, in being 'dead without being dead', he now looks at things simultaneously from below, above and beyond – trampled into the dust:

> . . . I'll be buried in the King's highway,
> Some way of common trade where subjects' feet
> May hourly trample on their sovereign's head,
> For on my heart they tread now, whilst I live,
> And buried once, why not upon my head?
>
> (3.3.154–8)

In *Richard II* these paradoxical tropes of self-erasure and omniscience necessarily open out on to a political dimension – one which is acutely overdetermined by the doctrine of the King's two bodies;[23] yet, as Hugh Grady recently reminds us, in the extreme dislocation of his exile and suffering Richard also anticipates the emergence of what we might term a poetic subjectivity: 'an unfixing of identity and the construction of alternative but unfixed subjectivity' effected in the play as a 'self-severing, or disinterpellation, from a previously taken-for-granted world of legitimated values and ideologies', a process which, in the case of Richard, Grady argues, is synonymous with 'a new idea of subjectivity' and of the emergence of the new category of an autonomous aesthetic in Western culture. Such subjectivity Grady reminds us is coded as 'unfettered, aimless, disconnected and alienated – but also suffused with libido and creative of some of the most remarkable insights, poetry and dramatic moments of these great plays'.[24] While cultural materialism and new historicism have offered us the reductive functionalism of an 'automaton-like' subject determined by an Althusserian or Foucauldian matrix of ideology and power, Grady argues that we need to think of the creative and transfigurative potentials of Richard's selfhood as a direct precursor of aesthetic modernity.

Yet interestingly Richard's poetics of grief also simultaneously invokes an earlier legacy of lament that predates Shakespearean drama,[25] as, in casting himself as a sacrificial victim and in inviting us to 'peer into heart of nothing' his appeal is already directly reminiscent of the radical reflexivity of an earlier Christian tradition, where the path to a 'saving self-knowledge' simultaneously locates an increasing 'bemusement' concerning the self, so that, as Augustine puts it in his *Confessions*: 'I became a great riddle to myself.'[26] As such Richard's appeal is already curiously outmoded – reminiscent of the lyrical suffering evoked by antecedents of poetic subjectivity in sources as wide-ranging as hagiographic writing and courtly romance (also overlooked by cultural materialism) and especially in terms of the 'confessional Augustianism' of Petrarch and other poets (see Aers, 'A Whisper in the Ear').

In short, Shakespeare's 'lamentable tragedy', *Richard II*, is a Passion play, where the legacy of an incomprehensible grief and the aporetic configuration of its interiority are entwined with the homilectic *exemplum* – we are confronted with the sublime alterity of our own being configured as the 'inward beholding' of an external truth in which we now may acknowledge a share. As such, Richard's lyricism dramatises a process self-iconisation where Christological metaphors and allusions to sacrifice and martyrdom are painfully embodied in the act of performance itself:

> I'll give my jewels for a set of beads,
> My gorgeous palace for a hermitage,
> My gay apparel for an almsman's gown,
> My figured goblets for a dish of wood,
> My sceptre for a palmer's walking staff,
> My subjects for a pair of carved saints,
> And my large kingdom for a little grave

$$(3.3.146\text{–}52)^{27}$$

In his insistent apprehension of bereavement Richard eventually settles for casting himself in terms of those future commemorative practices that will canonise his memory and by which his anonymity will simultaneously guarantee his legacy: as the impossible object of his own grief. Yet the risk is that Richard's hyperbole will be taken literally, or rather as merely theatrical. And of course it is precisely in these terms that Richard is often accused by his latter-day critics of waxing too lyrical, his overt theatricalisation of grief drawing the accusation of improbability, the tears of a 'player king' re-enacting the terms of what Freud would term a 'hysterical' mourning – interminably immersed in sad events that 'occurred long ago'. However if the denial of Richard's grief by others only consolidates the process by which he is cast as irretrievable, it also offers an audience a position from which to redeem themselves. In short, the extent of Richard's over-dramatic isolation will in time also itself prove a measure or gauge of an audience's willingness to overcome their scepticism and to commit to the very rites of pilgrimage he envisages.

There is, Derrida reminds us, 'no culture without a cult of ancestors, a ritualisation of mourning and sacrifice' (*Aporias*, 43) and the history of a national culture is nothing more or less than the history of death to which he refers us. More recently of course the psycho-drama of mourning and melancholia which links 'sacrificial' national figures to the narration of national and communal identities has become more commonplace, especially in the wake of the death of Princess Diana.[28]

It is precisely because death, lyricism and grief are bound together in unsettling and complex ways that they remain culturally and poetically marginal yet politically and symbolically central. Richard, Gaunt, Hamlet (and indeed Diana?) each in some sense proves a thorn in the side of monumental history and each to some extent remains in exile without a monument, yet their exemplary or singular status also offers an audience the opportunity to shape a new politics of communal identity, where the nation is positioned as a form of futural or imagined identity – or as a form of 'writing the nation which has not yet come into being' (Brannigan, 'Writing DeTermiNation', 56).

Notes

1 Lisa Freinkel, *Reading Shakespeare's Will: The Theology of Figure from Augustine to the Sonnets* (New York: Columbia University Press, 2002), xxvii.
2 Graham Holderness, *Shakespeare: The Histories* (Basingstoke: Palgrave Macmillan, 2000), 13.
3 Jacques Derrida, *Archive Fever: A Freudian Impression*, trans. Eric Prenowitz (Chicago: University of Chicago Press, 1996), 39.
4 Stephen Greenblatt, *Shakespearean Negotiations: The Circulation of Social Energy in Renaissance England* (Oxford: Clarendon Press, 1988), 1.
5 Stephen Greenblatt, *Hamlet in Purgatory* (Princeton: Princeton University Press, 2001), 157; 258–61.
6 See Thomas Nashe, *The Unfortunate Traveller and Other Works*, ed. J. B. Steane (Harmondsworth: Penguin, 1978), 112–13.
7 See Derrida, *Monolingualism of the Other; or, The Prosthesis of Origin*, trans. P. Mensah (Stanford: Stanford University Press, 1998), 1–2.
8 For a detailed exposition of the term 'chronotope' see M. M. Bakhtin and compare his account of 'historical poetics' in *The Dialogic Imagination*, trans. Caryl Emerson and Michael Holquist (Austin: University of Texas Press, 1981), esp. 84–258.
9 In *Richard II* while the terms of this linguistic dispossession are insistent they are by no means uniform. Here, for example, is Mowbray on the verge of exile, taking his leave:

> The language I have learnt these forty years,
> My native English, now I must forgo,
> And now my tongue's use is to me no more
> Than an unstrung viol or a harp,
> Or like a cunning instrument cased up,
> Or, being open, put into his hands
> That knows no touch to tune the harmony.
> . . .
> What is thy sentence then but speechless death,
> Which robs my tongue from breathing native breath?
>
> (1.3.153–9; 166–7)

On the face of it Mowbray's plea is grounded as a claim for free speech although it is difficult to see how free speech could ever prevail in the political regime in which he locates himself. In speaking of 'nativity' in these terms Mowbray nostalgically equates locality and utterance, reminiscent in some ways of a harmonious prelapsarian Adamic language where, as part of their natural property, words are perfect in their equivalence to things. As a consequence, to be banished from the air of one's native breath is, as Terry Eagleton puts it in his summary of Mowbray's speech, 'to be drained of the breath of its language' (*William Shakespeare* (Oxford: Basil Blackwell, 1986), 9). This seems to be an extreme form of monolingualism then, one which secures a form of absolute ontological claim in so far as, in a rather fixed sense, there is no sense of differentiation between place, language and identity, it is as if 'native language were life itself'.

10 In dramatic terms alone Gaunt's is of course in every sense 'a strategic act of dying', certainly Shakespeare orchestrates a significant departure from the source here, so that, as Peter Ure reminds us, Gaunt's death is 'very simply noted by the chronicler': see Peter Ure, 'Introduction', in Peter Ure (ed.) *Richard II* (1956; repr. London: Arden, 1991), xxxiv. In remodelling the episode Shakespeare ensures that it now emerges as a pivotal scene in the play.

11 Jacques Derrida, *Aporias*, trans. T. Dutoit (Stanford: Stanford University Press, 1993), 8.

12 So that, as John Brannigan reminds us, 'death exists outside the borders of the nation' then it also constitutes the threshold space of and for future national determination: 'As the end of "people living" death marks the end of nation and thereby constitutes the space of the nation in its very otherness to that space . . . the nation *is*. It lives. And yet only becomes apparent at the border, when the difference against which the nation is constituted is waiting "on the other side" . . . Death is the other nation, what lies outside the border, "the undiscovr'd bourn" consciousness of "ourselves" as "people living" is made possible only by a certain movement or step at the border, a movement at the threshold.' See 'Writing DeTermiNation: Reading Death in(to) Irish National Identity', in J. Brannigan, R. Robbins and J. Wolfreys (eds) *Applying: To Derrida* (Basingstoke: Macmillan, 1996), 55–70, p. 56.

13 See *The Times*, 28 January 2002 'Building Site Grave Could Solve Mystery of Richard II'.

14 See Benedict Anderson, *Imagined Communities: Reflections on the Origin and Spread of Nationalism* (London: Verso, 1983), 9.

15 Cf. Derrida, *Monolingualism of the Other*, passim; and cf. Geoffrey Bennington, 'Double Tonguing: Derrida's Monolingualism', www.usc.edu/dept/comp-lit/tympanum/4/bennington.html, 5.

16 Walter Benjamin, 'Theses on the Philosophy of History', trans. H. Zohn, in *Illuminations*, ed. H. Arendt (London: Fontana, 1968), 245–55, p. 249.

17 Jacques Lacan, 'God and the *Jouissance* of the Woman', in Juliet Mitchell and Jacqueline Rose (eds) *Feminine Sexuality: Jacques Lacan and the École Freudienne* (New York: Norton, 1981), 137–48, p. 147 as cited in Homi Bhabha, 'Aura and Agora: On Negotiating Rapture and Speaking Between', in Richard Francis (ed.), *Negotiating Rapture: The Power of Art to Transform Lives* (Chicago: The University of Chicago Press, 1996), 8–17, p. 8.

18 See Bhabha, 'Aura and Agora' and see also Jacques Derrida, *Specters of Marx: The State of the Debt, the Work of Mourning and the New International*, trans. P. Kamuf (London: Routledge, 1994), 6 and Derrida, *The Gift of Death*, trans. D. Wills (Chicago: University of Chicago Press, 1995), 91.

19 See Philippe Lacoue-Labarthe, 'On the Sublime', in *ICA Documents 4: Postmodernism* (London: ICA, 1986), 11–18, p. 17.

20 See, for example, Francis Barker, *The Culture of Violence* (Manchester: Manchester University Press, 1993).

21 See Jay M. Bernstein, *The Fate of Art: Aesthetic Alienation from Kant to Derrida and Adorno* (Oxford: Polity Press, 1992), 175.

22 See Bernstein's 'Autonomy and Solitude', in Keith Ansell Pearson (ed.) *Nietzsche and Modern German Thought* (London: Routledge, 1993).

23 Cf. Ernst Kantorowicz, *The King's Two Bodies: A Study in Mediaeval Political Theology* (Princeton: Princeton University Press, 1957).

24 See Hugh Grady, 'On the Need for a Differentiated Theory of (Early) Modern Subjects', in John J. Joughin (ed.) *Philosophical Shakespeares* (London: Routledge, 2000), 34–50, p. 47; see also Hugh Grady, *Shakespeare, Machiavelli and Montaigne* (Oxford: Oxford University Press, 2002), esp. pp. 58–125.

25 See for example W. H. Clemen, *English Tragedy Before Shakespeare: The Development of Dramatic Speech* (London: Methuen, 1961), 253–86.

26 Cited in David Aers, 'A Whisper in the Ear of the Early Modernists; Or, Reflections on Literary Critics Writing the "History of the Subject" ', in David Aers (ed.) *Culture and History, 1350–1600: Essays on English Communities, Identities and Writings* (Detroit: Wayne State University Press, 1992), 177–202, p. 182; and cf. Charles Taylor, *Sources of the Self: The Making of the Modern Identity* (Cambridge: Cambridge University Press, 1989), 131.

27 Here as elsewhere Richard bears a striking resemblance to Walter Benjamin's description of the German *Trauerspiel* or mourning play, where again as George Steiner remarks: 'It is not the tragic hero who occupies the centre of the stage, but the Janus-faced composite of tyrant and martyr of the Sovereign who incarnates the mystery of absolute will and of its victim (so often himself)'. Steiner in his 'Introduction' to Walter Benjamin, *The Origin of German Tragic Drama*, trans. John Osborne (London: Verso, 1992), 16.

28 Cf. Adrian Kear and Deborah Steinberg (eds) *Mourning Diana: Nation, Culture and the Performance of Grief* (London: Routledge, 1999), 60 and passim.

History, mourning and memory in *Henry V*

The texts of *Henry V*

Is *Henry V* better understood as a 'memory play' than as a 'history play'? The former category has helped to define the concerns of modern (and postmodern) drama; it may prove equally fertile for Renaissance theatre.[1] Perceiving Shakespeare's play as 'memorial' would supplant some traditional and contemporary emphases in its interpretation. It would stress, for example, its interest in conflicting processes of remembrance rather than assuming that it presents a uniform vision of the past associated with the 'history play'. *Henry V* may well extol the potential of English or 'British' nationhood especially as it is inspired by charismatic kingship; an audience's enthralment at this spectacle is undoubtedly sustained by influential acts of memory. Principally, this involves the recollections of the king, but he is aided by other voices, especially that of the Chorus who provides awestruck testimony to the scale of his endeavours. But are these memories to be trusted? A range of characters reminisce in very different modes throughout *Henry V* and these often contradict the account of national posterity advanced by the monarch. In this respect, Shakespeare explores the relationship between memory and history: the play considers how rival traditions of memory are subsumed by a far-reaching, if still far from inclusive, conception of 'history'.

Yet, before considering whose memory we trust in the play it is important to establish which version of the text we trust. *Henry V* is often assumed to be a unified work completed and performed between January and June 1599. The Chorus preceding the final act contains the famous reference to the Earl of Essex's imminent return from his Irish campaign in September of that year and from this, and other evidence, a detailed understanding of the play and its context has been elaborated.[2] *Henry V* exists, however, in both a quarto and folio printing; these are radically different. One way of foregrounding their distinctiveness is to consider the different weight each grants to memory and this enriches understanding of their particular visions of history.[3]

Broadly, we can conceive of the quarto as a history play where the emphasis falls squarely on action and event, although this work possesses its own complex mode of representation. In the folio version, recollection is granted great scope and complexity; it becomes, in short, a 'memory play'. Furthermore, memory also takes on a sorrowful quality constituting, in significant part, the act of mourning. It is best understood, I will suggest, through Walter Benjamin's recovery of the Renaissance *Trauerspiel* or 'mourning play'. This aspect of the folio *Henry V* is also a pervasive feature of Shakespeare's other history plays and it is crucial to their presentation and evaluation of historical experience. In *The Life of Henry the Fift*, mourning questions the king's exposition of historical destiny; this is exposed as involving the distancing and destruction of the past. Such an analysis runs against the grain of more celebratory accounts of *Henry V* insomuch as these have obscured the tragic idea of history in the folio version.

Henry V was first printed as an anonymous quarto, *The Cronicle History of Henry the fift* (1600), a text republished two years later and then again in 1619 with minor amendments.[4] With the publication of the First Folio in 1623, *The Life of Henry the Fift* emerged, and this has long been familiar to modern readers, critics and playgoers as presenting Shakespeare's complete realisation of the work. It supersedes the quarto not least by being twice its length, including some of its most famous material: the opening ecclesiastical dialogue, the 'four captains' scene, Henry's inspirational incitement to return to the breach in the walls at Harfleur (and the bulk of his later more graphic threats against its populace), Burgundy's lament for France in the final scene and, most obviously, the prologue, choruses and epilogue. Memory has been seen as playing an important role in the production of these two texts. The allusion to Essex is included only in the folio, offering powerful testimony that this longer version existed in 1599. Consequently, the seemingly truncated condition of the quarto was attributed to flawed recollections on the part of those minor and 'disloyal actors' who roughly assembled this text without authorial sanction.[5]

Recent textual scholarship, however, has discredited this enduring understanding of the quarto's origins in faulty plebeian memories. An exhaustive recent study concludes, that far from being an unreliable reconstruction, *The Cronicle History* has a 'very good verbal texture'.[6] Indeed, the opposition between 'good' authorial texts and derivative 'bad' ones has been subjected to wide-ranging critique, and previously 'debased' versions of plays are now recognised as distinct and meaningful works in their own right.[7] The most forceful accounts of the *Henry V* quarto now interpret it as 'an authoritative players' text' (Gurr, *First Quarto*, 9). It presents valuable evidence of how the longer folio text was reshaped for performance in 1599 by the Lord Chamberlain's Men. In this light, the earlier quarto represents 'a *later* stage of the text' (Taylor, *Henry V*, 26) and there is no reason why Shakespeare would not have been involved in its construction.

Perceiving *The Cronicle History* as a later theatrical version of *Henry V* certainly grants it a new integrity. Yet understanding the relationship between the two texts is not straightforward and the process of composition that Shakespeare undertook has provoked continuing speculation. The apparent allusion to Essex has been queried as being equally (if not more) applicable to the Earl of Mountjoy, allowing for both an earlier and a later date of composition and intriguing questions have been raised as to whether the folio text includes revisions, perhaps for the revival that took place at court on 7 January 1605.[8] Nothing survives, after all, of the manuscript that existed 'behind' these printed texts nor can we be sure of its subsequent fate. Assessing the extent and rationale of the theatrical adaptation that took place in 1599 is not clear-cut when comparing the quarto with a version that appeared only more than two decades after its apparent successor and, furthermore, without any knowledge of what was actually performed. Even the seemingly 'authorial' folio text is a collaborative product of Heminge and Condell's decision (at least) to reinstate material which had undergone an unknowable degree of mediation in the intervening time.[9] According to Andrew Gurr, the 'four captains' scene, or at least the roles of Macmorris and Jamy, 'do seem to be late inserts in the manuscript which was used to print the First Folio text'; how late?[10] Further research may well renew attention to these questions.

Uncertainty about the priority and status of the quarto and folio suggests that both require significant attention and that their relationship needs to weigh more heavily in interpretative debate. As Andrew Murphy has observed, searching questions are asked of unity and reliability when these are construed as ideological issues in *Henry V*, but 'the text is not imagined as having a past of its own, as possessing any history which might in itself be subjected to historicist analysis, or which might yield evidence relevant to the critic's analytical project'.[11] Is this because of the play's stature as a 'history play', a formative contribution to national memory? For readings that have emphasised its assertive expression of imperial identity and for contemporary critiques of this, the stability of the text has been largely unquestioned. Yet if *Henry V* offers a divided textual legacy, its relationship to issues of national heritage becomes more difficult to classify. How the political as well as the formal differences between the two texts might best be discerned is my next subject.

The quarto text of *Henry V* has been perceived as more chauvinistic in temper than the folio, more humorous in tone and more episodic in construction. Annabel Patterson argues that the abbreviated text represents 'a tactical retreat from one kind of play to another, from a complex historiography that might have been misunderstood to a symbolic enactment of nationalistic fervor'.[12] Perhaps the strongest version of this argument appears in Lukas Erne's recent contention that Shakespeare's longer and more 'literary' versions of his plays were intended for the more educated taste of readers. In the case of *Henry V*, the folio was 'designed for a reception in which the intellect is much involved', consequently it 'puts up greater resistance to the reader's mind than the short, theatrical text'. The quarto appeals to jingoistic emotions and 'seems designed to work as a theatrical event that draws upon and activates collective English memories and passions' (Erne, *Shakespeare as Literary Dramatist*, 232; 233). The more distance Shakespeare achieved from his fellow actors, from the activity of performance and from his audience, the more artistically intrepid and the less ideologically partisan, it appears, he became.

Yet, is the text printed in 1600 so simplistic? Exploring this question fully would require more scope than this chapter allows, but some of the difficulties it presents can be noted. For example, the abrupt transitions in the quarto are amongst its most notable features and these are conducive to a wide range of theatrical interpretations and responses. The play's pace is rapid and scenes succeed each other in ways that result in sharp, even jarring contrasts. This involves the experience of interruption and collision that Walter Benjamin characterised as 'epic theatre' and that he admired in Shakespeare's work as well as Brecht's. The 'basic form', Benjamin argues, 'is that of the shock with which the individual, well-defined situations of a play collide'; this provokes astonishment and alarm at even the most familiar events and situations.[13] Much of the quarto version of *Henry V* is susceptible to performance in this manner, complicating a widespread understanding of it as a work dominated by comic episodes and romance motifs.[14] Consider this moment in the midst of Agincourt:

KING   I blame you not,
     For hearing you, I must convert to tears.

                                     Alarum sounds

     What new alarum is this? Bid every soldier kill his prisoner.
PISTOL   *Couple gorge!*

                                       Exit omnes

FLEWELLEN   God's plood! Kill the boys and the luggage!
                               (15.30–2; 16.1)[15]

This complex dramatic passage involves startling switches in tone, mood and perspective, and its intentions are not easily assessed. Henry's grief at the outset follows Exeter's long speech of chivalric apotheosis as he describes the deaths of Suffolk and York. Yet this mood is quashed in an instant by the 'alarum' that triggers his order to massacre the French prisoners. Does Pistol's '*Couple gorge!*' express shock at this decision, the bloodthirsty desire to participate in the slaughter or merely frustration at the imminent loss of his newly acquired French captive? It is only after this that Fluellen discovers that the French have killed the boys, a disturbing sequencing of events preserved in both texts. As Graham Holderness and Bryan Loughrey have argued in their edition of the quarto, Henry V is enmeshed in events without the exalted vision of the Chorus and he is to be judged on an equal rather than a mythic basis (Holderness and Loughrey, *The Cronicle History*, 23–8). The apparently 'popular' or 'theatrical' disposition of the quarto is not necessarily synonymous, therefore, with political simplification and whether it supports a 'collective' memory of events is open to question. According to Benjamin, the task of epic theatre was to reveal rather than reproduce conditions and the quarto is certainly capable of performance in accordance with this aim. However, one crucial disparity between the formal and thematic concerns of quarto and folio is evident: the forceful, even provocative, pace of the quarto allows little space for the representation of memory and the radical extension of this interest in the latter text is brought out strongly by comparison.

Two examples help to suggest the significance of this contrast: firstly, the treatments of Falstaff's illness and death and, secondly, the representation of the French. The former can be construed in both texts as an instance of what William E. Engel terms 'monitory' memory. This form of homiletic recollection reminds us of truths we often forget. Construed as a *memento mori*, Falstaff 'stands as a warning of the eventual presence of one's own death and dissolution' and this helps to regulate present and future conduct.[16] His imminent and then actual passing is unforgettable in both versions; its effect, however, upon the memory of the characters is not the same. In the quarto, the news of Falstaff's mortal illness has little impact upon his quarrelsome companions (2.51–73); in the folio, this has more gravity. In both texts, for example, the Hostess comments that Falstaff will 'yeeld the Crow a pudding,' but in the folio she adds 'the King has kild his heart' (TLN 587). Similarly, between the Hostess's concluding plea to remember Falstaff, that 'poore heart' ('soule' in the quarto) and Nym and Pistol's terse agreement to go and 'condole the Knight,' the following appears in the folio:

> NYM   The King hath run bad humors on the Knight, that's the even of it.
> PISTOL   *Nym*, thou hast spoke the right, his heart is fracted and corroborate.
> NYM   The King is a good King, but it must bee as it may: he passes some humors and carreeres.
> PISTOL   Let us condole the Knight, for (Lambekins) we will live.
>   (TLN 619–26)

One response to these additions would be to follow Annabel Patterson's suggestion and construe the folio version as retrieving detail that undermines a heroic version of events. A Brechtian performance of the quarto might stress, in contrast, that the refusal to be duly admonished possesses its own integrity given Falstaff's own highly selective memory as well as his exploitative behaviour in the past. What the folio introduces, however, is an insistently sorrowful quality to these recollections: Falstaff's condition provokes melancholy reflection upon the cruelty they have witnessed. Now the impulse to 'condole' the knight derives from a shared recollection of ruined hopes and the peremptory, unfeeling ways of power. This may also provoke the audience's recollection of Falstaff's compelling presence (as well as his ultimate rejection) in *1* and *2 Henry IV*. The potential for pathos in this form of recollection is then realised exquisitely in the Hostess's great speech of lament for Falstaff as she recounts his passing to '*Arthurs* Bosome', a passage that is expanded substantially in the folio (TLN 832–47).

This scene does not represent the only reckoning of mortality in *The Life of Henry the Fift*. As has been mentioned, the play also includes the rapturous account of York and Suffolk's sacrifice. We might compare this with the Archbishop of Canterbury's earlier and equally inspiring, recollection of how Henry's exalted ancestor, the Black Prince, 'play'd a Tragedie' of unforgettable power at Crécy (TLN 253). This appeal to selfless heroic example needs to be located, however, within the play's crosscurrents of memory. In the folio's French court we find a very different memory of this battle and this deepens understanding of its tragic dimensions. Again, to modern readers or theatregoers, this scene appears abbreviated in the quarto consisting of only 86 lines to the folio's 154, but the sequence of incident remains largely the same. But in one crucial respect the scene is altered. *The Life of Henry the Fift* includes an important dimension of historical memory; the French king's stricken recollection of Crécy:

> The Kindred of him hath beene flesht upon us:
> And he is bred out of that bloodie straine,
> That haunted us in our familiar Pathes:
> Witnesse our too much memorable shame,
> When Cressy Battell fatally was strucke,
> And all our Princes captiv'd, by the hand
> Of that black Name, *Edward*, black Prince of Wales:
> Whiles that his Mountaine Sire, on Mountaine standing
> Up in the Ayre, crown'd with the Golden Sunne,
> Saw his Heroicall Seed, and smil'd to see him
> Mangle the Worke of Nature, and deface

The Patternes, that by God and by French Fathers
Had twentie yeeres been made.

(TLN 940–52)

Does this speech demonstrate that the folio is more or less heroic in tone? Perhaps this speech intensifies, for an English audience, the radiant memory of national conquest. The French king perceives history, however, in an idiom of lament with which we are growing familiar: the past appears as fatality, that which visits catastrophe and vanquishes hope. Witnessing how a generation of life was destroyed in a moment of 'memorable shame' transforms the French king's awareness of the past and present. To have seen one's countrymen used as carrion to be 'flesh'd upon' whilst others grow in strength, accomplishment and reputation circumvents any temptation for hubris. Such considerations might well be immaterial on a London stage, but this strain of lament at nature despoiled and French lives squandered sounds again in the folio with Burgundy's mourning for the ruin of France after Agincourt (TLN 3010–54). As Edward Pechter has suggested, the rhetorical expansiveness of folio texts can also intensify, in important respects, their dramatic power and their political complexity; this can include their attentiveness to common or popular experience.[17] In *The Life of Henry the Fift*, memory is exercised most expansively when it is devoted to, in Fredric Jameson's formulation, 'what hurts'.[18] This has important repercussions not only for the understanding of the past presented by this play but also for the genre of historical drama.

The Life of Henry the Fift and the *Trauerspiel*

Shakespeare's history plays have long been understood as dramas which create an influential form of national myth and, more recently, as narratives which stage processes of exclusion and inclusion from this.[19] In this respect, the genre can be defined as a sustained example of 'monitory' memory commemorating past sacrifice and endeavour. One influential formulation of this approach can be found within the period, in Thomas Nashe's famous commendation of the spectacle of Talbot's death in *1 Henry VI*. Nashe argues that the history play bestows a more discerning awareness of exemplary action upon those who might otherwise fritter away their time (although Nashe acknowledges that not everyone is suitably inspired):

> How would it have joyd brave Talbot (the terror of the French) to thinke that after he had lyne two hundred yeare in his Tomb, he should triumph againe on the Stage and have his bones new embalmed with the teares of ten thousand spectators at least, (at severall times) who in the Tragedian that represents his person, imagine they behold him fresh bleeding.[20]

This vision of history appears to enlist the audience's sympathy for the virtues of martial nationalism and it privileges masculine aristocratic will as both self-less and heroic. What matters about the past and what needs to be restored to memory, is the significance of the lives (and deaths) of great men; such a reading has not proved so commendable to much contemporary criticism.[21]

Nashe evokes this experience in an intense, even disconcerting way, however, that discloses another aspect of its impact. Paradoxically, what is most affective (and most memorable) about this history play is that Talbot is raised from the dead only to die again; what seems most permanently affecting about his life is its transience. To witness history in this mode is to witness its tragic, rather than its triumphalist, dimension. Nashe stresses the corporeality of Talbot's death, his 'bones,' his 'bleeding' and the emotive impact of his passing culminates in the 'tears' of the spectators. These are compelled by the actor's personation of this figure: 'the Tragedian that represents his person'. At the centre of this history play is the suffering body rather than a simple, inspirational myth of past national grandeur. It could be added that Talbot's death also marks the destruction of a chivalric ethos as his noble memory is swept away by the faction and self-interest that courses through political life in *1 Henry VI*. For the audience, in contrast, the fate of Talbot can become a 'memory-place' where the nature of historical experience and the powers that shape it are exposed to critical understanding. Such a tragic understanding of the past is common in Shakespeare, its presence has already been glimpsed in *The Life of Henry the Fift* and it is often expressed through sorrowful memory, as figures such as Constance in *King John*, Richard II and Lady Percy in *2 Henry IV* demonstrate. Each of these characters is distinctive and open to multivalent understanding, but their presence, at least, allows us to note how often the historical action of these plays is arrested and then subjected to tragic reflection through acts of recollection and lament. Such a mode of understanding history derives, in part, from Shakespeare's indebtedness to the ethos and conventions of the *Trauerspiel*, one of the most significant dramatic traditions of early modern Europe.

In his formidable exegesis of *The Origin of the German Mourning Play* (*Ursprung des deutschen Trauerspiels*) (1928), Walter Benjamin argued that this mode was central to Renaissance tragic theatre and he identified Shakespeare as its supreme exponent.[22] Benjamin's recovery of the *Trauerspiel* provides us with several clues for interpreting the expanded role of memory in the folio *Henry V* and for reconsidering the genre of the history play. In particular, Benjamin illuminates the preoccupation with human frailty and mortality in the *Trauerspiel* and this pervades *The Life of Henry the Fift* through acts of recollection.

For Benjamin, the mourning play was a form of historical drama: 'the historical subject was particularly suited to the *Trauerspiel*,' although it was equally committed to a free handling of plot (Benjamin, *Origin*, 120). Furthermore, the boundary between such drama and historical life was a porous one: 'the word *Trauerspiel* was applied in the seventeenth century to dramas and to historical events alike' and its pattern 'could be directly grasped in the events of history itself; it was only a question of finding the right words' (Benjamin, *Origin*, 63). Benjamin elaborates the idea of the mourning play not as a prescriptive genre, therefore, but as a way of comprehending history within theatrical works where idioms of mourning and lament prevailed or possessed an unusual degree of force.

One specific aspect of Benjamin's analysis of *Trauerspiel* lies in the distinction between 'first' and 'second nature'. This has a crucial bearing on the vision of history disclosed within *The Life of Henry the Fift* and within other Shakespearean histories especially in terms of their treatment of memory. 'First nature', for Benjamin, denotes the material, sensual world 'including the human body, whose physical well-being was the proper concern of the materialist. This was the concrete, particular nature to which the course of history did violence.'[23] 'Second nature' denotes those social traditions and conventions that explain how the body is 'placed' in history, what resources it is allotted, what demands are made upon it and the ways in which these might be justified. Emphasising 'first nature' offers a way of assessing political actions and experiences in terms of their impact upon the body. One way of sustaining this, and here we arrive at the significance of the *Trauerspiel*, is to see the world under the aspect of historical becoming, to perceive it as open-ended. History could take many courses and offer the body many different fates, but in the *Trauerspiel* the world was compelled unjustly towards catastrophe and the genre demanded reflection upon this tragic outcome. Benjamin's interest in this aspect of the Renaissance mourning play gathered and intensified around its presentation of bodily suffering; this was incurred by the contingent and often violent process of being 'placed' in history, especially by the will of the prince. In this form of drama, witnessing the inequity and suffering endured by the body dispels the power of 'second nature'. Not even the most potent ideological justification or evasion could withstand the lamentable passage of history as revealed by the *Trauerspiel*, a perspective we can see at work in the presentation of Talbot's passing in *1 Henry VI*.

The mourning play presented history as a subject for lamentation. This was elicited by witnessing the physical suffering and broken illusions of those who found themselves trammelled up by the (illusory) progress of history, a movement forever marshalled in the interests of the few. The imperatives of the latter are exposed most fully in their disregarding of the body's testimony: 'the body is the physical witness to the happening of an event; the event lives on, visibly, through the bodies of those who have been affected by it'.[24] It was from this attentiveness to mortality that the neglected tradition of *Trauerspiel* derived its power. This mode of theatre insisted that historical aspirations and achievements are also viewed in terms of their costs. Equally, any attempt to develop a unifying tradition of remembrance is shattered in the mourning play by the melancholy recollection of loss, unfulfilled promises and the unappeased wants that follow in the wake of historical endeavour. The apparent pessimism of this vision also provides a crucial source of hope. Historical life is presented as truly open-ended within the *Trauerspiel* as it unmasks how the deficient state of the world is shaped by decisions that were (and were not) taken. Witnessing what happens is the subject for lament, but it does not represent the only possible outcome; memory is one powerful reminder of this. Recollection offers a way in which protagonists find the 'right words' to name their experience and, in so doing, they articulate values and experiences that contrast strongly with the way in which history is being determined.

Memory and mourning in *The Life of Henry the Fift*

Benjamin remarks that in the mourning play, 'Everything about history that, from the very beginning, has been untimely, sorrowful, unsuccessful, is expressed in a face – or rather in a death's head' (Benjamin, *Origin*, 166). It is one of the key characteristics of memory in *The Life of Henry the Fift* that it discloses this vision of history amidst Henry's difficult, but ultimately triumphal progress. This can be detected even in the Chorus, a rhetorical presence often deemed to provide the most enthusiastic advocacy of the king's enterprise. In the concluding Epilogue, for example, the Chorus draws upon another source of memory by recalling Shakespeare's previous historical drama as testimony to the ruin that awaits Henry V's endeavours. As Robert Weimann has suggested, Shakespeare can appeal to the audience's powers of recollection in especially sensitive ways at the conclusion to his dramas, authorising them 'to recollect, discuss and reappropriate the performed play after its theatrical transaction is over'.[25] Ironically, this devastating reminder may never have been heard in Shakespeare's theatre. Its presence in the folio is consistent, however, with the Chorus's habit of recollecting the paucity of the theatrical medium: 'The flat unraysed Spirits, that hath dar'd, / On this unworthy Scaffold, to bring forth / So great an Object' (TLN 10–12). The play's realisation of history will be successful only with the audience's active imaginative participation, just as Henry must inspire his followers with the faith that insurmountable odds can be overcome. It is unclear whether this reiterated disparagement of performance is intended to be ironic. For the Chorus to fulfil its claims the stage would need to attain identity with its object of historical representation. This would allow the king to 'Assume the Port of Mars' (TLN 7), the actors to become their characters and the theatre a kingdom. In contrast, the Chorus insists on the finitude of its aspirations and on the non-identity between the present means at its disposal and the irretrievable magnitude of past events. The play's ability to recreate the myth of Agincourt depends on actors securing a consistent response in the unpredictable present. Hence, the play will only 'disgrace' the memory of Agincourt with 'most vile and ragged foyles' engaged in 'brawle ridiculous' (TLN 1838; 1839; 1840). At its conclusion, the Chorus judges that the play has succeeded only in 'Mangling by starts the full course of their glory' (TLN 3371) and this heightens awareness of the remoteness of these events. The Chorus can never forget that its task also lies in 'remembring you 'tis past' (TLN 2893). The melancholy strain of recognition that runs throughout these speeches culminates in the perception that these are 'things, / Which cannot in their huge and proper life, / Be here presented' (TLN 2854–56).

The continuous recollection of physical limitations by the Chorus is typical of the way memory functions more broadly in the play. It discloses material that proves recalcitrant to an idealised response and this is grounded in the realist perspective associated with 'first nature'. The Chorus discloses that what is 'untimely, sorrowful, unsuccessful' will be of real concern to the play and this awareness is suffused with the tragic concept of time presented by the *Trauerspiel*. This stressed the fundamental non-identity between past and present. As Howard Caygill notes, the mourning play possessed a strong sense of the past as a burden whose objects, beliefs and values could only be diminished, travestied or destroyed as they were bequeathed.[26] The relationship to the past presented by the *Trauerspiel* presumed the incomplete nature of any attempt to retrieve its fullness and this provided further evidence of the limitations that attend current historical endeavour. Hence, the past testified to ruination as much as continuity: 'In order for the past to be handed over to the present,' Caygill suggests, 'it has to be destroyed, made into a different kind of object, one which is past' (Caygill, 'Benjamin, Heidegger', 18–19). Furthermore, what was remembered and restored as material for edification or admiration could take only a misshapen form as it reflected the enduring priorities of the powerful. The *Trauerspiel* offered a critical image of how tradition always betrays its object as the past is subjected to the same damaged motivations that distort human experience in the present. Hence, the Chorus's strenuous and ever-incomplete attempt to inspire and govern memory collides with the simultaneous recollection of ruinous enterprises and the indifference of time associated with the *Trauerspiel*.

With this understanding of the unpredictable and discomfiting power of remembrance in the folio version, we can return to the play's specific interest in the attempt to shape memory. This aspect of *The Life of Henry the Fift* is also in accord with the mourning play's concern with the sovereign as 'the representative of history', attempting to hold 'the course of history in his hand like a sceptre' (Benjamin, *Origin*, 65). In the king's inspirational appeal before Agincourt, Henry repossesses Crispin Crispian day as an enduring testimony to English audacity and heroic will shaped by his guidance. He offers to both the living and the dead the promise of futurity. Their sacrifice will ensure they are gathered up into the artifice of the eternal 'memory-nation', shaping their own best recollection of themselves and inspiring others:

> This story shall the good man teach his sonne:
> And *Crispine Crispian* shall ne're goe by,
> From this day to the ending of the World,
> But we in it shall be remembred

(TLN 2299–302)[27]

Here, storytelling is compelled to serve an orthodox sense of affiliation – 'dedicated to *one* hero, *one* odyssey, or *one* battle'[28] – that Benjamin saw as an important tendency in modern traditions of memory. In the folio *Henry V*, however, recollection is a wide-ranging process that tells a variety of stories. Many of these concern the fate of common bodies that are degraded rather than fulfilled by war. The Boy recognises that '*Bardolfe* and *Nym* had tenne times more valour' than Pistol, 'this roaring divell i' the olde play' (TLN 2449–50); Pistol, in turn, knows that '*Doll* is dead I' the Spittle of a malady of France', provoking his own melancholy moment of self-awareness: 'Old I do waxe, and from my wearie limbes honour is Cudgeld' (TLN 2976–7; 2978–9); the people of France are reduced, in Burgundy's astonishing account, to desolation and barbarism after Agincourt, growing 'like Savages, as Souldiers will, / That nothing doe, but meditate on Blood' (TLN 3046–7).[29] This emphasis on the cost of history threatens to be submerged by an increasingly prominent account of English (or 'British') national 'tradition' with the king at its apex and determining its form. These perceptions constitute, however, a rich counter-narrative of historical experience that insistently advance the claims of 'first nature'. The effect of this checks, for example, Fluellen's constant use of classical prescription as providing the only adequate touchstone for discernment. This is brought up sharply against his indifference to Bardolph's living body as Pistol appeals to save him from execution: 'let not Hempe his Wind-pipe suffocate' (TLN 1491). Fluellen can see Bardolph only as an opportunity for the exercise of 'monitory memory', a chance to correct Pistol's deficient understanding of Fortune. Yet, in a striking reversal, it is Fluellen who recalls Bardolph again in the vivid account he offers to the king of his death; this illuminates, in turn, the latter's selectivity of memory.[30] Fluellen asks 'if your Majestie know the man' (TLN 1549–50) and receives only the most abstract, moralising response. This is an instance of the 'intricate pattern of forgetting' that

Jonathan Baldo has identified as 'intimately connected to the exercise of power' in *Henry V* (Baldo, 'Wars of Memory', 149). As the king evacuates his memory, so he makes it the more serviceable for the uncluttered pursuit of dynastic as well as national endeavour. This establishes what Benjamin calls elsewhere 'homogenous, empty time',[31] a streamlining of the past demanded in the name of progress that spirits away traditional associations, customary memories and local traditions.

Yet as Baldo also notes, the folio *Henry V* is 'a minefield of counter-memories' (Baldo, 'Wars of Memory', 143). Again, even the loyal Fluellen provides further instances of how the king's promulgation of a unifying national memory gives way to reminders of those who have been affected by this enterprise. During Agincourt, Fluellen compares the king to another classical analogue, Alexander, who 'did in his Ales and his angers (looke you) kill his best friend *Clytus* . . . so also *Harry Monmouth* being in his right wittes, and his good judgements, turn'd away the fat Knight with the great belly doublet' (TLN 2561–3; 2569–72). Fluellen can recollect Falstaff's physical presence and the manner of his speech ('jests, and gypes, and knaveries, and mockes') but he has forgotten his name; Gower remembers this: 'Sir *John Falstaffe*' (TLN 2572–3; 2574). Fluellen distinguishes between Alexander's wilfulness and Henry's self-command, but both result in undeserved destruction. Henry's subjection of himself to the same process of reformation he demands from his kingdom is depicted as having ambivalent consequences.

This pattern of allusion, speech and memory culminates in Michael Williams's astonishing evocation of the victims of war which portrays the 'heavie Reckoning' the king will be subject to from a very different kind of memory, when

> all those Legges, and Armes, and Heads, chopt off in a Battaile, shall joyne together at the latter day, and cry all, Wee dyed at such a place, some swearing, some crying for a Surgean; some upon their Wives, left poore behind them; some upon the Debts they owe, some upon their Children rawly left
>
> (TLN 1983–9)

Here, the anticipated memory of Agincourt is couched in the idiom of lament not celebration. It includes the words and wounds of those who will suffer for it as victory or defeat; a very different vision to the king's stark, preclusive summary of those commoners who constitute the war-dead: 'None else of name' (TLN 2824).

Thirty years ago, Anne Barton read *Henry V* against the grain as embodying Shakespeare's tragic understanding of historical life.[32] This argument can now be extended in the context of comparing the quarto and folio versions of the play and in terms of the latter text's engagement with memory. Shakespeare was not simply writing against naive 'lesser' dramatists who were susceptible to the wish-fulfilment offered by romance, as Barton suggested, nor did he construe tragedy as deriving solely from the prince's struggle with the demands made by the two bodies of kingship. In his stricken soliloquy before Agincourt, Henry does disavow the empty 'prowd Dreame' of 'Ceremonie' and sees through the ritual, costume and iconography that present the king's authority as sacred and superhuman. This moment of discovery is not as levelling as it appears, however, as it serves also to distinguish Henry as possessed of truly sovereign insight through his exposure of ceremony: 'I am a King that find thee' (TLN 2019–134, 2109). In contrast to this, the tragic quality of historical life in the folio version derives also from those who endure the consequences of the king's will and who are forgotten or disparaged by him. Henry's guilt-stricken recollection of Richard II in this soliloquy is preceded by his contemptuous dismissal of the 'wretched Slave' who possesses only a 'vacant mind' and a 'grosse braine' (TLN 2118–19; 2132). Memory endows subjects with a more powerful capacity for reflection than this verdict allows in *The Life of Henry the Fift*, enabling them to evaluate in a fuller way the tragic consequences of dynastic dilemmas and aspirations.

As Benjamin Griffin notes, Shakespeare and Marlowe turned towards tragic form in their historical drama although other generic modes, principally romance, remained open to them.[33] Walter Benjamin's understanding of the *Trauerspiel* helps to illuminate the reasons for this. Recurrently in Shakespeare's historical drama and that of his contemporaries, time is experienced as desolate and this weighs heavily in understanding political life from the viewpoint of bodily suffering. Such a perspective is especially prominent in the process of recollection included within these works. If history plays are interpreted as 'memory plays', works that are interested in how the past is created and recreated dynamically from a variety of perspectives, their openness to a history that is tragically rather than providentially conceived becomes clear.

Notes

All citations to the quarto and folio versions of *Henry V* are to Andrew Gurr (ed.) *The First Quarto of King Henry V* (Cambridge: Cambridge University Press, 2000) and to *The Life of Henry the Fift* from Charlton Hinman's facsimile edition of *The First Folio of Shakespeare* (New York: Norton, 1968; reissued 1996). I have adopted Hinman's 'through line number' (TLN) for reference to this text and standardised contemporary uses of 'u' / 'v', 'i' / 'j' and long 's'. Gurr's edition of the quarto is modernised and this exacerbates the contrast with quotation from the folio; however, the other recent (and unmodernised) edition of the quarto, by Graham Holderness and Bryan Loughrey (noted below), does not include line numbers.

1 See, for example, Jeanette R. Malkin, *Memory-Theater and Postmodern Drama* (Ann Arbor: University of Michigan Press, 1999); Garrett A. Sullivan, *Memory and Forgetting in English Renaissance Drama* (Cambridge: Cambridge University Press, 2005). For an outstanding analysis of the significance of memory for Shakespeare's play see Jonathan Baldo, 'Wars of Memory in *Henry V*', *SQ*, 47 (1996), 132–59.

2 See, for example, Jonathan Dollimore and Alan Sinfield, 'History and Ideology: The Instance of *Henry V*', in John Drakakis (ed.) *Alternative Shakespeares* (London and New York: Methuen, 1985), 206–27; Joel B. Altman, ' "Vile Participation": The Amplification of Violence in the Theater of *Henry V*', *SQ*, 42 (1991), 1–32.

3 For a reading that compares the texts in terms of their differing treatment of gender see Carol Banks, 'Shakespeare's *Henry V*: Tudor or Jacobean?,' in Mike Pincombe (ed.) *The Anatomy of Tudor Literature: Proceedings of the First International Conference of the Tudor Symposium* (Aldershot: Ashgate, 2001), 174–88.

4 See Gurr (ed.) *The First Quarto of King Henry V*, 6–9.

5 A. R. Humphreys (ed.) *Henry V* (Harmondsworth: Penguin, 1968), 222.

6 Laurie E. Maguire, *Shakespearean Suspect Texts: The 'Bad' Quartos and Their Contexts* (Cambridge: Cambridge University Press, 1996), 257.

7 For a concise analysis of the scholarship involved in this enduring debate with reference to *Henry V* see Lukas Erne, *Shakespeare as Literary Dramatist* (Cambridge: Cambridge University Press, 2003), ch. 8.

8 See Warren D. Smith, 'The *Henry V* Choruses in the First Folio', *Journal of English and Germanic Philology*, 53 (1954), 38–57; G. P. Jones, ' "Henry V": The Chorus and the Audience,' *Shakespeare Survey*, 31 (1978), 93–104; Keith Brown, 'Historical Context and *Henry V*', *Cahiers Elisabéthains*, 29 (1986), 77–81.

9 Paul Werstine suggests that early modern play texts underwent adaptation and revision from multiple sources: 'Narratives About Printed Shakespeare Texts: "Foul Papers" and "Bad Quartos" ', *SQ*, 41 (1990), 65–86.

10 Andrew Gurr (ed.) *King Henry V* (Cambridge: Cambridge University Press, 1992), 4; Gurr provides a full textual analysis at 213–25.

11 Andrew Murphy, ' "Tish ill done": *Henry the Fift* and the Politics of Editing', in Mark Thornton Burnett and Ramona Wray (eds) *Shakespeare and Ireland: History, Politics, Culture* (Basingstoke: Macmillan, 1997), 213–34, p. 218.

12 Annabel Patterson, *Shakespeare and the Popular Voice* (Oxford: Basil Blackwell, 1989), 77. Similar judgements are made by Gurr, *First Quarto*, 9 and Gary Taylor, *Modernizing Shakespeare's Spelling* (by Stanley Wells) with *Three Studies in the Text of Henry V* (Oxford: Clarendon Press, 1979), 103n.

13 Walter Benjamin, 'What is the Epic Theater? (II)', trans. Harry Zohn, in *Walter Benjamin: Selected Writings, Volume 4: 1938–1940*, eds Howard Eiland and Michael W. Jennings (Cambridge, Mass. and London: Harvard University Press, 2003), 302–9, p. 306. For an insightful exposition of 'epic theatre' and Shakespeare see Peter Womack, '*Henry IV* and Epic Theatre,' in *Henry IV, Parts One and Two*, ed. Nigel Wood (Buckingham and Philadelphia: Open University Press, 1995), 126–61.

14 See, for example, Graham Holderness and Bryan Loughrey (eds) *The Cronicle History of Henry the Fift* (Hemel Hempstead: Harvester Wheatsheaf, 1993), 23–8.

15 I have not adopted Gurr's modernisation of the quarto's 'Flewellen' as 'Llewellyn'.

16 William E. Engel, *Mapping Mortality: The Persistence of Memory and Melancholy in Early Modern England* (Amherst: University of Massachusetts Press, 1995), 57.

17 Edward Pechter, 'What's Wrong with Literature?,' *Textual Practice*, 17 (2003), 505–26. Pechter's judgement that the quarto is a politically simplified or 'dumbed down' version of the folio is hasty: see 509–11, 517–18.

18 Fredric Jameson, *The Political Unconscious: Narrative as a Socially Symbolic Act* (London: Methuen, 1981), 102.

19 See, for example, Richard Helgerson, *Forms of Nationhood: The Elizabethan Writing of England* (Chicago: University of Chicago Press, 1992), ch. 5.

20 Thomas Nashe, *Pierce Pennilesse his supplication to the Divell* (1592; repr. Menston: Scolar Press, 1969), 26r.

21 See, for example, Jean E. Howard and Phyllis Rackin, *Engendering a Nation: A Feminist Account of Shakespeare's English Histories* (London: Routledge, 1997).

22 'Calderón and Shakespeare created more important *Trauerspiele* than the German writers of the seventeenth century', Walter Benjamin, *The Origin of German Tragic Drama* (1928), trans. John Osborne (1998; repr. London and New York: Verso, 2003), 127.

23 Susan Buck-Morss, *The Origin of Negative Dialectics: Theodor W. Adorno, Walter Benjamin and the Frankfurt Institute* (Hassocks: The Harvester Press, 1977), 55.

24 Angelika Rauch, 'The Broken Vessel of Tradition', *Representations*, 53 (1996), 74–96, p. 76.

25 Robert Weimann, 'Thresholds to Memory and Commodity in Shakespeare's Endings', *Representations*, 53 (1996), 1–20, p. 1.

26 Howard Caygill, 'Benjamin, Heidegger and the Destruction of Tradition', in Andrew Benjamin and Peter Osborne (eds) *Walter Benjamin's Philosophy: Destruction and Experience* (1994; 2nd edition, Manchester: Clinamen Press, 2000), 1–30, esp. pp. 12–21.

27 This speech is included in the quarto, although its 'memorial' aspect is less expansive; see 12.23–48.

28 'The Storyteller: Observations on the Work of Nikolai Leskov', trans. Harry Zohn, in *Walter Benjamin: Selected Writings, Volume 3: 1935–1938*, eds Howard Eiland and Michael W. Jennings (Cambridge, Mass. and London: Harvard University Press, 2002), 143–66, p. 154.

29 The speeches by the Boy and Burgundy do not appear in the quarto. In the latter text, Doll is only 'sick' according to Pistol and no mention is made of the 'Spittle' or his own age and exhaustion; see 19.35–43.

30 Initially, Bardolph's execution is anticipated by both speakers, but upon the king's entrance it has occurred: 'his nose is executed and his fire's out' (TLN 1553–4). These exchanges are virtually identical in the quarto; see 9.15–81.

31 Walter Benjamin, 'On the Concept of History', trans. Harry Zohn, in *Walter Benjamin: Selected Writings, Volume 4*, 389–400, p. 395.

32 Anne Barton, 'The King Disguised: Shakespeare's *Henry V* and the Comical History', in Joseph G. Price (ed.) *The Triple Bond: Essays in Honour of Arthur Colby Sprague* (Pennsylvania: Pennsylvania State University Press, 1975), 92–117.
33 Benjamin Griffin, *Playing the Past: Approaches to English Historical Drama, 1385–1600* (Woodbridge: D. S. Brewer, 2001), ch. 5.

There is a history in all men's lives: reinventing history in 2 *Henry IV*

In recent years we have become accustomed to the idea that the fictional arts of narrative are an integral component of historiography.[1] However, it should not be forgotten that the initial heretical force of this proposition lay in its overturning of a long tradition of antipathy between these two 'arts'. Generations of historians have felt compelled to protect the purity of their discipline by defining this in opposition to poetry or, more generally, to the imaginative recasting of facts. Commenting on the antiquity of this 'internecine strife between history and storytelling', Michel de Certeau notes that the historian at once 'delimits his proper territory' and asserts his privileged relationship to the 'real' by distancing himself from 'genealogical storytelling, the myths and legends of the collective memory and the meanderings of the oral tradition'.[2] A version of this age-old struggle, I shall argue, is enacted in 2 *Henry IV*. For most of the play's duration the 'high' political history, centred on issues of dynastic succession, affairs of State and military conflict, that had formed the staple of the Tudor chronicles and of Shakespeare's previous English history plays is displaced by the meanderings of the oral tradition in which the past is typically reconstituted in anecdotal form through the informal medium of rumour, hearsay, gossip and personal reminiscence. It is only following Hal's accession to the throne in Act 5 that these unauthorised constructions of the past are once more consigned to the disreputable underbelly of 'official' history. More is at stake here, I would suggest, than a nostalgic wish to recover and commemorate a popular tradition of storytelling that was already in decline when the play was written. By tapping into alternative sources of historical memory within folk culture, 2 *Henry IV* could be seen as participating in an enquiry into dynastic historiography and its adequacy. Hence we might speculate that Shakespeare placed these competing models in contention with one another precisely in order to pose the question of what constitutes 'history'.

Rumour's many tongues

The play's indebtedness to popular tradition is flagged at the very outset by
Rumour's delivery of the Induction.[3] Although his role as the play's tutelary
spirit has been widely discussed, its significance may still bear reassessment.
Entering in his costume 'painted full of tongues', Rumour launches into
twenty-two lines of consciously redundant self-description since the audience's familiarity with his identity and 'office' is archly assumed:

> Open your ears; for which of you will stop
> The vent of hearing when loud Rumour speaks?
> I from the orient to the drooping west,
> Making the wind my post-horse, still unfold
> The acts commencèd on this ball of earth.
> Upon my tongues continual slanders ride,
> The which in every language I pronounce,
> Stuffing the ears of men with false reports.

$$(1.0.1–8)$$

History is implicitly redefined in this speech as carried in oral narrative (it is
Rumour who 'unfold[s] / The acts commencèd on this ball of earth'), as het-
eroglossic (full of 'tongues' speaking 'in every language'), radically unstable
and not to be trusted. Rumour's self-anatomising pointedly evokes the more
negative features of his classical prototypes, recalling both the fleetness and
monstrosity of Virgil's Fama (variously translatable as rumour, fame, public
opinion and idle talk) with her multiple ever-vigilant eyes and ears and
voluble tongues, as she flies over the earth disseminating scandalous stories.
Similarly, Rumour's malicious delight in stirring up fears or allaying them
with 'smooth comforts false' (40) plays upon the same hypostatised psychological traits – 'Credulity', 'hot-headed Error', 'groundless Joy', 'craven
Fears' and 'Seditions newly born' – that inhabit Ovid's House of Fame (or
Rumour).[4] Overlaying these classical allusions is another familiar, if more
contemporary, construction of rumour's *modus operandi*. When its
Shakespearean embodiment likens himself to an instrument through which
the fickle opinions of 'the blunt monster with uncounted heads, / The still-
discordant wav'ring multitude' (18–19) are broadcast, thereby aligning the
grotesqueness of his own multilingual existence with that of the common
sort, he panders to the early modern belief that rumours originated in, or
were fanned by, the credulity of the vulgar multitude. The authorities, in particular, took the view that the innate gullibility, ignorance and volatility of the
lower orders made them peculiarly susceptible to 'false report', more likely
to 'noise abroad' slanderous tales about their political masters and to use such
stories to whip up social discontent. 'How redy vulgare peple ar to be abused
by such and ar disposed to dispearse sedycyous rumors therby to procure

trobles and mocons', complained Elizabeth I in a letter written to the Earl of Shrewsbury in 1565.[5] This prejudice had material consequences. As Adam Fox has shown, those below the rank of gentry were disproportionately liable to be prosecuted under the statutes instituted by successive Tudor and Stuart administrations in an attempt to clamp down on any instance of idle or defamatory talk deemed to undermine the stability of the regime.[6] Government officials were equally nervous of the popular appetite for prognostication; although seditious prophecies circulated freely through every level of early modern society, it was their capacity to trigger plebeian uprisings that generated most anxiety.[7] Following Rumour's example, the political elite of 2 *Henry IV* are only too willing to exploit these fears, as is shown by the Archbishop of York's transparently self-serving attempt to displace responsibility for the latest outbreak of political unrest on to the 'giddy' loyalties and engorged appetites of the 'fond many' (1.3.87–100).

The play's critics have tended to accept at face value the concatenation of paranoid images of rumour deployed in the Induction, seeing this as setting the register for 2 *Henry IV*'s dystopian vision of political instability and moral decay flowing from Bolingbroke's act of regicide.[8] Much is made in these readings of Falstaff's jocular reference to having 'a whole school of tongues in this belly of mine' (4.2.16–20), which identifies his propensity for libellous gossip, for self-misrepresentation and, by extension, for riotous behaviour with the standard iconography of rumour. This has been taken as conclusive proof of the play's endorsement of the presumptive link between false reporting and lawlessness. However, in focusing on Falstaff's role as Rumour's surrogate, we risk overlooking the play's larger affiliations with oral history, of which the renegade knight, despite his multiple associations with popular culture (owing to his indulgence in festive misrule, irreverent wit, love of ballads and tall tales), is by no means the sole nor necessarily the most important representative. We also collude with Hal in placing a negative symbolic burden on Falstaff that is scarcely warranted by his defamatory remarks about the royal family or his self-aggrandising lies at Shrewsbury and Gaultres, which are presented as being more of an irritant than a genuine threat to the Lancastrian regime.

This is but one of the various ways in which stereotypical representations of rumour are subtly qualified even as they are paraded in the play's Induction and opening scenes. Take its social provenance. In the first scene Northumberland and his well-born political associates are shown to be every bit as avid for the latest 'news' from the battlefield and quite as liable to be taken in by the flow of disinformation, as the imagined occupants of the 'peasant towns' through which Rumour has 'noise[d]' his 'false reports'. This reflects ironically on Lord Bardolph's attempt to authenticate his (as it transpires) apocryphal report of Hotspur's victory at Shrewsbury by citing 'a gentleman well bred and of good name' as its source and his concomitant assumption that the true account relayed by Northumberland's servant must have been gleaned from 'some hilding fellow' who 'spoke at a venture'. The King's political vulnerability also makes him over-receptive to rumours about the opposing forces which 'doth double, like the voice and echo, / The numbers of the feared' (3.1.92–3). Indeed he is as quick to fasten upon popular gossip about Hal's wild behaviour as Northumberland is to credit the 'bruited' news of his son's death before it has been confirmed. Both these lords are also inclined to indulge in mystifying prophecies of the 'rotten times' to come, finding a perverse satisfaction in projecting the future in 'forms imaginary' that are luridly apocalyptic (1.1.150–60; 4.3.54–66, 241–65). And while we hear talk of plebeian 'old folk' finding ill omens in aberrant natural phenomena (4.3.121–8), what we actually witness onstage is the king's twin fixations with Richard II's prediction regarding Northumberland's treachery, superstitiously treated by him as a fated 'necessity', and with the prophecy that he 'should not die but in Jerusalem' (4.3.363–8), both of which he vainly misconstrues.

While the play does not dispute the perceived connections between rumour-mongering, war and political instability, it rapidly becomes apparent that it is interested as much in the psychological conditions that foster receptivity to 'false report' as in the political effects they enable. If characters from across the social spectrum succumb to the lure of rumour and prophecy, this would seem to be largely attributable to the way such fictions resonate with their deepest wishes, expectations and forebodings. Presented with conflicting news bulletins from the battlefield, Northumberland is careful to enquire after sources (1.1.23–4), but the reason why he intuitively credits Morton's 'tragic' tale even before it is uttered is not because it is based on an eye-witness account rather than hearsay, but that it 'seals up' his guilty expectation regarding the son whom he abandoned to his fate. A nagging sense of guilt and fear of retribution for his part in the deposition and murder of Richard II also feeds Bolingbroke's irrational conviction that the realm will be plunged into 'headstrong riot' after his death. Similarly, Falstaff's hubristic prophesying of 'pleasant days' to come under the new king stems from his refusal to admit that any intimacy they once enjoyed has long since cooled. What makes these imaginative projections of past and future so irresistible, we might infer, is their capacity to speak to the repressed thoughts and feelings their authors or recipients dare not acknowledge even to themselves. Evidence that the pathology which breeds such fictions cuts across normal hierarchical divisions lends retrospective weight to Rumour's opening rhetorical question which provocatively interpellates the audience as *his* punters: 'Open your ears; for which of you will stop / The vent of hearing when loud Rumour speaks?' Here and again when Rumour ironically presupposes that there is no need 'my well-known body to anatomise / Among my household' (ll. 20–2), we are being challenged to recognise ourselves, 'high' and 'low', players and spectators alike, as members of his disreputable entourage. With its implicit demand that we see the predisposition to invent or credit fantastic stories not as being solely the function of a stigmatised, inferior 'other' but as an integral aspect of our own particular histories, the Induction initiates a sustained reappraisal of the status of rumour and its relation to recorded history.[9]

Modern commentators generally regard rumour and other cognate expressions of the popular historical imagination as an elusive, transient and marginalised body of social testimony that forms a shadowy counterpart to the authority of written historical records. Rumour, it would seem, is destined always to inhabit 'a historical "side-room" of the great events about which [it] speak[s]' since it 'evades the clutches of traditional history'.[10] But in 2 *Henry IV* traditional history is conspicuously absent. Most of the political and military incidents given so much prominence by the sixteenth-century chroniclers in their accounts of Bolingbroke's troubled reign are either omitted or pushed to the periphery of the play: Glyndwr's marauding along the Welsh borders, the constant harassment of England's territorial possessions in France and the suppression of Northumberland's uprising at Bramham Moor in 1408 along with numerous other conspiracies. It is hard to escape the inference that Shakespeare deliberately emptied out the final decade of Bolingbroke's rule, which was in actuality no less eventful than his previous four years in office (covered in *Part One*), in order to create the effect of a political hiatus as the march of history is temporarily suspended while the ailing king's subjects await the demise of the old order. One way to interpret Rumour's supplanting of Bolingbroke (whose disquisition on the evils of civil conflict opens *Part One*) as the symbolic source and focus of historical report would be to read this as commenting on the tendency for idle talk to thrive in times of political uncertainty. Holinshed notes in passing the steady drip of rumour (usually claiming that Richard II was alive and poised to reclaim the throne), 'vaine prophesie' and other 'forged inventions' that added to Bolingbroke's woes.[11] Expanded from these brief references, the play's recreation of an atrophied, rumour-ridden regime is likely to have had strong topical resonance for the play's original audiences who had experienced the climate of gossip and feverish speculation that attended Elizabeth's last years. Given the play's interest in unsettling definitions of history, though, we might also see Rumour's 'usurpation' as giving notice of the dramatist's wish to try his hand at writing a different type of historical drama. Sidelining political events allows various types of fictionalised narrative about the past that flourished within popular culture but were generally deemed too inconsequential to merit inclusion within the narrower

purview of dynastic historiography to be brought centre stage. The evacu-
ated space of Bolingbroke's reign is thereby transformed into a vast echo-
chamber resembling Ovid's House of Fame whose 'whole structure [was] of
echoing brass ... repeating noises and giving back the sounds it hears'. From
within this resonating structure a cacophonous plethora of voices spanning
the full social and geographical range of fifteenth-century English life and
each striving to narrate its own version of the past, compete to be heard.

Remembering 'the times deceased'

The world of 2 *Henry IV* is dominated by the senior generation. Figures
'blasted with antiquity' – Falstaff, Bolingbroke, Northumberland, the Lord
Chief Justice, Mistress Quickly, Justices Shallow and Silence – monopolise
the scene, while youth, in the person of Hal especially, is forced to bide its
time. This generational imbalance in favour of the older characters offers
important clues not only to the forces that drive the play's incessant retrospection but to the nature of its relationship with oral history. Although 'in
early modern England the prevailing ideal was gerontocratic', Keith Thomas
argues that in practice men and women tended to lose much of their status
with advancing years. Aged citizens were frequently satirised in the literature of the period on account of their acquisitiveness, peevish manners, gar-
rulity and tedious preoccupation with the good old days of their youth.[12] To
some extent 2 *Henry IV* participates in this tradition of unflattering depictions of the elderly. At every opportunity the audience is reminded of the
many evils attendant on becoming old, including senility, physical decrepitude and diminishing 'wit' (cf. 1.2.169–80). Falstaff, who comically enrols
himself in 'the vanguard of . . . youth', is particularly eloquent on the shortcomings of old age which he equates with covetousness, disease and lying
(1.2.222–7; 3.2.276–80). On the other hand, in a society where, notwith-
standing the rapid advance of literacy, it remained the case that 'the principal means by which the people received their knowledge about the past . . .
was by word of mouth' rather than via the written or printed word, the
proverbial fondness for reminiscence ascribed to old men like Shallow
bestowed on them a vital role in the transmission of history and, with this,
a compensatory authority within the community.[13] For, as Thomas points
out, 'in a semi-literate society, still much dependent on oral tradition, it was
the old who controlled access to the past. They were the repositories of
history and custom, of pedigree and descent.'[14] It was their acknowledged
status as the 'custodians of communal memory' that made the ancient inhab-
itants of rural and, to a lesser degree, civic communities such an invaluable
resource for the burgeoning antiquarian movement of the late sixteenth and
seventeenth centuries. When scouring the land for vestiges of England's

Roman and medieval past, this new breed of cultural historians frequently mined the personal recollections of the common folk, especially old men and women, as the best, and in many cases the only, available source of information about historical traditions, customs and anecdotes pertaining to the locality. The distinguished antiquary John Aubrey recalled that 'when a Boy, he did ever love to converse with old men, as Living Histories' and he would continue to rely heavily upon the oral testimony of ancient informants, many of whom were passing on knowledge acquired by word of mouth from previous generations.[15]

Popular versions of history purveyed by the common folk diverged from historiographical conventions in various ways. Adam Fox notes that many of the tales spun about the past that circulated within the oral tradition 'were too narrow in interest, or too local in scope, to make the recording of them either necessary or desirable . . . It was events which were significant to the community that were remembered, while historical incidents or individuals of national renown tended to be conceived of within a familiar setting.'[16] Matters of national importance were thus transformed in the process of being refracted through the lens of local concerns. Little care was taken to discriminate between historical and legendary figures; both were liable to be jumbled up in the popular imagination with home-grown heroes and their exploits identified with particular neighbourhood landmarks.[17] As is typical of cultures with a strong oral tradition, these popular, localised histories were generally characterised by an absence of fixed temporal markers or definite sense of chronology as well as a tendency to compress or omit entire sections of the past. Nor were those who relayed such tales as preoccupied with factual accuracy as the official chroniclers of the period. On the contrary, the memories from which oral history was woven were usually high selective in what they retained or discarded from the past; they embodied an idiosyncratic perspective on bygone ages that rarely coincided with establishment views and that tended to become further distorted and embellished in the process of oral transmission.[18] In this sense, popular historical narratives were never bound by the same protocols as their written or printed counterparts.

The 'old folk' of *2 Henry IV* also assume the mantle of unofficial historians in their accepted capacity as 'time's doting chronicles' (4.3.126). With political events shunted to the margins of the play, individual acts of remembrance or, more specifically, the stories which the older generation tell themselves and others about their past lives become the principal source from which history is generated. In consequence the types of oral reportage deployed in the play's opening scenes are subtly modified. Repetition, identified by Ovid as the underlying dynamic of rumour's 'voice and echo', becomes internalised as the private reminiscence of characters who experience an inner compulsion to engage in a continual rehearsal or imaginative revisiting of the past. In Act 3 Scene 2, we are introduced to the provincial Justice of the Peace, Shallow, on his Gloucestershire estate as he is about to launch himself into a rambling monologue regarding his youthful adventures at the Inns of Court:

> SHALLOW A must then to the Inns o' Court shortly. I was once of Clement's
>   Inn, where I think they will talk of mad Shallow yet.
> SILENCE You were called 'lusty Shallow' then, cousin.
> SHALLOW By the mass, I was called anything; and I would have done any-
>   thing indeed, too and roundly, too. There was I and little John Doit of
>   Staffordshire and black George Barnes and Francis Pickbone and Will
>   Squeal, a Cotswold man; you had not four such swinge-bucklers in all
>   the Inns o' Court again. And I may say to you, we knew where the bona-
>   robas were and had the best of them all at commandment. Then was
>   Jack Falstaff, now Sir John, a boy and page to Thomas Mowbray, Duke
>   of Norfolk.
> SILENCE This Sir John, cousin, that comes hither anon about soldiers?
> SHALLOW The same Sir John, the very same. I see him break Scoggin's head
>   at the court gate when a was a crack, not thus high. And the very same
>   day did I fight with one Samson Stockfish, a fruiterer, behind Gray's Inn.
>   Jesu, Jesu, the mad days that I have spent! And to see how many of my
>   old acquaintance are dead.
> SILENCE We shall all follow, cousin.
> SHALLOW Certain, 'tis certain; very sure, very sure. Death as the Psalmist
>   saith, is certain to all; all shall die. How a good yoke of bullocks at
>   Stamford fair?
>
>   (3.2.11–35)

Despite his position as a minor officer of the Crown, Shallow's discourse locates his mental world at a distant remove, both socially and geographically, from the centres of power. Yet his recollections of his misspent youth recognisably qualify as 'history' in its root sense, still current in this period, of a 'narrative of past events, account, tale, story' (*OED*). Moreover, these memories are given an anecdotal interest and a vivid particularity that, together with Shallow's vagrant mode of narration, hold their own compelling power for the play's audiences and readers.

Probing the source of their appeal a little further we find that it stems precisely from those qualities in Shallow's discourse that align it most closely with the oral tradition. The almost hallucinogenic immediacy with which the past is resuscitated in Shallow's speeches may be partly explained by the extremely localised nature of his recollections which, in a play riddled with such precise topographical allusions, attach themselves to specific sites in and around London: Clement's Inn, Gray's Inn, the windmill in Saint George's Field, Mile-End Green, Turnbull Street, the tiltyard at Whitehall.

Even Shallow's 'old acquaintance' are identified by their place of origin or familiar haunts. The strong probability that Shakespeare was familiar with many of the places in London and the Cotswolds mentioned in the play reinforces the sense of local, concrete knowledge with which these citations are imbued. Cumulatively, these local topographical references construct a map of the realm that is in many ways at variance with the largely symbolic political geography of seats of baronial power, battlefields and territorial conquest that overlays them in the play. But the immediacy of Shallow's memories is also a product of his belief in the immanence of the past which maintains itself as a living presence in his mind. Throughout this scene he struggles to comprehend the passage of time that has resulted in the death or decrepitude of his contemporaries. His telling insistence that the Falstaff he is about to meet after an interval of more than half a century is 'the same Sir John, the very same' whom he recalls breaking Scoggin's head while still a boy reflects the sense in which past and present exist for him only as parts of a single unbroken continuum. (Compare this with the way he speaks of Jane Nightwork as though she were still the feisty prostitute he once lusted after until forcibly reminded of her age (3.2.183–94).) Mortality may be much in his thoughts, but this arguably attests more to his reluctance to accept the inevitability of its onset and his sententious disposition than to any real grasp of chronological time. Shallow's difficulty in distinguishing past from present is paralleled by other categorical confusions that violate traditional principles of historical decorum. As his thoughts shuttle back and forth between the madcap days of his youth and present demands on his attention, nostalgic reverie is jarringly brought up against mundane practicalities: 'How a good yoke of bullocks at Stamford fair?' Important historical figures from the ranks of the English aristocracy, like Thomas Mowbray and John of Gaunt who in their previous Shakespearean incarnations had been leading players in Richard II's downfall also reappear here in a new, strangely domesticated guise, imaginatively transplanted to a milieu where they are forced to rub shoulders with such vulgar local personalities as Samson Stockfish and Francis Pickbone.

Perpetuating oral customs and traditions was not solely a male prerogative; 'ancient beldams' also played a pivotal role in this process owing to their legendary skills as storytellers. Whether they were regaling youngsters with tales of the supernatural, narrating romantic fables from England's past, or simply gossiping about goings-on in the community, old women were famed for their capacity to spin out a potentially interminable thread of discourse. Patricia Parker has argued that the production of copious, expansive and dilatory narratives that defer closure, traditionally encoded as a feminine art, achieves its ultimate figuration in Falstaff's 'great belly' and the 'throng of words' that issues from him in the *Henry IV* plays.[19] Another and perhaps more likely candidate for this emblematic role is thus passed over. Mistress Quickly's apparently unstaunchable loquacity and relish for disseminating stories about her neighbours as well as for divulging her own history already endow her in this play with the classic lineaments of the gossip that were more fully fleshed out in *Merry Wives of Windsor*.[20] In the midst of petitioning the Lord Chief Justice to support her 'action' against Falstaff, Quickly is unexpectedly diverted into reminiscing about the occasion when the latter allegedly made her a marriage proposal:

> Thou didst swear to me upon a parcel-gilt goblet, sitting in my Dolphin chamber, at the round table, by a sea-coal fire, upon Wednesday in Wheeson week, when the Prince broke thy head for liking his father to a singing-man of Windsor – thou didst swear to me then, as I was washing thy wound, to marry me and make me my lady thy wife. Canst thou deny it? Did not goodwife Keech the butcher's wife come in then and call me 'Gossip Quickly' – coming in to borrow a mess of vinegar, telling us she had a good dish of prawns, whereby thou didst desire to eat some, whereby I told thee they were ill for a green wound? And didst thou not, when she was gone downstairs, desire me to be no more so familiarity with such poor people, saying that ere long they should call me 'madam'? And didst thou not kiss me and bid me fetch thee thirty shillings? I put thee now to thy book-oath; deny it if thou canst.
>
> (2.1.79–94)

The Hostess's tale shares with Shallow's monologue some striking linguistic features known to be characteristic of oral storytelling: its reiteration and redundancy, its digressive narrative structures that shape themselves around the speaker's anecdotal view of the past and a paratactic syntax that strings together simple clauses to produce an unsophisticated additive effect.[21] The degree to which Quickly's memories are genetically dependent on a specific location (the Dolphin chamber and all its paraphernalia) also concurs with Shallow's topographical sense of the past, just as the very intensity of her powers of recall serves, much like his, to blot out ironic discrepancies between the semi-mythologised past of her imagination and present realities.

For modern audiences, however, the real interest of this old wives' tale is likely to arise from the intriguing glimpse it seems to offer into the everyday existence of common folk in the fifteenth (or, more accurately perhaps, late sixteenth) century. This 'reality-effect' is generated chiefly by the astonishing elasticity of the syntactical forms used by Quickly which contrive, by heaping up prepositional phrases and adverbial clauses, to accommodate more and yet more, superfluous circumstantial detail of the most mundane sort until life, in all its random contingency and material density, appears to be caught in their grasp. What might be construed as an irrelevant detour from the linear syntax of political history, a copious digression that postpones its inexorable movement towards the glorious accession of Henry V, thus reveals itself, from a different standpoint, as a door opening briefly on to areas of social history that were largely occluded by the state-centred focus of most Tudor historiography but that we have since come to value.[22] Importantly, women as much as men held the key to this largely forgotten, because rarely recorded, world of popular culture, a fact appreciated by anti-quarian researchers. This was in pointed contrast to the status accorded them by the written historical tradition where, as Phyllis Rackin has argued, women were either marginalised in ways that prevented them from 'tell[ing] their own story' or were 'defined as opponents and subverters of the . . . his-toriographic enterprise, in short as anti-historians'.[23]

Pierre Nora's suggestive analysis of the different modes of thought that have shaped modern historical consciousness and what he calls 'memory-history' offers a useful schema that may enable us to bring into sharper focus the competing models of 'history' at issue in 2 *Henry IV*.[24] Nora argues that the encroachment of a self-critical historiography has led to the erasure of folk traditions long preserved in the collective memory, the shrunken rem-nants of which are now entrusted to *lieux de mémoire* (memory sites). Communal traditions have been displaced by a historical sensibility that, in its commitment to ideas of change and progress, sustains a quite different relationship to the past, one typified by a sense of rupture and alienation rather than retrospective continuity. Whereas our modern society perceives itself as divided from bygone ages by an unbridgeable gulf, 'memory-history' is predicated on the assumption that the community's ancestral past is always retrievable. Hence the customary rituals of popular culture were designed to arrest the passage of time through their daily resuscitation of the past in involuntary, unselfconscious acts of remembrance. Indeed the factor that essentially distinguishes 'living memory' from 'history', for Nora, is its refusal to acknowledge the *pastness* of a past that is experienced as a 'per-petually actual phenomenon' – that is to say, the total absence of that sense of anachronism whose 'discovery' in the fifteenth century is generally believed to mark the inception of modern historiography. The spontaneous reminiscence of Shallow and Quickly exhibits precisely this desire to halt time's advance, to deny temporality itself, through their compulsive repeti-tion of the past. In fact, we shall find that the same pattern of recurrence shapes the play's conception of 'memory-history' at every level, from the rhetorical trope of *epizeuxis* (the reiteration of words with no intervening space) that punctuates the discourse of these two garrulous narrators down to its larger dramaturgical structures.[25]

Rooted in material realities and practices, in 'spaces, gestures, images and objects', 'memory-history' is distinguished by its relationship to place as well as time. Nora asserts that 'it is the exclusion of the event that defines *lieux de mémoire*. Memory attaches itself to sites whereas history attaches itself to events'. The precedence granted to specific locations, and the memories inextricably tied up with them, over events in 2 *Henry IV* would certainly seem to bear this out. That places are capable of being amplified into *lieux de mémoire* is evidenced not only by the context-bound recollections of particular characters but by the way these memories provide a point of entry into and hence a means of recovering, a whole cultural environment. Nora's insistence that folk memories are never solely the property of the individual but always social and collective, in the sense that they represent a shared understanding of the past, might usefully adjust our sense of how memory functions in this play. Of course it is tempting to dismiss the reminiscences of Shallow and Quickly as the inconsequential outpourings of foolish minds. For there is undeniably a rich vein of comic irony in their manifestly partial and self-interested recollections; if Shallow screens out the seedier aspects of his sojourn at Clement's Inn highlighted by Falstaff's conflicting memories of that era, Quickly has forgotten Falstaff's exploitative treatment of her in a haze of nostalgic reminiscence. But we should perhaps be cautious about viewing these tales as just one more example of wilful self-delusion in a play where the wish is father to most thoughts. As we noted above, popular forms of historical consciousness tend to present a highly mediated version of the facts characterised by varying degrees of selectivity, suppression and distortion. Nora's observation that 'memory-history', inasmuch as it 'only accommodates those facts that suits it', displays its fictiveness more candidly than 'official' history, which lays claim to 'universal authority', suggests that such features may constitute an alternative way of making sense of the past. This possibility might help to prise us away from a restrictively moralising response to the characters' imaginative representations of 'former days' by relocating them within an identifiable cultural tradition.

The need to reassess the productive role of memory in generating different forms of historical knowledge (some sanctioned, others not) is emphasised by its omnipresence in 2 *Henry IV*. For, like the interest in rumour and prophecy, reinventing the 'times deceased' is a pastime that extends well beyond the lower orders. Shallow's entrance onstage in 3.2 is preceded by that of another credulous old man given to skewed forms of retrospection, the King himself. Cloistered in his bedchamber, mentally as well as physically removed from the unfolding crisis of the Scrope rebellion, Bolingbroke's thoughts turn instead to the past as he ruminates on events surrounding the deposition of Richard II eight years earlier. Reciting his predecessor's prophetic warning that the Percys would betray their new master, he discreetly revises the version given in Shakespeare's *Richard II* in ways that are clearly designed to mitigate his own culpability. At another crucial political juncture when the possibility of negotiating a truce between the rebel faction and the King's army hangs in the balance, the dramatic action is again disrupted by a flow of reminiscence. For twenty-seven lines (4.1.111–37) the business in hand is brought to a standstill while Mowbray and Westmorland become absorbed in a dispute over their conflicting recollections of the aborted trial-by-combat between Mowbray's father and the as-yet-uncrowned Bolingbroke (also previously staged in *Richard II*). The recurrence of such moments when the urge to rehearse the past disrupts the teleological progression of the plot exposes the fatuity of the Archbishop's optimistic forecast that the King, tired of the cyclical violence born of his subjects' inability to forget their Ricardian heritage, will 'wipe his tables clean, / And keep no tell-tale to his memory / That may *repeat* and *history* his loss / To new remembrance' (4.1.199–202, my emphasis); this is grammatically underlined by the eliding of 'history' (used here as a nonce verb) with the very processes of mnemonic repetition whose disappearance the Archbishop so confidently predicts. Far from appearing to be in retreat, the desire to spin tales about what is 'past and to come' is shown to be a socially pervasive force within the national community, not so much a marginalised counter-history as the life-blood of history itself.

Reforming historical consciousness

Until Act 5, that is, when Hal's coronation appears to signal the demise of 'memory-history'. Prior to this the characters' unauthorised constructions of past and future have been allowed to flourish virtually unchecked. However, the relentless sequence of dramatic *peripeteia*, extending over the last two acts, which one by one dashes the false expectations of the rebels, Bolingbroke, Doll, Quickly, Falstaff and Shallow, heralds a changed moral and political climate in which such imaginative projections will no longer be tolerated. Determined to succeed where his father failed, the new king makes it his mission to wipe clean the tables of both individual and collective remembrance. Thus he begins his reign by announcing his intention to purge the realm of vulgar errors:

> My father is gone wild into his grave,
> For in his tomb lie my affections;
> And with his spirits sadly I survive
> To mock the expectation of the world,
> To frustrate prophecies and to raze out
> Rotten opinion, who hath writ me down
> After my seeming.

> (5.2.122–8)

In place of the orally disseminated rumours, prophecies, gossip and fantastic stories that proliferated under his father's rule, Hal imposes upon his subjects a new style of historical discourse whose authority is enforced with the full weight of the paternal law (figured by the Lord Chief Justice). The self-consciously 'formal majesty' and hieratic tenor of this discourse, like its burden of dynastic and nationalist concerns (cf. 5.2.101–44), aligns it more closely with chronicle history than anything we have yet heard in the play. The banishment scene is the logical culmination of this shift in direction. Falstaff's overdetermined connections with popular culture have encouraged some critics to read his expulsion allegorically as signifying a wholesale rejection of this cultural tradition that is tacitly endorsed both by the play and by the playwright.[26] However, this interpretation is problematised as soon as we take into account the ironic framing of this event within its particular dramatic context. Ever since the Prince divulged his plans in the second scene of *Part One*, we have been conditioned to view the long-awaited rejection of Falstaff as a strategic exercise in political symbolism directed at specific ends. Apart from allowing Hal to stage his own 'reformation' by displacing responsibility for his former rebelliousness on to the renegade knight, his repudiation of Falstaff (whose lawless behaviour has conveniently tainted popular traditions by association) provides the ideal platform from which to publicise his resolve to reassert centralised State control over his subjects' illicit memories and the multiplying histories they have spawned.

In its drive to rid the kingdom of 'rotten opinion', Hal's 'reformation' of self and commonwealth presents striking parallels with the so-called English historiographical 'revolution' that was gathering pace at the turn of the sixteenth century.[27] The generation of humanist-trained 'politic' historians that came to prominence in the final years of Elizabeth's reign sought to impose a stricter decorum on their 'art' by limiting its proper scope to an analysis of 'eyther the government of mighty states, or the lives and actes of famous men'.[28] Demonstrating that the 'conquest and eradication of memory by history' described by Nora is not a uniquely twentieth-century phenomenon, this definition of history was clearly framed to exclude the admixture of legend, hearsay and anecdotal material that sometimes found its way into the chronicles. More rigorous standards of historical scholarship also militated against the use of informal types of historical narrative. An emerging consensus that truth could be established only through the critical evaluation of sources made historians less inclined to rely upon, or give credence to, evidence derived from oral testimony. Even the antiquaries, for all their greater responsiveness to the 'common voice' as a valuable source of historical knowledge, increasingly placed their trust in written records in preference to the uncertain authority of hearsay.[29] Consequently, the popular legends, tales and traditions that survived in the collective memory came more and more to be regarded by the elite as trivial, vulgar and erroneous fabrications of no historical interest other than as objects of curiosity. John

Florio's indiscriminate denunciation of the products of oral tradition as 'flim flam tales, old wives fables, a ribble rabble discourse, idle words, speeches of no worth' is fairly indicative of the educated opinion of his day.[30] Another crucial factor that contributed to this devaluation of oral culture was the Reformation. As Fox points out, the growing mistrust in the reliability of popular histories was reinforced by their association with a medieval legacy of fraudulent legends perpetrated by monkish chroniclers bent on exploiting the credulity of the common people. For Elizabethan audiences the whiff of Romish superstition that clung to the oral tradition may perhaps have accentuated the latent Protestant connotations of Hal's programme of 'reform'.[31] In any event, the new King's public offensive against 'rotten opinion' clearly participates in the concurrent impulse within late Elizabethan and Jacobean culture to secure the boundaries of a national historiographical tradition, grounded in the unimpeachable authority of documentary evidence, by expelling local memory from the precincts of 'proper' history.

Yet, just as these abjected folk traditions continued to interact with and thrive on the margins of, 'official' historiography, so Hal's reformed history remains more beholden to the force of rumour, fictitious report and popular myth than he cares to admit. After all, his newly acquired political capital depends on the skill with which he manipulates his assiduously cultivated reputation for dissolute living as well as the false expectations it has instilled in his subjects. In fact, Hal's personal transformation requires, on a grander scale, more of the same aptitude for expedient reinvention of the past that he displayed in 4.2 by misreporting the sentiments he expressed when taking the crown from his dying father's pillow. Moreover, the banishment scene makes visible the cost of establishing a new historical model. If Nora's thesis holds true, 'history' has achieved dominance only through deliberate acts of amnesia involving the erasure of that shared fund of cultural memory which binds us imaginatively to the past. By the same token, the only way that Hal can set his kingdom on a progressive course towards a brave new future of national self-assertiveness is by cutting it loose from the past and, more particularly, from the repetitive rhythms of individual and collective remembrance. Having tried to bury the people's memories of the contentious origins of his claim to the English throne along with his father's corpse, he must also disown his 'former self' (in the shape of his erstwhile companion, Falstaff) as nothing more than a distasteful 'dream'. But, as Freud has taught us, even the most draconian repression of the past can never be watertight. In the play's sequel, the King's composure on the eve of battle will be disturbed by the intrusive memory of his father's regicide; while the ghostly presence of the now deceased Falstaff returns to destabilise *Henry V's* triumphal vision of dynastic history, ironically through the irreverent gossiping and reminiscence of his former tavern associates (*Henry V,*

2.1.73–80, 106–16; 2.3.3–37). Effective though it may be as political theatre, Hal's 'fresh start' serves in another way to illustrate the impossibility of excising communal memories from the heart of political life.

If Hal's campaign to transform the nation's historical consciousness is only partially successful, what of the play's attempts to reconfigure the way we think about history? Its revisionist tendencies in this regard are perhaps most fully encapsulated by the bold decision to juxtapose at the play's centre (Act 3) two old men ruminating on their respective pasts in the semi-privacy of their domestic surroundings – their entrances temporally synchronised so that the insomniac King in his bedchamber blends almost seamlessly into the provincial Justice taking the early morning air in his orchard. By showing history as it is being produced in such individual yet shared acts of remembrance, rather than through the momentous political developments taking place offstage, the play invites us to identify this with the fictional narratives we invent in order to make the past intelligible (and palatable) to ourselves. The scenic intercutting between Bolingbroke and Shallow simultaneously serves here to underline the 'semblable coherence' between the royal master and his servant in terms of their obsessive retrospection, postulating an implied ontological equivalence between their imaginative reshapings of the past. These devices contribute to the dramatic articulation of a radically devolved, socially levelling, local and domesticated vision of history – one grounded in the belief, to adapt Warwick's point, that 'there is a history in all men's lives' (3.1.80). Inasmuch as these scenes foreground the constitutive role of memory in the representation of the past, they also help to establish the play's status as a *lieu de mémoire* in its own right. That 2 *Henry IV* becomes a repository for 'memory-history' will be apparent from its instrumental role in conserving forms and idioms of the popular historical imagination that were passing into obscurity, the intensity of its 'feel' for the poetics of oral culture and for the enormous vitality and circumstantial richness of local memory. Ultimately, though, the play's function as a *lieu de mémoire* does not rest entirely on its popular sympathies or its staging of particular recollections; at a more fundamental level, it is encoded in the play's dramatic rhythms and structures which are implicated in the same cyclical dynamic of repetition and retrospection that governs the lives and thoughts of its characters. It has long been recognised as a peculiarity of 2 *Henry IV* that it redeploys, in an altered key, images, speeches and whole scenes from the two previous plays in the tetralogy, just as it consciously reworks popular plays and legends about Hal's prodigal youth and parodically echoes the dramatic 'hits' of the 1570s and 1580s in Pistol's bombastic rant. Instead of deploring this high incidence of dramatic recycling as a sign of Shakespeare's depleted creativity or the play's parasitic dependence on *Part One*, we might wish to view such repetition as integral to the process of redefining the parameters of the dynastic history play in 2 *Henry IV* through its assimilation of a popular cultural heritage it had tended to ignore.

Notes

1 See, for example, Hayden White, 'The Historical Text as Literary Artifact', in *Tropics of Discourse: Essays in Cultural Criticism* (Baltimore: Johns Hopkins University Press, 1978), ch. 3.

2 Michel de Certeau, 'History: Science and Fiction', in *Heterologies: Discourse on the Other*, trans. Brian Massumi (Manchester: Manchester University Press, 1986), 199–221, pp. 200–1.

3 For the complex relationship between popular culture and oral tradition see, for example, the Introductions to Barry Reay (ed.) *Popular Culture in Seventeenth-Century England* (London: Croom Helm, 1985) and Tim Harris (ed.) *Popular Culture in England, c. 1500–1800* (Basingstoke: Macmillan, 1995); and Adam Fox, *Oral and Literate Culture in England 1500–1700* (Oxford: Clarendon Press, 2000).

4 See Virgil, *The Aeneid*, trans. David West (London: Penguin, 1990), Book IV, p. 86; and *The Metamorphoses of Ovid*, trans. Mary M. Innes (Harmondsworth: Penguin: 1955), Book XII, p. 269.

5 Quoted in Fox, *Oral and Literate Culture*, 339.

6 *Ibid.*, 339–40.

7 See Keith Thomas, *Religion and the Decline of Magic* (London: Weidenfeld and Nicolson, 1971), 128–50 and Fox, *Oral and Literate Culture*, 358–67.

8 See, for example, Richard Knowles, 'Unquiet and the Double Plot of 2 *Henry IV*', *Shakespeare Studies*, 2 (1966), 133–40; Richard Abrams, 'Rumour's Reign in 2 *Henry IV*: The Scope of a Personification', *ELR*, 16 (1986), 467–95; and David Bergeron, 'Shakespeare Makes History: 2 *Henry IV*', *SEL*, 31 (1991), 231–45.

9 Dermot Cavanagh has argued that the 'illicit' discourse of rumour is similarly reclaimed as a source of historical insight in *King John*. See *Language and Politics in the Sixteenth-Century History Play* (Basingstoke: Palgrave Macmillan, 2003), ch. 4.

10 Hans-Joachim Neubauer, *The Rumour: A Cultural History*, trans. Christian Braun (London and New York: Free Association Books, 1999), 25, 32.

11 Raphael Holinshed, *The Third Volume of Chronicles* (1587), 519–21, 525, 530, 533, 539, 541.

12 Keith Thomas, 'Age and Authority in Early Modern England', *Proceedings of the British Academy*, 62 (1976), 205–48, p. 207.

13 Fox, *Oral and Literate Culture*, 214, 220–2.

14 Thomas, 'Age and Authority', 233–4.

15 *Aubrey's Brief Lives*, ed. Oliver Lawson Dick (London: Secker and Warburg, 1949), xxv.

16 Fox, *Oral and Literate Culture*, 215.

17 See Keith Thomas, *The Perception of the Past in Early Modern England*, Creighton Trust Lecture (London: Weidenfeld and Nicolson, 1984), 4.

18 *Ibid.*, 6–7.
19 Patricia Parker, *Literary Fat Ladies: Rhetoric, Gender, Property* (London: Methuen, 1987), 20–2.
20 The order of composition of these two plays is still disputed: see Rene Weis's introduction to the Oxford edition of *2 Henry IV* (1997), 10–13.
21 See, for example, Walter Ong, *Orality and Literacy: The Technologizing of the Word* (London: Methuen, 1982), 39–41; Laura Wright, 'Syntactic Structure of Witnesses' Narratives from the Sixteenth-Century Court Minute Books of the Royal Hospitals of Bridewell and Bedlam', *Neuphilologische Mitteilungen*, 96 (1995), 93–105.
22 Compare Richard Helgerson's analysis of 'Murder in Faversham: Holinshed's Impertinent History', in Donald R. Kelly and David Harris Sacks (eds) *The Historical Imagination in Early Modern Britain* (Cambridge: Cambridge University Press, 1997), 133–58.
23 Phyllis Rackin, *Stages of History: Shakespeare's English Chronicles* (London: Routledge, 1990), 147–8.
24 See Pierre Nora, 'Between Memory and History: *Les Lieux de Mémoires*', *Representations*, 26 (1989), 7–25.
25 On the ubiquitous use of this rhetorical figure and its structural analogues in *2 Henry IV* see Parker, *Literary Fat Ladies*, 71–3.
26 See, for example, Bergeron, 'Shakespeare Makes History', 233 and Richard Helgerson, *Forms of Nationhood: The Elizabethan Writing of England* (Chicago: Chicago University Press, 1992).
27 See F. Smith Fussner, *The Historical Revolution: English Historical Writing and Thought 1580–1640* (London: Routledge and Kegan Paul, 1962) and F. J. Levy, *Tudor Historical Thought* (San Marino, Cal.: Huntington Library, 1967).
28 John Hayward, *The First Part of the Life and Raigne of Henrie the IIII* (1599), Preface to the Reader.
29 See D. R. Woolf, 'The "Common Voice": History, Folklore and Oral Tradition in Early Modern England', *Past and Present*, 120 (1988), 26–52.
30 Florio, *A Worlde of Wordes* (1598), 125. Quoted in Fox, *Oral and Literate Culture*, 175.
31 First used to denote the Protestant movement in 1563, according to the *OED*, the word 'reformation' is employed by Hal in *Part One*, 1.2.201 and 'reform' in 5.5.66.

Good sometimes Queen: *Richard II*, Mary Stuart and the poetics of queenship

In Shakespeare's *Richard II*, the tragic protagonist is noted for his addiction to narrative. His narcissistic tendency to 'sit upon the ground, / And tell sad stories of the death of kings' (3.2.151–2) results in the loss of his Crown. His deposition, far from being a cautionary lesson, encourages him to expand his project of self-narrativisation. Richard plans to export his tragic biography, entreating his queen to absent herself from felicity awhile, in order to tell his story:

> Good sometimes Queen, prepare thee hence for France.
> Think I am dead, and that even here thou tak'st,
> As from my death-bed, thy last living leave.
> In winter's tedious nights, sit by the fire
> With good old folks, and let them tell thee tales
> Of woeful ages long ago betid;
> And ere thou bid goodnight, to quit their griefs
> Tell thou the lamentable fall of me,
> And send the hearers weeping to their beds;
> Forwhy, the senseless brands will sympathise
> The heavy accent of thy moving tongue,
> And in compassion weep the fire out;
> And some will mourn in ashes, some coal black,
> For the deposing of a rightful king.
>
> (5.1.37–50)

These remarkable lines draw attention to the play's own memorialising project in playing out the tragedy of Richard II. For early modern spectators closely attuned to the climate of religious controversy surrounding Elizabeth's succession, they would also allude to a darker purpose in *Richard II*. As well as offering a detailed examination of the politics of leadership, the play explores the politics of self-fashioned martyrdom. The speech's form of address, to a French-born 'Good sometimes Queen' and its striking references to brands, to fire extinguished with sympathetic tears and to mourning in ashes or coal black, all evoke a tradition of Catholic martyr-dom at the hands of Elizabeth, headed by the most powerful recent martyr-figure, Mary Stuart, Queen of Scots.

Richard's speech begins 'Good sometimes Queen', an apt title for Mary, who actively ruled Scotland for only six years of her forty-four-year life. She was a minor and absentee ruler for the first nineteen years and was deposed in favour of her son James and imprisoned in England for the last nineteen.[1] Shakespeare's play uses the feminine Isabella to represent the French dimen-sion of Mary Stuart's identity, but it is Richard who figures her role as tragic protagonist in Scotland and England.

Paul Budra has argued that Richard II fashions himself within the provi-dential pattern of *de casibus* historical tradition: the 'sad stories' in which kings die tragically. In this pattern, 'the self is formed by the constraints of history: its own self-awareness of history predetermines its fate'.[2] Even within that teleological framework, however, the historical subject has the power to shape the stories or histories that surround him or her. Indeed, that imperative is all the stronger if one is confined, as Richard and Mary are, to a tragic role. Richard's desire to heighten his story into tear-jerking tragedy and create a sympathetic audience by the fireside in France is a typical example of his deliberate strategy to transform present impotence into his-torical significance. Harry Berger Jr perceptively notes that Richard always 'keeps one eye on the future perfect tense that has the power to undo the Richard he knows he is and to impose the Richard he performs on all the future generations of wide-eyed playgoers'.[3] The good old folks who tell tales 'of woeful ages long ago betid' are such playgoers: the popular audi-ence whose sense of history relies more on familiar patterns of parable, as displayed in *A Mirror for Magistrates* (1559–87), than on detailed historical knowledge gained from reading Holinshed's *Chronicles* (1577; 1587). Richard's speech recreates the spectators watching *Richard II* as an audience more attuned to sad stories of the death of kings than historical 'facts'.

Like Richard, Mary Stuart had fewer and fewer options for writing herself into history in the final months of her imprisonment. Once the order for her execution arrived, she too endeavoured to construct a future within histor-ical narrative. Mary charged her doctors and waiting women to retell *her* final hours to listeners at the French court: 'leur commandant de . . . porter bon & fidelle tesmoignage de sa mort en la religion ancienne, saincte & Catholique [commanding them to bear true and faithful witness to her death in the old religion, holy and Catholic].[4] Writing her last-living leave to her brother-in-law Henry III, six hours before she was executed, she tells him 's'il vous plait de croire mon médecin et ces autres miens désolez serviteurs, vous oyrez la vérité, et comme, grâce a Dieu, je mepris la mort et fidellement proteste de la recevoir innocente de tout crime, quand je serois leur sujette'[5] [If you please to listen to my doctor and my other grieving servants, you will have the truth and how, by the Grace of God, I scorned death and faithfully protested my innocence of all crime, as their subject]. Mary constructed herself as a triumphant subject scorning death, martyred for her religion, in the 'lamentable tale of me' that she entrusted her servants to tell. By comparing her words with Richard's, we can see that both deposed monarchs try to control the retellings of their lives. Richard and Mary offer images of the living author who is conscious of his own death in the representations that will follow.

Mary's servants were detained at Fotheringay and then in London, but, when they did reach Paris in October 1587, their stories *were* the foundation of a profusion of literature on their saintly royal mistress. The discussion of storytelling in *Richard II* may be Shakespeare's own self-conscious allusion to the literary retellings of Mary's fate amongst the Catholic community that presented her as a martyr for the faith. Adam Blackwood's *Martyre de la Royne d'Escosse*, published in five editions between 1587 and 1589 was accompanied by *La Mort de la Royne D'Escosse*, with at least four editions between 1588 and 1589. Tragedies by Jean de Bordes (in Milan) and Adrian Roulers, schoolmaster of the Jesuit seminary at Douai, moved the story into a new genre. Indeed, Roulers's play, published in 1593, was written to be performed by the schoolboys.[6] If Shakespeare was brought up as a Catholic and had close contact with the Jesuit Counter-Reformation mission, he may have been aware of these dramatic precedents. Another appropriation of Mary's martyrdom, much closer to home, may have influenced the composition of *Richard II*. The year 1595 saw the execution of the Jesuit priest Richard Southwell, a distant cousin to Shakespeare, whose poems included a ventriloquisation of Mary:

Alive a Queene, now dead I am a sainte;
Once Mary called, my name nowe Martyr is;
From earthly raigne debarred by restraint,
In liew whereof I raigne in heavenly blisse.[7]

Southwell's death perhaps reawakened sad stories of the death of Queens for the playwright. Any oblique representation of Mary Stuart in *Richard II* is, however, far from the clear celebratory picture offered by the Jesuit martyr. Perhaps as a result of Shakespeare's own turbulent relationship with forms of Catholicism, it is deeply ambivalent.

It was, of course, Elizabeth I rather than Mary Stuart who proclaimed 'I am Richard II, Know ye not that'.[8] Through a cross-gendered representation, Shakespeare's play explores the nineteen-year struggle between two queens who both had to cope with the political challenge of identifying themselves as princes rather than women. In the absence of automatic male authority to command, Mary Stuart and Elizabeth I cultivated a specialised poetics of queenship, interweaving emblems, images, verbal and non-verbal languages, as Jennifer Summit has noted.[9] They enacted the same style of government as the poet-king of the play, whose mastery depends primarily on an invisible (and absent) divine paternal authority that must be invoked through language and symbol.

The queens regnant relied on their ability to fashion themselves through metaphor. Both had the ability to communicate in several languages and, like Richard, were well known for expressing themselves through verse. On the death of her husband, King Francis II, Mary wrote his sad story in a poem that won the praise of both Ronsard and Brantome. With Ronsard as her literary mentor, she was seemingly well fitted with a 'moving tongue' to present herself as a commanding figure. Her poem 'The Diamond Speaks', written to Elizabeth sometime in 1562 offers an astute assessment of the techniques required for female rule, but also the desire for female solidarity in the world of male government.[10] The verse was to accompany a 'ring with a diamond fashioned lyke a heart', passed as a symbol of unity and equality between two queens.[11] Mary's French original is lost, but Thomas Chaloner's 1579 Latin translation and Robin Bell's English translation of it, suggest the artful terms in which Mary conceived of her role as queen.

The poem claims that the diamond's sparkling power surpasses the strength of flame and brand and its many facets display the cunning craft behind its creation. The heart-shaped jewel, with its feminine associations of beauty and tenderness, is here reconstructed as a metaphor for hard-headed female government. Skilful self-fashioning and brilliant display can surpass the power of material force (or biology). The second part of the poem expands the metaphor, imagining each queen as such a diamond, mounted on a common band of iron (signalling strength in loyalty). Sisterly unity would amaze and blind all enemies:

> *Tunc ego perstingam tremulo fulgore coruscans*
> *Adstantum, immisis lumina seu radu.*
> *Tunc ego seu pretio, seu quae me provocet arte,*
> *Gemma, adamas firmo robore prima ferar.*

> [Then with my glitt'ring rays I should confound the sight
> Of all who saw me, dazzling enemies with my light.
> Then, by my worth and by her art, I should be known
> As the diamond, the greatest jewel, the mighty stone.]

In Shakespeare's play, Richard II's power relies on the same dazzling inscrutability. When he returns from Ireland to confront the military threat posed by Bolingbroke, Richard compensates for his lack of military power with an elaborately crafted poetic performance, drawing on the conventional imagery of kingship to style himself as a heavenly sun who 'darts his light through every guilty hole', to expose and shame all rebels into submission, 'bare and naked, trembling at themselves' (3.2.39; 42). Richard employs an image of omnipresent blazing power, a royal sun that can look everywhere but cannot be looked at. The exact strength of the King is invisible to the trembling foe who blushes before the poetically crafted appearance of majesty. Mary's image of the queenly diamond dazzling enemies with its light is refracted in this dramatic representation. As we will see, Elizabeth took up the same idea of majestic inscrutability and turned it back on Mary when she fled to England. Both queens can therefore be aligned with the poet-king Richard, whose ability to sustain his position in the first part of the play relies as much on his ability to tell his own stories (and silence others like Gaunt) as on his divine right.

While Elizabeth sustained this regal poetic with consummate skill throughout her reign, Mary Stuart followed Richard's sad story of misgovernment and fall from power. She was a nightmarish example of what could happen to Elizabeth. At Flint Castle, Richard's failure to sustain the rhetoric of command is clear when he publicly stages his own abdication by subjecting himself to Bolingbroke:

> What must the King do now? Must he submit?
> The King shall do it. Must he be deposed?
> The King shall be contented. Must he lose
> The name of King? A God's name let it go.

$$(3.3.142-5)$$

Mary Queen of Scots' surrender of herself to Bothwell offers a striking parallel to Richard II's words, though it lacks his irony. By marrying her abductor, the Queen disastrously compromised her position, not just because she had implicated herself in the murder of her husband Darnley, but because she had forgotten her royal identity and effectively rewritten herself as a wife subjected to her husband's authority. (In relation to Darnley, she had remained the primary signatory of all royal documents.)[12] George Buchanan's translation of love sonnets supposedly written by Mary to Bothwell and used as evidence against Mary at the 1568 Conference of Westminster, emphasised her low-status role:

> In his handis and in his full power
> I put my sonne, my honour and my lyif,
> My contry, my subiects, my soule al subdewit

We do not know whether Mary wrote the original French poems herself and, importantly, Buchanan's case for the overthrow of a queen regnant was not presented in terms of her sex. Instead, Buchanan based his argument on the notion of a Scottish tradition of elective monarchy, where individuals rule at the pleasure of their electors, the nobility.[13] Nevertheless, the queenly voice, as published in Buchanan's translations, is one example of Mary losing control of her story. She is ventriloquised as unsuitable to rule in lines like 'I haif no wealth, hap, nor contentation / But to obay and serve him truly'.[14] Rewritten as a saintly model of wifely duty she can no longer be a queen.

It was only natural that this woman should submit to the Scottish lords at Carberry Hill and ultimately abdicate. Calderwood reports how, as Mary was marched into Edinburgh, in 1567 she was jeered and 'could skarse be holdin upon horsebacke, for greefe and faintnesse, So soon as she recovered, she burst furth in teares, threats, reporaches, as her discontent moved. All the way she lingered, looking for some helpe. She came to Edinburgh about ten hours at night, her face all disfigured with dust and teares.'[15] Mary's sense of public humiliation is perhaps recalled in the Duke of York's account of Richard's dismal return to London, where 'No joyful tongue gave him his welcome home; / But dust was thrown upon his sacred head' (5.2.29–30).

Richard II refigures the struggle between Mary and Elizabeth in the roles of Richard and Bolingbroke, though in a deliberately ambiguous way. Mary is both the illegitimate usurper threatening Elizabeth and the weak monarch, forced to give up Crown and regal identity. In the deposition scene Bolingbroke and Richard face each other on opposite sides of the Crown, as Mary and Elizabeth had to during the long years of Mary's imprisonment. Richard tells Bolingbroke:

> Here, cousin, seize the Crown.
> Here, cousin. On this side my hand, on that side thine.
> Now is this golden Crown like a deep well
> That owes two buckets filling one another,
> The emptier ever dancing in the air,
> The other down, unseen and full of water.
> That bucket down and full of tears am I,
> Drinking my griefs, whilst you mount up on high.

> (4.1.172–9)

The mirroring of opposites exposes sameness. Mary's role as the fallen queen of tears was a feminine image which always haunted Elizabeth's power as Prince. When Mary appealed to her sister Queen for help, reminding her of the ring gift,[16] Elizabeth, suspicious of the Catholic plots surrounding Mary, turned against her as an enemy rather than uniting with a weaker sister diamond. Elizabeth's sonnet 'The Doubt of Future Foes' was written c. 1570, in the wake of the Northern rebellion and probably during the trial of Thomas Howard, Duke of Norfolk.[17] It is an expression of panoptic queenly power. The Queen, fearing that her Catholic 'subjects faith doth ebb', claims foreknowledge of 'future foes'.[18] Like Richard's royal sun in *Richard II*, Elizabeth is able to dart her 'light through every guilty hole' (2.3.39), with the help of 'worthy wights' such as Walsingham and the members of his secret service. She cautions Mary that she already knows of future plots and will undo these before they come to fruition.

> The top of hope supposed the root upreared shall be,
> And fruitless all their grafted guile, as shortly ye shall see.
> Then dazzled eyes with pride, which great ambition blinds,
> Shall be unsealed by worthy wights whose foresight falsehood finds.
> The daughter of debate that discord aye doth sowe
> Shall reap no gain where former rule still peace hath taught to know.
> No foreign bannished wight shall anchor in this port;
> Our realm brooks not seditious sects let them elsewhere resort.
> My rusty sword through rest shall first his edge employ
> To poll their tops that seek such change or gape for future joy.
>
> (ll. 7–16)

The 'foreign bannished wight' and 'daughter of debate' who sows civil unrest is Mary Stuart. Elizabeth warns that she is able to see through all their 'grafted guile' and will use her sword to execute such rebellious or unruly plants.

The poem's horticultural imagery – 'root upreared', 'fruitless', 'grafted', 'sow', 'reap' – follows a popular trope: the garden as kingdom. As Frances Teague has remarked, Elizabeth's lines 'remind one of the garden scene in *Richard II*'[19] which draws on the same trope from Livy.[20] The Gardener's instructions are charged with political significance:

> Go thou, and, like an executioner,
> Cut off the heads of too fast-growing sprays
> That look too lofty in our commonwealth.
> All must be even in our government.
> You thus employed, I will go root away
> The noisome weeds which without profit suck
> The soil's fertility from wholesome flowers.
> FIRST MAN   Why should we, in the compass of a pale,
> Keep law and form and due proportion,
> Showing as in a model our firm estate,
> When our sea-wallèd garden, the whole land,
> Is full of weeds, her fairest flowers choked up,
> Her fruit trees all unpruned, her hedges ruined,
> Her knots disordered and her wholesome herbs
> Swarming with caterpillars?
>
> (3.4.34–48)

The allegorical nature of Act 3 Scene 4 makes it stand out like a highly decorated illustration in the play's narrative. Taken in isolation, its echoing of the garden trope in Elizabeth's poem could be coincidental. However, further investigation suggests that Shakespeare's 'illustrative panel' may have offered a particular encrypted message for Catholic spectators or those familiar with Counter-Reformation propaganda. The gardeners' lines replay the religious struggle between Mary and Elizabeth by reproducing the very allegories they used. Mary Stuart reworked the verbal images in Elizabeth's 'The Doubt of Future Foes' in her embroideries, in particular the central panel of the Oxburgh Hanging, which depicts a horticultural execution. The dangerous nature of these emblems was clear since they were produced as evidence of treason at the trial of the Duke of Norfolk, leading to his execution in 1571. They also incriminated Mary. The historian William Camden noted in his *Annales of England* (1615) that

> Suspitions were layd hold on, as if there were a plot already layd to set her at liberty: and that, by occasion of certaine *Emblems* sent unto her. Which were these: *Argus* with his many eyes, all his eyes lull'd asleep by *Mercurius* sweetly piping, with this short sentence, *Eloquium tot lumina clausit* that is *so many eyes have faire speech clos'd*: *Mercurius* cutting off *Argus* head which kept *Iô*. A scien grafted into a stocke and bound about with bands, yet budding forth fresh and written about, *per vincula cresco*, that is to say *through bands I grow*. A palme tree pressed downe but rising up againe, with this sentence, *Ponderibus virtus innata resistit*, that is '*Gainst weights doth inbred vertue strive*. This Anagram also *Veritas armata*, that is, Truth armed, according to her name Maria Stuarta, the letters being transposed, was taken in worse part . . . Neverthelesse, there crept forth certaine spies and letters were secretly sent as well fained as true, whereby her womanish impotency might be thrust on to her owne destruction.[21]

Mary's countering shots to 'The Doubt of Future Foes' in the queenly battle fought with pen and needle are clear. The eyes lulled by sweet piping and 'faire speech' suggest that Mary's professions of love and loyalty to 'ma chère soeur' were far from genuine, accompanied, as they were, by involvement in Catholic plots.[22] The gardening symbols are even more interesting since they show Mary's ability to turn a story inside out. The image of pruning implies Mary's ability to assassinate Elizabeth (undoubtedly the reading taken at Norfolk's trial), but, once the pruning glove is on the other hand, it also celebrates Mary's iconic power as a sacrificial figure executed by Elizabeth, suggesting that wounding or oppression will actually encourage further growth. The Latin motto on Mary's Oxburgh Hanging reads '*Virescit, Vulnere Virtus*': 'virtue flourishes through wounding'. 'A sentence is but a cheverel glove to a good wit,' says Feste in *Twelfth Night*, 'how quickly the wrong side may be turned outward' (3.1.10–12). Mary Stuart had a good poetic wit and, as her imprisonment continued, she could play both sides of the game, presenting a Bolingbroke-like threat of usurpation and a disturbing potential for martyrdom.

Read in the context of this war over emblems, the scene in *Richard II* takes a pragmatic but particularly Marian line on gardening. The lines above stress the necessity for pruning the too-fast-growing sprays. This is what a good king, an ideal Richard, should have done. Richard failed, as Mary failed to prune her nobles and was usurped (or fails to assassinate Elizabeth and is killed). So as not to fall into the same trap, Elizabeth had to execute rebels and finally, after nineteen years, uproot or decapitate Mary herself. However, the Gardener's second speech points out the inevitable (indeed, desirable) consequences of pruning: further growth. 'We at time of year / Do wound the bark' (3.4.58–9) he says, echoing the symbol from Mary's embroidery. The pruning images in *Richard II* offer a positive reading of Mary's execution as a cull that will produce fruit of greater Catholic support, more vigorous regrowth. Yet, as Elizabeth recognises in 'The Doubt of Future Foes', if she must poll the tops that gape for future joy, the execution of Mary will only make her cause flourish all the more strongly, threatening to turn the sea-walled kingdom into a wilderness of fast-growing sprays, an unweeded garden that will require constant attention.

Shakespeare could certainly have known Elizabeth's poem since it was a celebrated example of her literary skill in Puttenham's *Arte of English Poesie* (1589). Its political import was emphasised by Puttenham's discussion of Elizabeth's use of dark and figurative language in his 'Defence of the Honorable Sentence and Execution of the Queene of Scotes'.[23]

Whether Shakespeare would have had access to the details of Mary's embroideries is far more difficult to determine, although, if he was writing in the same circle as Robert Southwell, as has been suggested, it would have been highly likely. Southwell was chaplain to Anne, Countess of Arundel, to whom Mary bequeathed her prayer book, the veil she wore and rosary she carried at her execution. Anne Dacre, herself an accomplished needle-woman, was probably in possession of both the gardening panel sent to her father-in-law, the Duke of Norfolk and another panel which Mary embroidered for Anne's husband, Philip Howard, imprisoned in the Tower from 1585 to 1595.[24] The fact that the emblem of fruitful wounding was sent *to* Mary as well as being embroidered *by* her suggests these images formed a hieroglyphics of Catholic resistance. Southwell's poem 'Decease Release' presented Queen Mary celebrating her execution with the words 'The lopped tree doth best and soonest grow' and 'By lopping shot I up to heavenly rest'. Mary's view that the executioner's axe 'cutt off my cares from combred breste'[25] may follow from Thomas à Kempis's *Imitation of Christ* (a book recommended by Ignatius de Loyola and central to Jesuit thinking), which warned disciples 'If you wish to climb to this height, you must begin bravely and lay the axe to the root; pull up and destroy every movement toward self-centred, selfish desires.'[26] Another Southwell poem, 'Time Goes by Turnes', begins with the lines:

> The lopped tree in time may grow againe,
> Most naked plantes renew both fruit and flower:
> The soriest wight may find release of pain,
> The dryest soyle sucke in some moystning shower

(ll. 1–4)

The endurance of the metaphor, as well as Catholic resistance, was recognised in Sir Christopher Hatton's opening speech to Parliament in February 1589. Having rehearsed past dangers and 'the utter subversion and destruction of us all' in the plots surrounding Mary, Hatton goes on to warn that, although the Armada has been repulsed, the defeated Catholic forces remain dangerous: '*Arbor excisa pullulat*: we have lopte some of his boughs, but thei will sooner growe againe then we thinke of.'[27]

Mary's embroidery suggests that she recognised her death would be the beginning of a powerful iconography. Her personal motto, 'en ma fin est mon commencement', perhaps explains her enthusiasm for execution as a form of victory over Elizabeth.[28] In *Richard II*, Richard's self-conscious refashioning of himself as tragic martyr prepares for a death that, he knows, will be far more powerful than his life. Shakespeare depicts that post-mortem influence throughout the second tetralogy, culminating in Henry V's admission on the night before Agincourt that he has had Richard's body reinterred. Derek Cohen usefully points out that 'The murder of Richard looms over its own future, well into the age of Elizabeth. Those close to it recognise a need to position themselves in relation to it. Nothing less than the enveloping concept of the English nation is at stake.'[29]

Mary's execution, likewise, forced Scottish, English and European subjects to position themselves in relation to it and to the future of the English nation. In addition to the Armada, it prompted Jesuit negotiations with Prince Philip II to promote a Spanish claim to the throne in the early 1590s and hopes on the part of many moderate English and Scottish Catholics that James VI would be a monarch likely to tolerate Catholic sympathies. Persons's *Conference About the Next Succession* (1593), reprinted under Cardinal Allen's name in 1595, took a much stronger Jesuit line. Cyndia Susan Clegg (who has noted its strong connections with *Richard II*), observes that it claimed that the whole Tudor dynasty was invalid and that, since 'the lady Mary late Queene of Scotland' had been executed for plotting against Queen Elizabeth, her son James could not legally inherit as the son of a conspirator.[30] In 1602, Mary's name was still in circulation as a byword for Catholic hopes in the succession. *A Tract on the Succession*, copied in the Harington–Arundel manuscript, noted that, if a man had an enemy, it was enough to say he was a papist and 'praied for the Queene' and some would ask him 'which Queene, as though he might meane the Queene of Scotts'.[31]

Although Mary was not officially recognised as a martyr, accounts of her death inscribed her in a cult of Catholic sacrifice. Adam Blackwood's *Martyre de la Royne d'Escosse* (1589), presents Mary offering to spill her blood: 'J' offrois volontairement repandre mon sang en la querelle de l'Eglise Catholique' (p. 388). She represents a model of faithful endurance in the face of torture and death: 'elle n'a nullement fleschie & n'a rien rabbatue de la foy, qu'elle a jure a sa religion, non plus ne changera elle pour crainte de la morte pour peur de tourmens don't vous la menassez, ny pour l' infamie dont vous penses par vos calumnies la diffamer'[32] [She did not bend at all and did not change her faith a bit, which she swore as her religion, neither did she falter for fear of death, or of the torments with which you threatened her, nor from the infamy which you thought your slanders would cast on her]. English Catholics are explicitly invited to embrace the model offered by Mary Stuart in the text: a preliminary sonnet appeals to them thus:

> *Martyrs de Jesus Christ d' invincible courage*
> *Qui pour l'honneur de Dieu, souffrez tant de tourment,*
> *Catholiques Anglois, vois que journellement*
> *On bat, on frappe, on tue, on menace, on outrage:*
> *Ne vous desesperez, le beau temps suit l'ourage . . .*
>
> *La mort du bon Chrestien est principe de vie.*
> *Courage donc, amis, qui meurt pour Jesus Christ,*
> *Dompte en mourant l'enfer, le monde, & l'Ante-Christ,*
> *Le rage des tyrans, la mort mesme, & l'envie.*
>
> (B1v)
>
> [Martyrs for Jesus Christ of invincible courage
> Who, for the honour of God, suffer so much torment,
> English Catholics, who every day
> Are whipped, beaten, killed, threatened, wronged:
> Do not despair, faith weather follows the storm . . .
>
> The death of a good Christian is the beginning of life,
> Courage then, friends, who die for Jesus Christ,
> In dying, vanquish death, the world and the anti-Christ,
> The fury of tyrants, death itself and desire.]

The cult of martyrdom had refired the Catholic imagination in the 1581 execution of Edmund Campion, Jesuit leader of the Counter-Reformation. (Mary Stuart is supposed to have owned a reliquary containing remains of Campion.)[33] Henry Walpole, who was converted when he was splashed with Campion's blood, took the role of telling Campion's sad story, in a poem: 'Why do I use my paper, inke and penne / And call my wits to counsel what to say?' It circulated in manuscript copies until about 1650.[34] In 1595 (when *Richard II* may have been written), Walpole was himself executed in York, leaving the onus on other Catholic writers to tell his story in a culture where, as Arthur Marotti says, 'the reverence for lyrics began to migrate into print culture where the remains of a person were verbal'.[35] In the same year, the Catholic Earl of Arundel diëd in the Tower. His chaplain Richard Southwell, who had immortalised Mary's voice in verse and who had urged his 'loving cousin' (possibly Shakespeare) to 'begin some finer peece, wherein it may be seene how well verse and vertue sute together', was himself executed.[36] Could *Richard II* be an equivocal answer to that call?

In preparing the role of martyr, Richard II and Mary Stuart go through a process of self-dissolution: 'Nor I, nor any man that but man is, / With nothing shall be pleased till he be eased / With being nothing' (5.5.39–41). Richard's poetic meditations on time, self-recognition and dissolution are uncannily duplicated in Mary Stuart's 'Book of Hours', whose religious texts she embellished with marginal jottings, mainly poetry. Her life in prison becomes a clock to number the hours and days:

> Les heures je guide et le jour
> Par l'ordre exact de ma carrière,
> Quittant mon triste séjour
> Pour ici croitre ma lumière.

> [I guide the hours and guide the day
> Because my course is true and right
> And thus I quit my own sad stay
> That here I may increase my light.][37]

Through the bitterness, Mary recognises that 'ici croitre ma lumière' [here I may increase my light]. To increase her light in spiritual terms was to recognise, like Richard, the truth of her own insignificance. In a more worldly sense, it is the beginnings of self as story, a lasting fame, as long as men can live or eyes can see: 'Quittant mon triste séjour / Pour *ici* croitre ma lumière', dying to increase one's brightness on earth. One of Mary's poems captures the suggestion that self-dissolution may be only the gateway to a new identity as martyr:

> Un Coeur que l' outrage martire
> Par un mépris ou d'un refus,
> A le pouvoir de faire dire:
> Je ne suis plus ce que je fus.

> [A heart which is martyred with agony
> Through scorn, rejection and disdain

Still has the power and right to say:
What I was I no more remain.][38]

Richard II too ends with a powerful reassertion of the self: 'Mount, mount, my soul; thy seat is up on high, / Whilst my gross flesh sinks downward, here to die' (5.5.111–12). How are these lines to be read? Critics have noted Richard's ostentatious use of religious symbolism, as he offers to swap his jewels for a set of beads, his figured goblets for a dish of wood (3.3.146–53) and then goes on to compare himself to Christ, chastising his disobedient subjects as 'Pilates' who have 'delivered me to my sour cross' (4.1.230–1). Mary's repeated declarations that she was dying for her faith, rather than as a criminal, suggest a self-conscious manipulation of martyr-dom to match Richard's. (In one verse in the Book of Hours she imagines her enemies round her deathbed casting lots for her garments.)[39] She care-fully bequeathed silver boxes, cups and ewers, the golden rosary and the prayer book she took to the block in Fotheringay Castle. Elizabeth's offi-cers recognised that her possessions could easily be fetishised as the relics of a martyr and insisted they were all washed or burned, as Blackwood reports:

> de peur qu'au temps a venir ils servissent a superstition, c'est a dire, de peur qu'ils fussent recueillis par les Catholiques avec respect, honneur, & reverence, come les bons peres anciens avoient de coustume de garder les reliques & observer avec devotion les monuments des martyrs. (416)

> [for fear that in time to come they would serve superstition, that is to say, for fear that they would be collected by Catholics with respect, honour and rever-ence, according to the custom of the former good fathers, of keeping the relics and devotedly watching over the monuments of martyrs]

By pruning or wounding the self, both monarchs know their stories will flourish. They prepare their places in the future perfect historical narrative, as well as for the afterlife.

One could argue that Mary's verses, jotted in a personal prayer book, are private meditations. This turns out to be far from the truth. Amongst the leaves of the Book of Hours, in addition to Mary's lines, are the signatures of prominent members of the English court, including Francis Walsingham, Charles Howard, Thomas Radcliffe, Walter Devereux, Elizabeth Shrewsbury and Arbella Stuart. The signatures, penned between 1571 and 1610, suggest that the Book of Hours was being inspected by interested individuals during Mary's imprisonment and after her death. Could this circulation have given Shakespeare access to the verses inside? The answer to this intriguing mystery can only be speculative, but knowing that Mary Stuart was aware that her poems would be read by others is important. It makes us reassess the personal confessions in verse, as 'woeful tales' *and* worldly self-fashionings.

Like Mary Stuart's head, the pages of the Book of Hours have been bru-
tally cropped, so cutting off some of her words. At the bottom of folio 81v
she desperately observes:

Il faut plus que la renommée
Pour dire et publier . . .

[Never again in all my fame must I
Proclaim and tell . . .]⁴⁰

The sentence is unfinished. Did Shakespeare take up the story of the 'Good
sometimes Queen', retelling it in *Richard II* to send spectators to their beds
musing on the destructive and regenerative force of martyrdom? Mary's faith
in narrative may have reminded the playwright that each martyred monarch
or Jesuit needed 'the heavy accent of a moving tongue' to retell his or
her story.

Notes

1 Jenny Wormald, *Mary Queen of Scots: A Study in Failure* (London: George
   Philip, 1988), 19.
2 Paul Budra, 'Writing the Tragic Self: Richard II's Sad Stories', *Renaissance and
   Reformation*, 18 (1994), 5–15, p. 14.
3 Harry Berger Jr, *Imaginary Audition* (Berkeley: University of California Press,
   1989), 137.
4 Adam Blackwood, *Martyre de la Royne d'Escosse* (Edinburgh [Paris], 1589), 417.
5 Alexandre Labanoff-Rostovsky, *Lettres, Instructions et Memoires De Marie
   Stuart*, 7 vols (London: C. Dolman, 1844), VI, 492.
6 James Emerson Phillips, *Images of a Queen: Mary Stuart in Sixteenth-Century
   Literature* (Berkeley and Los Angeles: University of California Press, 1964),
   189–95.
7 Robert Southwell, *The Complete Poems of Robert Southwell, SJ*, ed. R. B.
   Grosart (London: Fuller Worthies' Library, 1872), 171–2.
8 J. E. Neale, *Queen Elizabeth I* (Harmondsworth: Penguin, 1967), 386–7. On the
   performance of a play about Richard II by Shakespeare's company, commissioned by followers of the Earl of Essex, see Richard Dutton, *Mastering the
   Revels: The Regulation and Censorship of English Renaissance Drama* (London:
   Macmillan, 1991), 117–20.
9 Jennifer Summit, '"The Arte of a Ladies Penne": Elizabeth I and the Poetics of
   Queenship', *ELR*, 26 (1996), 395–422. For further discussion of the queen
   regnant and the gendering of monarchy in *Richard II* and other history plays see
   Alison Findlay, *A Feminist Perspective on Renaissance Drama* (Oxford:
   Blackwell, 1999), ch. 5.
10 Labanoff Rostorsky, *Lettres*, I, 154–6.
11 See Thomas Finlayson Henderson, *Mary Queen of Scots: Her Environment and
   Tragedy*, 2 vols (London: Hutchinson, 1905), I, 205.

12 Antonia Fraser, *Mary Queen of Scots* (London: Weidenfeld and Nicolson, 1969), 238–9.

13 See Amanda Shepherd, *Gender and Authority in Sixteenth Century England* (Keele: Ryburn Publishing, Keele University Press, 1994), who points out that Buchanan's *De Jure Regni Apud Scotos* (1579) may have been written during the exclusion crisis of 1567 (p. 68).

14 G. Buchanan, *Ane Detection of the duinges of Marie Quene of Scottes* (1571), R3 and R4v. See also *Bittersweet Within My Heart: The Love Poems of Mary, Queen of Scots*, ed. and trans. Robin Bell (London: Pavilion Books, 1992), 44.

15 David Calderwood, *The History of the Kirk of Scotland*, eds T. Thomson and D. Laing, 8 vols (Edinburgh: Wodrow Society, 1842–49), II, 365, cited by Henderson, *Mary Queen of Scots*, I, 470.

16 Mary asked Elizabeth for help, 'tant pour la proximité du sang, similytue d'état et professée amitié' and reminded her of the ring: 'je vous envoyés mon cueur en bague et je vous ay aporté le vray et corps ensamble'. In Labanoff-Rostorsky, *Lettres*, II, 80–2.

17 Thomas Norton's *A Discourse touching the pretended match betwene the Duke of Norfolke and the Queene of Scottes* (1569) pointed out the unsuitability of the match, noting that Mary Stuart's *'aspiring minde'* could be seen in her public bearing of the English royal arms, which declared her *'a competitour of this crowne'* (A3).

18 Elizabeth I, 'The Doubt of Future Foes', in *The Paradise of Women: Writings by Englishwomen of the Renaissance*, ed. Betty S. Travitsky (Westport, Conn.: Greenwood Press, 1981), 93–4.

19 Francis Teague, 'Elizabeth I', in Katherina M. Wilson (ed.) *Women Writers of the Renaissance and Reformation* (Athens: University of Georgia Press, 1987), 529.

20 The image of Tarquin decapitating poppies as a covert death sentence appears in Livy's *History* (1.54), cited in H. J. Leon, 'Classical Sources for the Garden Scene in *Richard II*', *Philological Quarterly*, 29 (1950), 65–70, p. 65.

21 William Camden, *Annales, or the Historie of the Most Renowned and Victorious Princesse Elizabeth* (1635), trans. by R. N.; first published 1615.

22 See the range of letters to Elizabeth in Labanoff-Rostorsky, *Lettres*, III.

23 *Accounts and Papers Relating to Mary Queen of Scots*, eds Allan J. Crosby and John Bruce (1587–88). The British Museum Harl. 831 MS version says it is written 'for large satisfaction of all such persons both prince and private who by ignorance of the case or partiallitie of mind shall happen to be irresolute and not satisfied in the said cause'.

24 Margaret Swain, *The Needlework of Mary, Queen of Scots* (New York: Van Nostrand Reinhold Company, 1973), 102–3.

25 Grosart, ed., *Poems of Robert Southwell*, 171. Southwell's *Epistle of Comfort* (Arundel House, London, 1587) also uses the imagery of pruning to show God's good husbandry, in pruning the vine 'leaste all the force be unprofitable spente in leaves and the roote beinge therbye weackened' (21v–22r). See also 15v and 17r.

26 Thomas à Kempis, *The Imitation of Christ*, ed. William C. Creasy (Macon, Ga: Mercer University Press, 1989), 150.

27 *Proceedings in the Parliaments of Elizabeth I*, vol. II 1584–1589, ed. T. E. Hartley (Leicester: Leicester University Press, 1995), 416–17, p. 423.

28 This motto accompanied the image of a phoenix and, according to William Drummond of Hawthornden, was inherited from Mary's mother, Mary of Guise. See Fraser, *Mary Queen of Scots*, 413.

29 Derek Cohen, 'History and the Nation in *Richard II* and *Henry IV*', *Studies in English Literature 1500–1900*, 42 (1992), 293–316, p. 302.

30 Cardinal Allen, *Conference about the Next Successsion* (1595), Book 2, p. 17. Cyndia Susan Clegg, ' "By choice and invitation of all the realme": *Richard II* and Elizabethan Press Censorship', *Shakespeare Quarterly*, 48 (1997), 432–48.

31 York Minster MS XVI. L6, 235 *A Tract in the Succession to the Crown* (1602). I am grateful to Gerard Kilroy for this reference.

32 Funeral sermon preached in Paris, printed at the end of *Martyre de la Royne d'Escosse* and separately paginated, 29–30.

33 Richard Simpson, *Edmund Campion: A Biography* (London, 1867), p. 468.

34 Gerard Kilroy, 'Paper, Inke and Penne: The Literary *Memoria* of the Recusant Community', *The Downside Review* (April 2001), 95–124.

35 Arthur Marotti, *Manuscript, Print and the English Renaissance Lyric* (Ithaca: Cornell University Press, 1995), p. 53.

36 Robert Southwell, *St Peters Complaint with other poemes* (1595), Epistle dedicatory 'To His Loving Cousin' (A2v).

37 Labanoff-Rostorsky, *Lettres*, VII, 349. Translation by Bell, *Bittersweet Within My Heart*, 89.

38 Labanoff-Rostorsky, *Lettres*, VII, 350. Translation by Bell, *Bittersweet Within My Heart*, 91.

39 'En fainte mes amis changent leur bienveillance . . .' Labanoff-Rostorsky, *Lettres*, VII, 350.

40 *Ibid.*, 349.

II
Counter-histories

Strange truths: the Stanleys of Derby on the English Renaissance stage

It is a truism to say that English history plays concentrate on kings. But, like most other truisms, it is only partly true. In this essay I want to concentrate on the ways in which a number of English history plays represent the history of a dynasty which never ascended the English throne – the Stanleys, who, with their Tudor blood and kingship of the Island of Man, seem often to be seen almost as alternative kings, a role that was indeed contemplated for perhaps their most famous representative, Ferdinando Stanley, Lord Strange and subsequently Fifth Earl of Derby. My title comes from John Ford's late history play *Perkin Warbeck*, whose full title is *The Chronicle Historie of Perkin Warbeck: A Strange Truth*, but it will be my contention that a number of other plays tell Strange truths. Moreover, Lord Strange is not the only member of the family who finds himself represented or alluded to on the English stage: I will also be considering various Earls of Derby, at least one Sir Edward Stanley and two separate bearers of the name Sir William Stanley. Since it was '[t]he view of the torturer Topcliffe, voiced in 1592, that "all the Stanleys in England are traitors" ',[1] these plays, taken together, offer an alternative, dangerous and sometimes scurrilous counter-history of England which seems deliberately to position itself in opposition to the official truth.

It is not surprising that the emphasis should be on danger, because, celebrated and important though the Earls of Derby were, much of their fame was overshadowed by the notoriety of a quite different member of the family, Sir William Stanley, an officer in the English army in the Low Countries who in 1587 betrayed the English-held city of Deventer to the Spanish, but denied that his actions were treacherous because he said he had had permission from Leicester to use his discretion as to whether it was possible to hold the city. Nor was this the end of Sir William's adventures: in 1591 he proposed to seize the Channel Island of Alderney. Its 'lord', Thomas Chamberlain, was willing to hand it over, Stanley said, and his brother Captain Edward Stanley was ready to occupy it with two hundred men.[2] Stanley further tried to resurrect the idea in 1598 and 1599. He also had a more straightforward plan of invasion, this time involving the Derby family. To quote Ethel Seaton:

> By 1592, Stanley's plans of attack were maturing: sixteen ships were to invade England in April 'near Stanley's own country, where a great personage would be ready to help and take part with him, whose name was set down by the figure 19 (Earl of Derby) and (Lord Strange), a young one who he hoped would be ready to assist, by that of 14.'. . . The curious fact that neither Derby nor Strange was even secretly a Roman Catholic was no deterrent to the volatile Stanley, who evidently felt sure that they would be of the same mind as Henri IV.[3]

Seaton refers of course to Henri IV of France, but the title is one suggestive of wider applicability, for it was also that of the first Lancastrian king. The coincidence may perhaps encourage us to pay particular attention to the obsessive repetition in Shakespeare's *Richard II* of Henry's full range of titles – Henry of Hereford, Lancaster and Derby – and it may be worth remembering this when we turn later to *Perkin Warbeck*, which is obviously indebted to *Richard II* and which also floats the possibility that the succession to the Crown of England might move in unexpected directions.

I will come back to Sir William Stanley in due course, but I want first to turn to another member of the Stanley family, who may perhaps have been an influence on the representation of history in Marlowe's *Jew of Malta*. There does seem to be a definite connection between Marlowe and the Stanleys: quite apart from the problematic question of Marlowe's possible relationship with Lord Strange, to which I will return, John Poole – who Charles Nicholl suggests was the man who taught Marlowe how to counterfeit money – was the brother-in-law of the sixteenth-century Sir William Stanley, the betrayer of Deventer. I think this spills over into *The Jew of Malta* and inflects its representation of historical events. I have argued elsewhere that Marlowe's representation of the island of Malta is more accurate than is often appreciated. In particular, Marlowe may well, as Emily Bartels suggested some years ago, have known better than his editors when he implied considerable tension between the Knights of St John and the Spanish, who go so far as to threaten them with expulsion.[4] One Spaniard in particular, Don Garcia de Toledo, viceroy of Sicily, was a special bugbear of the Knights, most notably during the siege of 1565. Since the Maltese islands had been the gift of Spain and since Don Garcia's own territory of Sicily would be directly threatened if Malta was lost, the Knights looked repeatedly to him for support, but the help he provided was minimal. He hedged around every offer of assistance with impossible conditions and when he finally allowed the small relief force known as the Piccolo Siccorso (the 'Small Succour') to leave Sicily it was only with express orders that it was not to land unless the crucial fort of St Elmo were still in the Knights' hands; if it were not, they were to be abandoned to their fate. He did, however, leave his son, Frederic, as a pledge of his goodwill; the boy fought gallantly and was eventually killed in action during the siege.

There are, I think, a number of suggestive parallels between these events and Marlowe's play. The stark contrast between the heroism of young Frederic and the dilatoriness of his father may well seem quite closely analogous to the distance which separates the loving commitment of Abigail, dying alongside the nuns in the community which her father has destroyed, and Barabas's opportunism. The latter is a quality Barabas also shares with Don Garcia de Toledo, who, despite the pitifully small part he had played in events, was not slow to be publicly associated with the Grand Master after the Turks' eventual withdrawal. Don Garcia arrived on the island with the final Sicilian relief force and shared in a celebration banquet. Since provisions were naturally scarce, however, he brought his own food to it.[5] Again there is a parallel here with *The Jew of Malta*, this time with the rather unexpected reaction of Calymath to Barabas's invitation to a similar occasion:

> To banquet with him in his citadel?
> I fear me, messenger, to feast my train
> Within a town of war so lately pillaged,
> Will be too costly and too troublesome

> (5.3.20–3)

This seems an odd detail to include; but it, like the mining of the monastery, does offer a very close echo of the events of the later part of the siege, after the theatre of war moved from St Elmo to Birgu. And perhaps there is a reason for the closeness of the echo.

In order to understand what that reason might have been, it is necessary to grasp the strategic importance of Fort St Elmo to the siege. The Knights' headquarters, Fort St Angelo, was based in the town of Birgu, well inside what is now the Grand Harbour of Valletta. However, access to the harbour was entirely controlled by the much smaller Fort St Elmo, situated at its mouth. Consequently the Turks could not even begin the attack on Fort St Angelo until they had first subdued Fort St Elmo. The Turkish admiral Dragut expected to be able to do so within five days; instead, it resisted for almost a month, until every man in it had been slaughtered (and the bodies, in most cases, mutilated and sent downstream to St Angelo with their hearts cut out). The unexpected success of Fort St Elmo's defence turned the tide of the siege and the Turks eventually sailed away unsuccessful.

It was shortly after the Fall of St Elmo that the Chevalier Robles brought the Piccolo Siccorso to the aid of his beleaguered brethren in June, 1565 and there were two Englishmen with the force. One of them, Sir Edward Stanley, is almost certainly identifiable as the uncle of Ferdinando Stanley, Lord

Strange – by whose acting company *The Jew of Malta* was performed. This Sir Edward Stanley had been implicated in a plot in 1571 to rescue Mary, Queen of Scots, and take her to the Isle of Man and was 'listed as a recusant and a "dangerous person" in 1592'.[6] The Piccolo Siccorso arrived on the island at a crucial stage in the siege, immediately after the fall of Fort St Elmo. The loss of St Elmo triggered a complete change in the strategic situation and the conduct of the siege, which was now directed entirely at the peninsula towns of Senglea and Birgu and at Fort St Angelo, which are all on the other side of the Grand Harbour. The Piccolo Siccorso was, as remarked above, transported in Sicilian galleys which actually had orders not to land if Fort St Elmo was not still in Maltese hands, since possession of it was considered so vital that the island was to be written off as lost if it was gone; but the Knight of St John who was sent ashore to learn the situation lied to the Sicilian commander and the force was landed anyway. In fact, Turkish brutality to the captured defenders of St Elmo had been so monstrous that the loss of the fort had, if anything, stiffened the backbone of Maltese resistance; determined to avenge their dead brethren and heartened by the fact that this, their smallest fortress, had put up so lengthy a resistance (which had bought time for strengthening the fortifications of Senglea, Birgu and St Angelo), the Knights were grimly resolved to defend their position to the last man and the indigenous Maltese gave them complete support.

Sir Edward Stanley, then, arrived on Malta at a vital turning-point of the siege. Spared the lingering horrors suffered by the indomitable defenders of St Elmo, spared too the discussions attendant on the Grand Master's agonised decision to leave them to their fate, spared the sight of the decapitated bodies, their hearts gouged out of their chests, which the current wafted across to St Angelo, Sir Edward served not in the living hell of the tiny, ruined fort but in a large, well-supplied garrison fired by furious determination and, thanks to the length of the resistance offered by St Elmo, a reasonable chance of survival, which improved significantly with every extra day they could hold out. It would probably not have been easy for even Marlowe to be wholly cynical about the defence of Fort St Elmo, but the rest of the siege was indeed much more as Marlowe depicts it, with the Knights no longer in serious danger and politicking more to the fore than heroism. When the Turks finally did abandon the siege in September, two and a half months after he arrived, Sir Edward also witnessed the withdrawal of their humiliated army, in poor morale and devastated by the loss of some of their ablest commanders, and the ensuing jubilation and thanksgiving of the Knights, the Maltese and the Sicilians who had brought the final relief force. Since Sir Edward did not die until 1609, he would presumably have been well able to give evidence of his experiences.

When Marlowe wrote his play, then, he did so in the service of a patron whose own immediate family had almost certainly had significant experience of both the island of Malta in general and the great siege in particular. I have dwelt at some length on the probable experiences of Sir Edward Stanley because they seem to me to overlap in some significant respects with Marlowe's dramatisations of the siege, which, intriguingly, is represented in greater particularity towards its closing stages – precisely those which Sir Edward witnessed. Beyond any specific correspondences, however, is that *The Jew of Malta* is in many ways typical of what might be loosely classified as the Stanley view of history in insisting on the idea that behind the official version of events, which is presented as hypocritical and self-serving, there is a much darker and truer unofficial one.

Just as I suspect that *The Jew of Malta* reflects a congruence between Marlowe and the Stanleys, so I wonder if it may be possible to trace the break-up of that relationship, because I think *Edward II* reflects rather less favourably on the Stanleys and specifically on Lord Strange himself. Much is made in the play of the fact that Edward creates Gaveston 'King and Lord of Man' (1.1.155). Actually Gaveston was merely given the lordship of the island and was never its king, but the title King of Man was in fact held by the Earls of Derby and would in the course of time fall to Lord Strange. It therefore seems to me particularly interesting that the character in the play who is unhistorically made to share this title, Gaveston, dies at the hands of the Earl of Pembroke's men. The primary resonance here is of course that by the time of *Edward II* Marlowe – or so Kyd appears to hint – seems to have fallen out with Strange and switched theatre troupe to Pembroke's Men, so this might look like revenge. In the context of this apparent quarrel, it might also be tempting to look again at Nashe's reference to Ferdinando after his death as 'Jove's Eagle-born Ganimed'.[7] The Stanley badge was an eagle and child, but to link it with this particular child obviously does considerable ideological damage.

If Marlowe is indeed reflecting on the Stanley family, however, he is doing so only delicately. When we turn to Shakespeare's *Richard III*, it may look as if the Stanley family is much more openly represented, but actually I want to argue that much of what is being suggested about them is in fact being presented covertly and that here too there is a tension between official and unofficial versions of history. Shakespeare's telling of this story fits into a clutch of other sixteenth-century renderings of the relevant events, particularly those sponsored or authored by the Stanleys – of which there are so many that one might indeed speak of a sustained propaganda drive by the Stanleys and their agents to maximise their own importance in English history. The Stanleys were always acutely aware of the importance of disseminating information – in 1588 Henry, Fourth Earl of Derby, presided over the destruction of the Marprelate press in Manchester – and it is therefore unsurprising to find several anonymous ballads celebrating the way in which they won the battle of Flodden single-handed and a northern-authored account of their decisive intervention at the battle of Bosworth, which survives in both an early prose version and a later ballad one. (In real life, the Stanleys hung back at Bosworth; in *Bosworth Feilde*, this becomes masterly inactivity and the sole factor ensuring the victory of Richmond.) Most notably, there is 'The Stanley Poem', which was written in about 1560 by another Thomas Stanley, Bishop of Man. This is a naively charming poem with a number of splendid vocabulary items: I am particularly fond of its dismissal of one group of soldiers as not worth a 'dickeduckefarte' (Fitte Three, l. 208). It also glorifies the Stanleys in a number of ways. In the first place, they are invincible warriors, who not only won the battles of Flodden and Bosworth Field but also conquered the crucial frontier town of Berwick:

> Thus Barwicke became Englishe by therle Standelay,
> There is no true man that therto dare say nay;
> A thousand four hundred lxxij. no doubt
> Barwicke was made Englishe, or neere thereaboute.
>
> (Fitte Three, ll. 447–50)

Bishop Thomas is in some doubt here about the date, but he is quite sure who won the battle. Secondly, the Stanleys are irresistibly attractive to women, particularly in the case of Thomas, First Earl of Derby:

> Then he came in favour with Lady Margaret,
> That was doghter to the Duke of Somerset,
> And King Henry the Seaventh she was his mother,
> She would have Lord Standley, she would have none other
>
> (Fitte Three, ll. 89–92)

'The Stanley Poem' also refers to Henry VII's admiration of Lathom House, which he visited in 1495, five months after his execution of Sir William Stanley – on which occasion, Stanley legend has it, the king leaned over the roof to admire the view and the household jester whispered in the ear of Earl Thomas, Sir William Stanley's brother, 'Tom, remember Will!'[8] There is, not surprisingly, none of this in 'The Stanley Poem', but it does record proudly – and entirely erroneously – that Henry was so impressed that 'his haule at Richmond he pulld downe all, / To make it up againe after Latham hall' (Fitte Three, ll. 863–4).

Particularly notable are two specific references in Bishop Thomas's account of Stanley history. In the first place, he claims that the King gave the heir of John Stanley the manors of 'Winge, Trynge and Iving, in Buckinghamshire' (Fitte Two, l. 47). These three manors had acquired considerable symbolic importance because of a legend associated with their transfer. In the fourteenth century, the then lord of the three manors, Lord Hampden, is said to have slapped the Black Prince in a dispute about chivalry and Edward III therefore seized these three manors, as recorded in the jingle

Tring, Wing and Ivinghoe,
　Hampden did foregoe,
　For striking of a blow,
　And glad he did escape so.[9]

It was to recall this rhyme that Sir Walter Scott would later name his most famous hero Ivanhoe, deliberately alluding to Lord Hampden's refusal to accept what he saw as royal tyranny, and I think the mention of the three may well be performing something of a similar function in 'The Stanley Poem': it memorialises and asserts aristocratic independence from the Crown. This is even more the case with the second reference in 'The Stanley Poem' on which I want to pick up, which in this case departs entirely from other accounts:

Then therle of Darby without taking more reade,
Straighte set the crowne on King Harry the Seaventh his heade.
Sir William Standleyes tongue was somewhat to ryfe,
For a fonde worde he spake soone after he lost his lyfe,
Said, set it thine owne head, for nowe thou maye.
King Henry afterwarde hard tell of that saye:
In such cause it is not meete with princes to boorde,
Good service may be soone loste with a fonde woorde.

(Fitte Three, ll. 529–36)

The usual version of these events, as we shall see when we come to Ford's *Perkin Warbeck*, is that it was the impostor Perkin Warbeck whom Sir William was proposing to set on the throne; here it is his own brother, reinforcing the dangerous suggestion that the Stanleys in effect constitute an alternative royal family.

But it was not only in poetry that the Stanleys were involved; they took a keen interest in drama too. Thomas, Second Earl, had been a patron of the Chester players, and both the subsequent earls maintained the interest. William the Sixth Earl was even said to write plays himself at his home in Chester: 'two extant letters dated June 1599 speak of him "busy penning commedies for the common players", and in a later undated letter Lady Derby asked Robert Cecil to look with favour on Derby's Men, "for that my Lord taking delite in them, it will kepe him from moer prodigall courses"'. Earl William may also have been responsible for the erection of a playhouse in Prescot, near Knowsley.[10] Most notably, of course, there is the suggestion that either Earl William or his brother, Ferdinando the Fifth Earl, might in some way have been involved with Shakespeare (or occasionally that Earl William *was* Shakespeare, but that idea need not detain us here). E. A. J. Honigmann, for instance, thinks that

Shakespeare 'was one of Strange's Men before 1594' and that *Richard III*, *Love's Labour's Lost, Henry VI* and *A Midsummer Night's Dream* all bear the marks of the connection. He argues that 'Thomas Stanley, the first Earl of Derby, who established the family's fortunes, figures in *Richard III* . . . and Shakespeare rearranged history so as to make Stanley's services to the incoming Tudor dynasty seem more momentous than they really were' and that something similar is at work in *Henry VI*, where Queen Margaret rather than Lord Clifford, as in Hall, is blamed for the cruel killing of Rutland:

> Lord Strange was the son of Margaret Clifford and was therefore a direct descendant of the Cliffords represented in *Henry VI*; also . . . Ferdinando's 'Stanley' ancestors had not yet risen to prominence in the reign of Henry VI – if Lord Strange was to have the pleasure of identifying himself with any of the principal figures in Shakespeare's version of history it had to be through his mother's family.[11]

Honigmann is also prepared to entertain Dugdale's ascription of the epitaphs to Sir Edward Stanley of Winwick and Tong and his father Sir Thomas Shakespeare.[12]

Of particular interest for *Richard III*, though, is the relationship between the play and the ballad known as 'The Song of the Ladye Bessiye', which purports to tell the story of the events surrounding the battle of Bosworth from the perspective of Edward IV's eldest daughter Elizabeth of York, who subsequently married Henry VII, and was probably written by Humphrey Brereton, who actually appears as a character in the narrative. This work is clearly part of Stanley propaganda: Lady Bessy speaks to the Earl of Derby of how

> Sir William Stanley, thy brother deere
>   in the hol[t]e where he doth lye,
> he may make 500 fightinge men
>   by the marryage of his faire Ladye.

(IV, 65–8)

She also mentions George, Lord Strange, Edward and James Stanley, two other Stanleys and a nephew, Sir John Savage, and the familiar themes of Stanley reliability in battle and good relations with women are thoroughly worked over. There are, however, two rather more unusual emphases. In the first place, 'The Song of the Ladye Bessiye' is remarkable for the considerable stress it lays on Lady Bessy's literacy. The first thing we are told about her is that 'shee cold write, & shee cold reede, / well shee cold worke by prophesye',[13] and her literacy is also the first piece of information about her given to her prospective husband, when Humphrey Bretton tells him:

> shee is a Countesse, a Kings daughter,
>   the name of her is Bessye,

a lovelye Lady to looke upon,
    & well shee can worke by profecye.

(IV, 721–4)

She reads 'how shee shold bee Queene of England, / but many a guiltelesse man first must dye' (I, 167–8) in a book which, she declares, her father left her (I, 52) – suggesting that it has proper patriarchal endorsement, but further suggesting, of course, that it in some sense needs it, as if reading – particularly of a book of prophecy – is a questionable activity for a well-born young lady.

And so indeed it was, or at least for this young lady in particular, because to stress the literacy of Elizabeth of York might come close to glancing in the direction of something rather dangerous, which was the allegation made by Sir George Buc in his *History of Richard III* that Elizabeth of York exercised her literacy to quite different effect, by writing a letter not to Lord Stanley but to the Duke of Norfolk, expressing her desire to marry Richard III. In Buc's words,

> the Lady Elizabeth, being more impatient and jealous of the success than every one knew or conceived, writes a letter to the Duke of Norfolk, intimating first, that he was the man in whom she most affied, in respect of the love her father had ever bore him, & c. Then she congratulates his many courtesies, in continuance of which, she desires him to be a mediator for her to the King, in continuance of which, in behalf of the marriage propounded between them, who, as she wrote, was her only joy and maker in this world and that she was his in heart and thought; with all insinuating, that the better part of February was past and that she feared the Queen would never die.
>
> All of these be her own words, written with her own hand and this is the sum of her letter, which remains in the autograph, or original draft, under her own hand, in the magnificent cabinet of Thomas Earl of Arundel and Surrey.[14]

Given the circulation of this wildly contentious allegation and the two diametrically opposed versions of the conduct of Elizabeth of York, it is perhaps easier to account for Shakespeare's circumspect decision to exclude her altogether from the play and for the ambiguity which surrounds the behaviour of Elizabeth Woodville, whom the play does its best, in difficult circumstances, to exculpate.

Also interesting for the same reason is the contrast between the repeated mention of Lord Strange in 'The Song of the Ladye Bessiye' and the absolute silence on the subject in Shakespeare's play. First we are told in the poem that

King Richard made a messenger,
    & send into the west countrye,
bidd the Erle of Derbye make him readye

& bring 20000 men unto mee,
or the Lord stranges head I shall him send.

(V, 861–5)

The name 'Lord Strange' recurs twice more, the second time in conjunction with a reference to his wife and eldest son (V, 881–2 and VI, 977–86). 'Georg Lord Strang sonn & heire to Thomas Lord Stanley' is also identified in the margin of Sir William Cornwallis's *Encomium of Richard III*, of which one surviving copy may perhaps have been annotated by Shakespare's patron Southampton,[15] while 'The Stanley Poem' not only refers repeatedly to George Stanley as Lord Strange but also adds the detail that 'The lord Straung to be headded was brought out twise' (Fitte Three, l. 523). Shakespeare, however, never calls George Stanley Lord Strange, even though 'Strange' was a name often played with because of the obvious possibilities for punning and rhyming – Strange was for instance often rhymed with change, not least because Ferdinando's motto was *Sans changer ma verité*,[16] and 'The Stanley Poem' refers to the alleged origin of the eagle and child myth as 'the like so straunge a thing hath not beene seene' – (Second Fitte, l. 11). *Richard III* is, indeed, virtually the only Shakespeare play where the word 'strange' never occurs at all, and this may well have been because it would have embarrassed the Stanley family to mention that name in connection with the succession to the Crown and the replacement of one dynasty by another.

When we turn to John Ford's *Perkin Warbeck*, we revisit both the material of *Richard III* and the text of *The Jew of Malta*, since Marlowe's play was printed for the first time in 1633, the probable year of *Perkin Warbeck*'s composition. Moreover, not only was it both revived and published by Ford's friend Heywood, but it contains lines which sound rather more like Ford than like Marlowe:

Then take them up and let them be interred
Within one sacred monument of stone;
Upon which altar I will offer up
My daily sacrifice of sighs and tears

(3.2.29–32)

These are phrases of which Ford is fond – there are close, though not exact, variations on them in his play *Love's Sacrifice*, which was also going through the press that year – and I would not be at all surprised if there were some form of contamination or revision at work here in which Ford was involved. On the criteria newly legitimated by Gilles Monsarrat in his re-assignation of the 'Elegy for William Peter', I would certainly be tempted to ascribe these lines to Ford. Since Ford also seems to refer to Marlowe in *'Tis Pity She's a Whore*, I think we are at least dealing with a conscious revisiting of the Marlovian aesthetic as well as of the Shakespearean one.

The full title of *Perkin Warbeck* is, as I have already mentioned, *The Chronicle Historie of Perkin Warbeck: A Strange Truth*. Both the truth and the strangeness of it are usually taken to refer to Perkin Warbeck himself, but I want to argue that the play also encodes a rather different sort of strange truth. The unfolding of the main plot of the play is at various points conspicuously delayed and indeed at times almost derailed by an emphasis on the relatively unconnected story of Sir William Stanley, brother of Thomas, Earl of Derby and the trusted friend and adviser of Henry VII, and the revelation of the fact that he has been plotting against the king. In Act 1 Scene 3, Sir William Stanley is named (in full) six times in thirty lines, and there is also a striking episode where he makes the sign of the cross on the face of Clifford, the man who has revealed his treachery (2.2.84 SD). Although it is clear that Clifford is telling the truth, he is made to seem here almost more of a traitor than the man whose treachery he unmasks.

I wonder whether one reason for this insistence on the repetition of the name 'Sir William Stanley' is that the story of the fifteenth-century Sir William Stanley of the play is meant to recall that other, sixteenth-century Sir William Stanley, who in 1587 had betrayed Deventer to the Spanish and who died in Ghent on 3 March 1630, four years before the first publication of Ford's play. Several clues seem to me to point in this direction. In 1584 the sixteenth-century Sir William Stanley had been made sheriff of Cork; much stress is laid on the fact that one of the comic characters in *Perkin Warbeck* is a former mayor of Cork, and indeed the structure of the play is such that John a Water, the ex-mayor in question, could readily double the play's William Stanley. Moreover, at a number of points in *Perkin Warbeck*, there is reference to the Low Countries, which were the setting for the sixteenth-century Sir William Stanley's treason. The Spanish ambassador Hialas declares that

> France, Spain and Germany combine a league
> Of amity with England; nothing wants
> For settling peace through Christendom but love
> Between the British monarchs, James and Henry.
> DURHAM   The English merchants, sir, have been receiv'd
> With general procession into Antwerp;
> The emperor confirms the combination.
>
> (4.3.1–7)

Here, as with the numerous references to the Duchess of Burgundy, the Low Countries context is insisted on.

There is also another notable connection with the Stanleys which I think impacts on the meanings of *Perkin Warbeck*. The sixteenth-century Sir William Stanley married Elizabeth, daughter of John Egerton of Egerton; the

Egerton family was that for which *Comus* was written, and there appear to
be references to the Castlehaven affair in both *Perkin Warbeck* and *Comus*.[17]
In 1631 the Earl of Castlehaven was found guilty of sodomising one of his
servants, for physically assisting another servant to bugger the Countess and
for pandering his daughter-in-law to yet another servant;[18] *Comus*, it has
been suggested, with its insistence on the sexual purity of its participants,
was a conscious attempt to improve the reputation of the family, vicariously
tainted by association with their notorious relative. I have previously suggested a similar context for *Perkin Warbeck*, since the full name of the renegade peer was Mervyn Touchet, Lord Audley, Earl of Castlehaven, and an
earlier bearer of that title, James Touchet, Lord Audley, is prominently fea-
tured in *Perkin Warbeck* as one of the principal leaders of the Cornish revolt.
He is mentioned by name four times, and the final occasion is one that seems
virtually designed to bring to mind the recent, even more opprobrious, disgrace of another bearer of the Audley title:

> Let false Audley
> Be drawn upon an hurdle from the Newgate
> To Tower-hill in his own coat of arms
> Painted on paper, with the arms revers'd,
> Defac'd and torn; there let him lose his head.

(3.1.94–8)[19]

This possible allusion to the Castlehaven affair in *Perkin Warbeck* takes on
a sharp resonance because of a very odd historical fact. In 'The Stanley
Poem', Bishop Thomas Stanley begins his history of the family with some
startling information:

> I intend with true report to praise
> The valiaunte actes of the stoute Standelais;
> From whence they came, and how they came to that name,
> I shall plainely and truly declare the same.
> Theire names be Awdeley by very right dissent,
> I shall shewe you how, if you geeve good attente,
> As quickly as I can, without more delay,
> How the name was changed and called Stanley.
> In antique tyme much more then two hundred yeare
> Was on L. Audley, by stories does appeare,
> Audley by creation and by name Audley,
> Havinge a lordshippe is yeat called Standley,
> Which lordship he gave to his second sonne,
> For valiaunte actes that he before had donne.
> There this young man dwelling many a longe daye,
> And many yeares called Awdley of Standelay,
> After he maried the heyre of Sturton;

And when Sturton died thether he went to wonne,
And as in length of tyme thinges be lost and wonne,
All the countrey called him Standley of Sturtonn

(First Fitte, ll. 1–20)

This Audley of Stanley then married 'the daughter and heyre of Hooton' (First Fitte, ll. 23–5), acceding to the title later held by the traitor of Deventer. Of course at the time when Bishop Thomas wrote this there was no reason for anyone to shrink from association with the Audleys, but the Castlehaven scandal entirely altered the situation. By the time Ford was writing, therefore, his incrimination of the Audleys and semi-exculpation of Sir William Stanley could well have been a useful tactic for putting distance between the Stanleys and the now-undesirable Audleys with whom they had so unfortunately claimed identity.

The 'strange truth' of *Perkin Warbeck*, therefore, seems to me to be twofold. Firstly, it offers an exculpation of the Stanleys in general, and, secondly, it provides a palliation of an event which it presents as analogous to Sir William Stanley's betrayal and his subsequent plot to secure the succession of his cousin, Lord Strange. Perhaps the point is that Perkin is a lost king, as English Catholics thought Strange was – an attractive but doomed alternative ruler. Perhaps, indeed, we are meant to ask who the true king should be.

More widely, though, I think we are also meant to ask how kings in general should behave. There seems to have been something of a precedent for using the figure of the fifteenth-century Sir William Stanley to question the justice of more recent kings. He is, for instance, mentioned in William Warner's *Albion's England*, where we read that

> *Perken* was hang'd, and hang may such: but that the Earle should die
> Some thought hard law, save that it stood with present pollicie.
> Sir *William Stanley* dide for this (oft King law is doe thus)
> Deserving better of the King: but what is that to us?[20]

Sir William Stanley occurs too in Thomas Gainsford's 'The true and wonderful History of *Perkin Warbeck*, proclaiming himself *Richard the Fourth*', where we are told that

> Sir William Stanley swore and affirmed, that he would never fight nor bear Armour against the young Man *Peter Warbeck*, if he knew of a Truth that he was the undoubted Son of *Edward the Fourth*, whereupon arose a conjectural Proof, that he had no Good-will to King *Henry*.[21]

Epistemological certainty is initially evoked here only to disappear like smoke: we go from the absolutes of 'swore and affirmed' to the doubt implicit in 'if he knew of a truth' and ultimately to the darkly uncertain 'whereupon arose a conjectural Proof'. The progression is markedly from apparent knowledge to avowed ignorance, and yet it is also clear that, terrifyingly, the more exiguous the evidence, the more extreme is the action taken on the basis of it. On the basis of the 'conjectural Proof', Sir William Stanley will lose his head.

Gainsford's clever rhetoric here makes it clear that he regards the category of treason as a highly dubious one, and there are many other instances of this during the course of his long 'History'. Also *à propos* of Sir William Stanley, he says that

> The Searcher of Hearts was weary of his Humours and Ingratitude and so took the King's Cause in Hand and upon good Inforcement thrust him into the House of Destruction. Otherwise he could not choose but remember, how, not twenty Years before, the Law had interpreted the profuse and lavish Speeches of a Grocer, named *Walker*, dwelling at the Sign of the *Crown*, in *Cheapside*, who bad his Son learn a pace and he would make him Heir of the *Crown*, meaning his House he dwelt in, for which he was adjudged to die . . . Thus you see there is no Jesting with Princes. (523)

You do indeed – but you also see that this might well be because not all princes are fit to rule.

The suitability of specific princes is, of course, the matter that lies at the nub of the Stanley-oriented counter-history at which I have tried to gesture here. In particular, it is hard to forget in any account of the Perkin story that, if Perkin *were* the king, the treason would, in a kind of world-upside-down motif, be the other way about: the name of traitor would, inevitably, be the name due not to those who follow Perkin but of those who fight against him. This is made clear in Ford's *Perkin Warbeck* when Durham says that Sir William Stanley believes that York's title is better than that of Lancaster:

> Which, if it be not treason in the highest,
> Then we are traitors all, perjured and false,
> Who have took oath to Henry and the justice
> Of Henry's title.[22]

Here, treason takes on an eerie reversibility, reminiscent of the inverse proportions of proof and punishment in Gainsford: either the traitor must be proved wrong – and, implicitly, punished accordingly – or, hideously, we find ourselves in a world in which *everyone else* is a traitor. Although the fact is never mentioned outright, it is clear that Ford's play is haunted by the possible alternative title of *Richard the Fourth* – and that would give rise to a very different view of history in which all polarities of loyalty and sedition would be exactly reversed. It also, of course, raises the whole idea of history as a contingent rather than an inevitable force, a tactic which had often been espoused by discontented groups – as with the Tacitean approach favoured by the Earl of Essex's circle – and used to question royalist politics. Eight years after Ford's play was published, the advent of the Civil War would show only too vividly how right he had been to wonder whether there was still any consensus over the nature of treason. *Perkin Warbeck* showed Ford's prescience in this and it showed, too, how useful the mention of the Stanley family could still be in raising this very question and that other, far more important question of how much truth there is in the histories that we are told.

Notes

1 Charles Nicholl, *The Reckoning: The Murder of Chrisopher Marlowe*, 2nd edition (London: Vintage, 2002), 276.
2 Albert J. Loomie, S. J., *The Spanish Elizabethans: The English Exiles at the Court of Philip II* (New York: Fordham University Press, 1963), 147–8.
3 Ethel Seaton, 'Marlowe, Robert Poley and the Tippings', *Review of English Studies*, 5 (1929), 273–87, p. 285.
4 Emily Bartels, *Spectacles of Strangeness: Imperialism, Alienation and Marlowe* (Philiadelphia: Pennsylvania University Press, 1993), 90.
5 Ernle Bradford, *The Great Siege: Malta 1565* [1961] (Harmondworth: Penguin, 1964), 222.
6 Charles Nicholl, *The Reckoning: The Murder of Christopher Marlowe* (London: Jonathan Cape, 1992), 227.
7 J. J. Bagley, *The Earls of Derby 1485–1985* (London: Sidgwick & Jackson, 1985), 75.
8 *Ibid.*, 21, 32, 26.
9 G. F. Northall, *English Folk Rhymes* (London: Kessinger, 1892), 8.
10 Bagley, *Earls of Derby*, 76.
11 E. A. J. Honigmann, *Shakespeare: The 'Lost Years'* (Manchester: Manchester University Press, 1985), 60, 62–4, 154.
12 E. A. J. Honigmann, *John Weever* (Manchester: Manchester University Press, 1987), 69–70.
13 'Ladye Bessiye', Part One, ll. 17–18.
14 George Buc, *History of Richard the Third*, ed. A. N. Kincaid (Gloucester: Alan Sutton, 1979), 128. For discussion of the letter's authenticity see for instance Alison Hanham, 'Sir George Buck and Princess Elizabeth's Letter: A Problem in Detection', *The Ricardian*, 7, 97 (June 1987) and A. N. Kincaid, 'Buck and the Elizabeth of York Letter: A Reply to Dr Hanham', *The Ricardian*, 8, 101 (June 1988).
15 Sir William Cornwallis the Younger, *The Encomium of Richard III*, ed. A. N. Kincaid (London: Turner & Devereux, 1977), 27, vii.
16 Honigmann, *Weever*, 65.
17 This was first suggested in Barbara Breasted, 'Comus and the Castlehaven Scanuar', *Milton Studies*, 3 (1971), 201–4.
18 Frances Dolan, *Dangerous Familiars: Representations of Domestic Crime in England 1550–1700* (Ithaca: Cornell University Press, 1994), 80.

19 The other references to Audley in the play are at 3.1.133, 3.1.48 and 3.1.75. See my 'Touching Touchets: Perkin Warbeck and the Buggery Statute', *Renaissance Quarterly*, 52, 2 (summer 1999), 384–401.

20 William Warner, *Albions England*, book 7, ll. 268–71.

21 Thomas Gainsford, *The true and wonderful History of* Perkin Warbeck, *proclaiming himself* Richard the Fourth (London, 1618), 523.

22 John Ford, *The Chronicle History of Perkin Warbeck*, in *'Tis Pity She's a Whore and Other Plays*, ed. Marion Lomax (Oxford: Oxford University Press, 1995), 2.2.18–20. All further quotations are from this edition.

A sea of troubles: the thought of the outside in Shakespeare's histories

Because of his crippling deformity, he liked to feel 'the heat of the sun' on his back, so that he would always throw a shadow before him, rather than hold his 'face into the cold'; but those who punningly nicknamed him the 'arch enemy', from his bent shape, never forgot that 'beneath the black cloak, his back was hunched', nor that it was proverbially considered 'an unwholesome thing to meet a man in the morning which hath a wry neck, a crooked back or a splay foot'. His spinal curvature has, in fact, been diagnosed as caused by a fall from his nurse's arms; but he was also called *diabolus* by some who swore that his hump, 'bumbasted legs' and outsize head were devil's signs. Devil, Judas, Toad, Elf, Dwarf, Gobbo, Crookback, Pigmy, Hog: his nicknames were legion precisely because he was so despised and feared. Yet according to modern biographers, 'as soon as he was old enough, he learned to adjust himself to the repugnance' he provoked and 'bore with it by masking his feelings'. Though 'he could not join in oudoor sports . . . and could never dance', the effect of his hunchback and 'the loneliness it thrust upon him, was that he was acutely self-conscious', with 'a self-awareness that was . . . often ironical, for he seldom gave himself away . . . he was always fully in control of himself, a control learnt when he bit back tears of humiliation and pain in childhood'. As his kinsman Francis Bacon wrote in the essay *Of Deformity* – where, it was said, 'he painted his little cousin to the life' – such ridicule gave him 'a perpetual spur to rescue and deliver himself', in the way that all 'Deformed persons are commonly even with nature: for as nature hath done ill by them, so do they by nature . . . it stirreth in them industry and especially to watch and observe the weakness of others . . . for they will, if they be of spirit, seek to free themselves from scorn, which must be either by virtue or malice'.[1] No wonder, then, that with these paranoid characteristics, and an indifference to idle pastimes, 'the little hunchback', Robert Cecil, had become, by the early 1590s, 'the greatest Councillor in England, without whose favour little can be done'

(Du Maurier, *The Winding Stair*, 152–3). Nor that, in such a superstitious
court, his deformity inspired in victims inevitable comparisons with the
hunchback and monstrous birth of Richard III, 'the stock bogeyman' of
Tudor demonology:

> Here lieth Robin Crookback, unjustly reckoned
> A Richard the Third: he was Judas the Second . . .
> Richard or Robert, which is the worse?
> A Crookback great in State is England's curse.
>
> > (*Ibid.*, 15–16)

'Whiles two RRs, both crouchbacks, stood at the helm', jeered one of the
rhymes circulated after Cecil's death in 1612, 'The one spilt the blood royal,
the other the realm'.[2] 'Richard or Robert', the 'Little Cecil' who in these
libels 'trips up and down' and 'rules both court and Crown . . . In his fox-
furred gown'; a 'monster sent by cruel fate / To plague his country and the
state' (De Luna, *Jonson's Romish Plot*, 1; 230), was so consistently associated by contemporaries with the hunchback Richard III that the question
posed by Shakespeare's play on the tyrannical upstart is not *whether* its audiences would have recognised there a portrait of Elizabeth's Machiavellian
minister, but just how the author was able to get away with such a cutting
comparison. The answer surely lies in the circumstances of the play's original
production, which, as editors infer, was almost certainly some time in 1593
by Strange's Men: the acting troupe patronised by Ferdinando Stanley, Lord
Strange, heir to Henry, Fourth Earl of Derby and the overlord of north-west
England. There, this so-called 'king of Lancashire' kept court in such magnificent style that his palace at Lathom had been copied for the royal one at
Richmond, while his household spent a colossal £1500 a year on food and
had 150 servants.[3] Because the family's power was so soon obliterated,
Shakespeare critics have underestimated the feudal wealth and significance
of the dynasty to which the young writer attached himself, but in 1593 the
house of Stanley was at the pinnacle of its prospects, which the Fourth Earl
had cemented with a royal marriage at Whitehall, attended by Queen Mary
and King Philip, to Margaret Clifford, great-granddaughter of Henry VII,
the victor of the Wars of the Roses. This meant that, under the terms of
Henry VIII's will, Ferdinando (named after his godfather, the Habsburg
Emperor Ferdinand, no less) and his brother William were raised as 'the only
unquestioned legitimate English heirs to the throne' and it was as such a
prince, who himself wrote poetry and acted in plays, that he was saluted by
Spenser as 'Amyntas . . . the noblest swain that ever piped'.[4] One consequence of Ferdinando's international status was that the plays commissioned
for his actors were outstanding for lavish troupes and costuming, but,
according to Scott McMillin, another was that they were politically

audacious.[5] And of all the works staged by Strange's Men it is *Richard III* which trumpets most loudly the role of the Stanleys in the Tudor epic, and the contrast between their Herculean grandeur and the meanness of a 'goose-quilled pen gent' like the hunchback clerk, 'St Gobbo' (Handover, *The Second Cecil*, 145; 230). With its exorbitant cast and masque-like processions, *Richard III* reads, by this light, like a professional continuation of the kind of pageantry the Stanleys staged in their own territories, such as that displayed in 1572 at the funeral of the Third Earl, when the family advertised its royal ambitions and, as one bystander recorded, 'it was as if Duke Hector, or Ajax, or Sir Lancelot were being buried':

> First came 100 poor men fitted out in black for the occasion. Behind them marched a choir of 40 in their surplices, followed by a knight on horseback bearing the late earl's standard. Next came 80 gentlemen of the earl, his 2 secretaries, 2 chaplains and 50 knights, the preacher, the Dean of Chester, the 3 chief officers and a knight on horse carrying the great banner. At this point appeared the splendid spectacle of four royal heralds riding horses with black trappings ornamented with escutcheons reaching to the ground. First came Lancaster carrying the Earl's gilt helmet, followed by Norroy with his shield topped by a coronet, Clarenceux with the Earl's sword, and finally Garter bearing his coat of arms. The heralds preceded the black draped chariot with the coffin, drawn by four horses and surrounded by ten hooded guards on horseback, carrying the arms of the distinguished families whose blood was mingled with that of the Stanleys. Behind the chariot walked the chief mourner, the new earl, with his two sons [Ferdinando and William] and eight other noblemen. Finally, the tail of this great procession was composed of 500 yeomen and the servants of all the gentlemen taking part in the ceremony.[6]

If Homer rewrote the *Odyssey*, exclaimed Thomas Nashe in 1592, he would model his hero on Ferdinando Stanley. Nashe's salute, at the end of *Pierce Penniless*, to 'Jove's eagle-born Ganymede, thrice noble Amyntas', compares this 'singular man of perfection, in whom all ornaments of peace and war are assembled', with those 'buckram giants, that having an outward face of honour set on them by flatterers and parasites' and 'painting themselves with church spoils', are stuffed with 'atheism, schism, hypocrisy and vainglory'. The Ganymede tribute plays on the Stanley badge (presumably worn by Rosalind in the Forest of Arden) of an eagle and child. But the eagle was also a Habsburg symbol and since Jove was code for the Pope and the insignia had been adopted by priests presuming on Ferdinando's faith, the poetic elevation of the Catholic-born aristocrat over Puritan clerks adds political and religious dimensions to the contrast of upstart nobility of the robe with true nobility of the sword. For a 'penniless' writer, though, the comparison is between two classes of patron. The parvenu is 'a clown that knows not how to use a scholar', too occupied 'with my Lord What call-ye-him' to reward the 'poor simple pedant in a threadbare cloak' for his labours. By contrast, Amyntas (whose name means 'defender') maintains 'Augustus' liberality, that never sent any away empty'. It is because they are 'mightily supported by your plentiful largesse', Nashe advises Stanley, that poets 'sing such goodly hymns of your praise'. This service has to be earned, he admits: 'for what reason have I to bestow my wit upon him that will bestow none of his wealth upon me?' But Strange's 'exceeding bounty and liberality' make him so 'magnificent a rewarder of virtue' that Spenser ought to devote to him a second *Faerie Queene*, having 'let so special a pillar of nobility pass unsaluted' the first time out of 'forgetfulness'. The joke locates Stanley patronage in antagonism to Protestant empire and so defines the literary field which Shakespeare enters with *Richard III* as one polarised between courtiers like the Cecils, for whom 'cap and thanks is payment' and 'countrymen that live out of the echo of the court', such as the 'far-derived' Stanleys, who secure 'zeal and duty' from artists with the beneficence of Homeric heroes.[7] No wonder, then, that so many writers of the early 1590s concur with Robert Greene in 'thinking nothing rare, view-worthy or sufficiently patronaged unless shrouded under the protection of so honourable a Maecenas' as Ferdinando.[8] For as Nashe records, the moment of Strange's Men, and so of *Richard III*, was when aspiring poets and players began to desert Elizabeth's regime, as he urged Spenser to do, for the 'bright stars of glittering nobility and glistering attendants on the true Diana', the revanchist Catholic aristocracy:

> Many writers and good wits are given to commend their patrons and benefactors . . . but if my unable pen should ever enterprise such a continuate task . . . I would embowel a number of those wind-puffed bladders and disfurnish their bald pates of the periwigs poets have lent them, that so I might restore glory to his right inheritance and those stolen titles to their true owners. Which, if it would so fall out (as time may work all things), the aspiring nettles, with their shady tops, shall no longer overdrip the best herbs, or keep them from the smiling aspect of the sun . . . none but desert should sit in fame's grace, none but Hector be remembered in the chronicles of prowess, none but thou, most courteous Amyntas, be the second mystical argument of the knight of the Red Cross. (Nashe, 'Pierce Penniless', 143)

'Now are our brows bound with victorious wreaths . . . Our stern alarums changed to merry meetings': Richard's analysis of the end of the War of the Roses could as well describe the difficulty facing England's war party in the wake of the Armada, when 'all the clouds that loured' upon the house of Cecil were 'In the deep bosom of the ocean buried' and its bellicosity sounded obsolete as 'dreadful marches' shifted into 'delightful measures' (*Richard III*, 1.1.3–8): like the Accession Tilt of 1590, in which 'Brave Ferdinand Lord Strange' capered to the 'lascivious pleasing' of George

Peele's 'Polyhymnia', 'Under Jove's kingly bird, the golden Eagle, / Stanley's old crest'.[9] The same symbol of Jupiter's eagle would reappear in *Cymbeline* as a sign of Roman pacification, and Ferdinando's pose of Ganymede proclaims his mission, as a papal favourite, to usher a 'piping time of peace'. So, if the fictional Crookback is a spitting image of Robert Cecil, it is apt that he is so 'rudely stamped' and curtailed of 'fair proportion' that he says he has 'no delight to pass away the time', and plans to wreck 'the idle pleasures of these days' in plots (1.1.1–32). This Puritan gargoyle starts, therefore, as the first of the theatre-haters who menace Shakespeare's stage, the prototype malcontent or 'pale companion' (*Dream*, 1.1.15) who 'reads much . . . loves no plays . . . hears no music . . . and smiles in such a sort / As if he mocked himself' (*Caesar*, 1.1.202–7). The irony, however, is that this opponent of 'sportive tricks' (1.1.14), who protests he 'cannot flatter and look fair' (1.3.47) since his 'tongue could never learn sweet smoothing word' (1.2.172), develops into 'Shakespeare's arch player',[10] a forerunner of later carnival-kings, who learns how to 'Play the maid's part' (3.7.51) as well as 'counterfeit the deep tragedian' (3.5.5). 'Associated remorselessly with the theatre', as Anne Barton observes, Richard 'seems to be regarded more as an example of the power wielded by the actor than a figure of evil'.[11] Yet theatricality, we are reminded by his role-play, 'is not set over against power but is one of power's essential modes'. And so the question that the play appears to pose, when set into Elizabethan context, is precisely the one confronting Strange's company as they acted it in 1593, of how to steal the thunder from a Protestant regime which had made the power of the actor, under the eyes of 'the little hunchback', such a propaganda instrument of its own (Handover, *The Second Cecil*, 55):

> Why, I can smile, and murder whiles I smile,
> And cry 'Content!' to that which grieves my heart,
> And wet my cheeks with artificial tears,
> And frame my face to all occasions.
> I'll drown more sailors than the mermaid shall;
> I'll slay more gazers than the basilisk;
> I'll play the orator as well as Nestor,
> Deceive more slyly than Ulysses could,
> And, like a Sinon, take another Troy.
> I can add colours to the chameleon,
> Change shapes with Proteus for advantages,
> And set the murderous Machiavel to school.
> (*Richard Duke of York* [*3 Henry VI*], 3.2.182–93)

Richard III is a play about defection arising from a defection on the London stage. For as Peter Thomson recounts in his résumé of Shakespeare's career, the literary field mapped by Nashe, with Protestant power pitted against papist patronage, would come to be organised as a duopoly of theatre troupes 'aligned on opposite sides of the political gulf', with Strange's (or, later, the Chamberlain's) Men tied to the party of toleration and Leicester's (or the Admiral's) Men to 'Robert Cecil and the conservative establishment'. By 1594, when Shakespeare is first known to have joined the Strange group, the 'jostling for supremacy' with the Admiral's Men had become a duel in which 'both troupes were bent on survival'. Thomson thinks it unlikely, therefore, that the companies ever admired each other's work.[12] And, in fact, their reper- toires were ideologically opposed, with Strange's support of subversive drama pitched against Lord Admiral Charles Howard's sponsorship of imperialist epics, like Marlowe's *Tamburlaine the Great*. But the two teams co-operated and periodically combined until just prior to *Richard III*, when a dispute over pay marked the parting of the ways. Significantly, the star actor, Edward Alleyn, had then threatened the theatre manager, James Burbage, with reprisals from the Privy Council and the impresario 'shouted that he cared nothing for the three "best lords of them all" '.[13] This professional divorce epitomised the collapse of consensus at the end of the Tudor century, since it divided audiences as well as actors, confining the Admiral's Men (at the Fortune theatre within the City) to a citizen public, but freeing the Chamberlain's Men (at the Theatre and then the Globe, outside the City walls) to innovate, according to Andrew Gurr, with plays that had 'particular appeal for law students and gallants' of the free-thinking Inns of court.[14] And editors detect signs of the rupture in the very part of the king in *Richard III*, where the Marlovian histrionics of Richard of Gloucester in *3 Henry VI*, written for Alleyn, are subdued into the 'subtle, false and treacherous' (1.1.37) tone of a new kind of 'gentle villain' (1.3.162).[15] This was the mode of Richard Burbage, the son of James and the actor who became so identified with the role that he took the king's crest of a boar's head as his own. For by the time the play was staged, Alleyn and the Admiral's Men had left and Shakespeare had chosen sides. From this moment of separation, it was Burbage and Lord Strange's Men who would always speak Shakespeare's lines.

In 1599 the Lancashire poet John Weever praised Shakespeare as creator of characters like Richard III in a book of *Epigrams* he claimed he wrote at university, before he ever went to London. Weever was also a Stanley protégé and, since most of the *Epigrams* are addressed to Lancastrian gentry, com- mentators speculate that this play could have been staged initially in the Earl of Derby's court theatre at Prescot in Lancashire.[16] What is certain is that *Richard III* is constructed around a series of tributes to the Stanleys that exaggerates their importance in the invasion of 1485 which brought the Tudors to power. Thus, when Richmond makes Sir William Brandon his standard-bearer, the Tudor banner is passed symbolically to Ferdinando himself, since it was from Brandon's son's marriage to Henry's daughter that his royal claim derived. In 1593, the episode implies, the flag of the 'valiant crew' was carried, on Henry's order, by Strange's Men themselves. And crucially, Shakespeare makes his climax an incident at the battle of Bosworth, reported in Holinshed, when Ferdinando's great-great-grandfather, Thomas Stanley, 'took the Crown of King Richard, which was found amongst the spoil in the field' and set it on Henry Tudor's head. As Ernst Honigmann notes, in the source there is no suggestion that Stanley found the Crown himself, whereas in the play he claims not only to have retrieved 'this long-usurpèd royalty' but to have 'plucked' it off 'the dead temples of this bloody wretch . . . to grace thy brows withal', so the effect is to inflate him as the literal 'king-maker', who can tell Henry: 'Wear it, enjoy it and make much of it' (5.8.4–7).[17] There seems no question that Shakespeare intended this rewriting of the Tudor founding moment to remind audiences how Elizabeth owed her Crown to the family who were now her heirs and that this motive lies behind his other manipulations of fact: as when Stanley is exempted from Queen Margaret's curse; remains the only Yorkist noble not to be deceived by Richard; urges Dorset to change sides; opens negotiations with Henry; and himself fights for the Tudors. In reality, as Honigmann points out, though 'as the step-father of Henry, the historical Thomas Stanley might have been expected to side with him, he was much more cautious' than his fictional counterpart; left it to his brother to lead his forces in the field; and, when asked by Henry to advance them into action, at first refused, saying 'he would come to him in time': a rebuff Shakespeare has him give instead to Richard.[18] And as if to expunge this hesitation and fix the Tudor debt to the Stanleys, Thomas is here called 'Earl of Derby' from the start: the title he won for deserting Richard, but which his descendants carried. So, when Henry takes the Crown, it must have been highly significant to the original audience that the very first act of his reign is to ask about the life and safety of the heir to the Stanleys:

> Great God of Heaven, say 'Amen' to all!
> But tell me – young George Stanley is he living?
>
> (5.8.8–9)

By making Henry VII's first thought as king concern for the boy who, when his father became Earl of Derby, was known as Lord Strange, Shakespeare concluded *Richard III* with a question that would have had sinister implications for Strange's actors and their audience. He found a source for this alarm in Thomas More's scathing analysis of Richard as a prototypical Renaissance dictator, where the king, suspecting Stanley plans to aid an invasion, 'in no wise would suffer him to depart before that he had left as a hostage in the court George Stanley, Lord Strange, his first begotten son and heir'.[19] But by repeatedly reminding us 'That in the sty of this most dreadful boar / My son George Stanley is franked up in hold' and that 'If I revolt, off goes young George's head', the fictitious earl not only provides an excuse for his family's fence-sitting in 1485 – since, as he says, 'The fear of that holds off my present aid' (4.5.2–5) – but he also depicts the lethal trap in which they were shut a century later by Burghley. 'In the sty of the most dreadful boar' might well define, indeed, the claustrophobic cage in which the whole of Catholic nobility was penned by the court of Wards operated by the Cecils, whereby guardianship of young heirs (like the poet's later patron, Henry Wriothesley, the Earl of Southampton) was used to defraud their estates and indoctrinate them in Protestant faith. But it would have had a special foreboding for Ferdinando, who was kept at court and made to dance in masques as surety for his father's conformity to the prevailing order. 'Caught in the Crown's financial web', their independence 'curtailed by court attendance' and their estates encumbered by massive debts, the Stanleys' patronage was itself a means to divert them from royal ambitions.[20] As the Countess of Derby assured Robert Cecil in 1599, when William, the sixth Earl was himself 'busy penning comedies for the common players', it was best for a Stanley to be plotting plays, 'for that my Lord taking delight in them, it will keep him from more prodigal courses'.[21] So, if Strange's Company flourished in symbolic protest at this incarceration, the fear that stalks *Richard III*, that young Strange should 'fall / Into the blind cave of eternal night' (5.5.14–15), reveals that the stakes in these artistic games were high. Shakespeare would further demonise the house of Burghley through the punning emblem of the 'foul, grim and urchin-snouted boar' in *Venus and Adonis* (l. 1105); and satirise the Cecilian system in his second tetralogy as a criminal racket run by 'minions of the moon' (*1 Henry IV*, 1.2.23) under the sign of the 'old frank' (*2 Henry IV*, 2.3.125). But it can only have been the situation in which Strange was being 'franked up to fatting' (*Richard III*, 1.2.312) in Cecil's sty which led him to sponsor an entire drama spun out of the nightmare Shakespeare puts into the mind of his forefather, when on the eve of Richard's coronation the Earl of Derby dreams that the Stanley crest is ousted by the same 'picture of an angry, chaffing boar' (*Venus*, 662):

HASTINGS   Cannot my Lord Stanley sleep these tedious nights?
MESSENGER   So it appears by that I have to say.
  First he commends him to your noble self.
HASTINGS   What then?
MESSENGER   Then certifies your lordship that this night
  He dreamt the boar had razèd off his helm.

                                                              (3.2.3–8)

For Catholic satirists, like Nashe, 'the blunt boar, rough bear, or lion proud' (*Venus*, 884) were Aesopian signifiers of their *bêtes noires*, Cecil,

Leicester and the Queen. And when Cecil later became an Earl, 'Richard D. of Glo. Robert E. of Salisbury', his enemies quipped, 'the anagram whereof is a silly burs'. This multiple play on 'boar' referred 'both to the hump he had in common with Richard III and to his bourse'.[22] But editors wonder why from the First to the Fifth Quartos of *Richard III*, printed between 1597 and 1612, Stanley's dream was said to be about a heraldic 'bear' (emblem of the deceased Leicester) and not a 'boar' and why the text was not corrected until 1622. Given the audacity of the play on Burghley's name, however, this alteration looks like prudence, rather than typographic error, which could be adjusted only after Cecil was safely dead himself. For though, in the play, Hastings mocks Lord Stanley's fears, he soon regrets that when 'Stanley did dream the boar did raze our helms . . . I did scorn it and disdain to fly' (3.4.83). In *Richard III*, we learn, the symbolism of the tyrant's badge of a white boar – 'the most deadly boar' (4.5.2), 'this foul swine' (5.2.10) – proves all too apt, when the heraldic bestiary comes true. It had been Elizabeth who dubbed Cecil her 'Pigmy', or 'My Pig', to denote his diminutive succession to the older swine, his father (at which he winced that 'I mislike not the name only because she gives it') (Handover, *The Second Cecil*, 34; 57); but the terror that haunts Shakespeare's text is that this young tusker will live up to its sire. 'Doth the old boar feed in the old frank?' asks Hal of pillagers with their snouts in the trough of 'the old church' (*2 Henry IV*, 2.2.124; 128); and this porcine imagery focuses the Catholic dilemma of whether attack is best defence from such a voracious predator, or if 'To fly the boar before the boar pursues / Were to incense the boar to follow us, / And make pursuit where he did mean no chase' (3.2.25–7). For while the 'dreadful boar' is a visual and verbal pun on the House of Burghley, Shakespeare directs the hunting metaphor which was a signature of Catholic resistance to the tactical problem he posed in *Venus and Adonis*: of how 'With javelin's point a churlish swine to gore' (616), when the animal is so fiercely armed and subterranean in intelligence that it forages through the branches of the nobility and roots among the gentry with such impunity and even the royal lion – the Queen herself – is intimidated:

On his bow-back he hath a battle set
Of bristly pikes that ever threat his foes.
His eyes like glow-worms shine; when he doth fret
His snout digs sepulchres where'er he goes.
   Being moved, he strikes, whate'er is in his way,
   And whom he strikes his crooked tushes slay.

His brawny sides with hairy bristles armed
Are better proof than thy spear's point can enter.
His short thick neck cannot be easily harmed.
Being ireful, on the lion he will venture.

> The thorny brambles and embracing bushes,
> As fearful of him, part; through whom he rushes.
>
> (*Venus*, 619–30)

'Good angels guard thee from the boar's annoy!' (*Richard III*, 5.5.105): if the 'foul boar's conquest' (*Venus*, 1030) depicted in such garish detail in these texts does encipher the irresistible rise of the 'bow-back' executioner, Robert Cecil, Shakespeare was being no more outspoken than other writers affiliated with anti-Cecilians, such as Peter Woodhouse, whose fable *The Elephant and the Flea* pitched the midget parasite against a giant Essex; Rowland White, who depicted Cecil as a lazy ass, bloodthirsty owl and poisonous scorpion; and John Day, who villified him as Dametas, a 'monstrous and deformed shape of vice' and 'the most misshapen suit of gentility that ever the court wore', in *The Isle of Gulls*. Day was, in fact, imprisoned in Bridewell for ridiculing not only Cecil, as 'a little hillock, made great with others ruins', but also his crippled daughter Francis as Mopsa, a 'frank' or pigsty of stinking swill.[23] For though Dekker disingenuously begged fellow-dramatists to 'despise him not for that deformity which fell upon him by misfortune', but to pity those 'spoiled by ill nurses, within a month after they come into the world', even Jonson bit the ministerial hand which fed him by harping, through the stunted physique of Cicero in *Catiline*, on Cecil's 'petty' size.[24] The object of this mocking 'refused to prosecute those whose malice was only towards his own person', taking a perverse pride that 'all our actions are upon the open stage and can be no more hidden than the Sun' (Da Luna, *Jonson's Romish Plot*, 146; Handover, *The Second Cecil*, 33). But if oppositional writers remained outside Cecil's reach, that was only so long as they were attached to patrons equally strong.[25] Thus, Nashe got away with satirising Leicester as 'the bear, chief burgomaster of all the beasts', a 'hungry usurper' and 'savage blood-hunter', who devoured 'whole herds of sheep, fat oxen, heifers, swine and young kids' and was hated by every animal save the lion, 'whose eyes he could blind as he list', when he was protected by the Earls of Derby and Southampton.[26] And it was the backing of the same crypto-Catholic patronage network which surely explains why Cecil was unable to stifle even such blatant allusions to his own inherited traits and physical condition as the curses of Queen Margaret in *Richard III*:

> No sleep close up that deadly eye of thine,
> Unless it be while some tormenting dream
> Affrights thee with a hell of ugly devils!
> Thou elvish-marked, abortive, rooting hog!
> Thou that wast sealed in thy nativity
> The slave of nature and the son of hell,
> Thou slander of thy heavy mother's womb,

Thou loathèd issue of thy father's loins,
Thou rag of honour . . .

(1.3.222–30)

As 'the second Cecil' climbed to power so grafitti were daubed across London walls excoriating him as 'an atheist, a Machiavel', or 'Robin with the red breast' of the hangman's apron. And at Christmas 1600, above his own door at Whitehall Palace there even appeared a sign that read, 'Here lieth the Toad' (Handover, *The Second Cecil*, 230). So, Shakespeare's caricature of 'this poisonous bunch-backed toad' (1.3.244) and his refrain that 'Never hung poison on a fouler toad' (1.2.147) drew on a cesspit of anti-Cecilian prejudice. But the sexual connotations of Richard's animalisation as a 'bottled spider, that foul bunch-backed toad' (4.4.81), as in the Duchess of York's revulsion, 'Thou toad, thou toad' (4.4.145), or Lady Anne's horror at all such 'spiders, toads, / Or any creeping venomed thing' (1.2.19–20), also offers a clue to the provenance of Shakespeare's play, since disgust with the *regnum Cecilianum* here seems keyed to reports in 1593 of Burghley's plan to steal the throne for his son by marrying him to royalty. In fact, Shakespeare's staging of the folktale of the frog-prince, in Richard's wooing of Anne, chimes with the attitude of Catholic exiles on hearing that 'England expects a new Queen and another Cecil'.[27] The 'Lady' wooed by 'the Toad' was Arbella Stuart, neice of Mary Queen of Scots and the next-best hope of English Catholics after Ferdinando. 'Sir R. Cecil intends to be King by marrying Arabella and now lacks only the name', according to rumours in Brussels at the time Shakespeare likewise fantasised the seduction of an heiress by a 'lump of foul deformity' (1.2.57). In the event, 'Lady A' earned Cecil's hate by spurning him as 'a little hunchback' (Handover, *Arbella Stuart*, p. 128; p. 55); but the possibility that she might succumb to this 'foul misshapen stigmatic, / Marked by the destinies to be avoided, / As venom toads' (*Richard Duke of York* [*3 Henry VI*], 2.2.136–8), was threatening for Ferdinando, whose claim also put him in Cecil's path. And it is when the play is most explicit about this fear that it comes nearest to identifying the 'hedgehog' (1.2.102) with the Secretary. For it is just as we are reminded how Henry Tudor's mother married Lord Stanley and so he called him father, that 'the sty of this most deadly boar' (4.5.2) is tracked precisely to the locale of the Cecil seat 'in the centry of this isle': at Burghley House, 'Near to the town of Leicester' (5.2.11–12). This is surely as sharp as any writer dared to be in criticism of the House of Cecil, but the peril in which his patron stood may have steeled Shakespeare to turn his analogy on the fact that the 'deadly boar' had been run to earth at Bosworth Field, so close to Burghley's famous pile. Thus, we see how it is the sworn enemies of the 'foul swine' with best claim to be the rightful heirs:

Bruised underneath the yoke of tyranny,
Thus far into the bowels of the land
Have we marched on without impediment,
And here receive we from our father Stanley
Lines of fair comfort and encouragement.
The wretched, bloody and usurping boar,
That spoils your summer fields and fruitful vines,
Swills your warm blood like wash and makes his trough
In your imbowelled bosoms, this foul swine
Lies now even in the centry of this isle,
Near to the town of Leicester, as we learn.
From Tamworth thither is but one day's march.
In God's name, cheerly on, courageous friends,
To reap the harvest of perpetual peace
By this one bloody trial of sharp war.

(5.2.2–16)

Henry's war-cry proves how he has learned the lesson of *Venus and Adonis* and heeded the warning issued to Stanley – 'where is your boar-spear, man? / Fear you the boar and go so unprovided?' (3.2.69–70). In fact, the similarity of its language to that of the poem is a key to its Elizabethan occasion. Like the Jesuit missionaries, these texts use harvest imagery to mean conversion and speak cryptically of the resister's urge to 'hunt the boar with certain of his friends' (*Venus*, 588) in retaliation for the persecution waged by the 'wretched, bloody and usurping boar' on those 'most loving friends, / Bruis'd underneath the yoke of tyranny'. As with 'the wide wound the boar had trench'd' to castrate Adonis (1052), the grue-some image of 'this foul swine' swilling warm blood and making its 'trough / In your embowell'd bosoms' seems, therefore, to be to the disembowelling of recent Catholic martyrs on orders of Burghley. In particular, it may honour the poet-priest who introduced such Baroque violence into English poetry and whose capture in 1592 was Cecil's greatest prize: Shakespeare's own possible kinsman, the Jesuit Robert Southwell. It had been the Jesuits who spoke of reaping English converts, as Henry does, like some 'harvest of perpetual peace'; but the arrest and torture of Southwell had been on a far more dangerous charge, for the dramatist, of treasonous conspiracy with his patron, Ferdinando. No wonder that in this play it is 'prayers of holy saints and wrongèd souls' which support the insurgents (5.5.195). According to informers, it was Southwell who had been directed to contact Ferdinando with a promise of support from Rome, should he fight to succeed the Queen. Surrounded by spies, Ferdinando had, in fact, camou-flaged his true faith, so that 'Lord Strange gives good countenance to reli-gion', Cecil was notified in 1590, 'when he is with us' (Devlin, *Hamlet's*

Divinity, 82); but the coded letter allegedly carried by the priest had pledged him most compromising aid, in the form of a regiment commanded by his kinsman Sir William Stanley. In 1587 this veteran soldier had changed sides by sensationally giving up the Flemish fort of Deventer to Spain and so made 'Stanley's regiment' a byword in London for perfidy. As Henry of Navarre epitomised opportunist betrayal of the Protestant cause in France – with his quip that 'Paris is worth a mass'[28] – so the Stanleys thus came to be confirmed as the turncoats of English history, whose 'boar-spear' might yet prove as decisive at the end of the Tudor dynasty as at its start, when Richard III had despatched 'To Stanley's regiment', as he does in the play, to 'Bid him bring his power' (5.5.13) and so challenged the loyalty of the 'king of Lancashire':

> Where be thy tenants and thy followers?
> Are they not now upon the Western shore,
> Safe-conducting the rebels from their ships?
>
> (4.4.411–13)

'*Sans changer ma verite*' – or, 'Without changing my truth' – some time around 1592 Ferdinando added this defiant rider to the Strange motto – 'God and my faith' – to protest the consistency of his allegiance; but with both *Richard III* and *Love's Labour's Lost*, it appears, Shakespeare wrote 'some strange pastime' (*Love's*, 4.3.351) to dramatise the predicament of those, like his patron, who must persuade themselves 'it is religion to be thus forsworn' (339), when accused of breaking faith. In the comedy, Ferdinando's namesake, the King of Navarre, is mocked for his plea that 'If I break faith, this word shall speak for me: / I am forsworn on mere "necessity"' (1.1.151); and critics of the history play find Stanley's promise that 'I never was, nor will be, false' (4.4.424) as unconvincing as does Richard (Hammond, *Richard III*, 298). 'Hoyday, a riddle!' (390): Crookback's sneer at the Earl's equivocation condenses all the contempt felt by the Cecils for Catholic subjects who evaded the 1588 test of loyalty which they framed, as it initiates one of the dramatist's recurring problems: the dilemma of the dissident subject trapped within a state that has become 'a wilderness of tigers' (*Titus*, 3.1.53). For if Shakespeare's historical plays have a dominant atmosphere, it is one of claustophobia, the suffocating constriction of a land 'bound in with shame, / With inky blots and rotten parchment bonds' (*Richard II*, 2.1.63–4), where 'Devouring pestilence hangs in [the] air' enough to force resisters to 'fly to a fresher clime' among the 'singing birds' of Catholic Europe (1.3.284–8), or to 'imitate the sun / Who doth permit the base contagious clouds / To smother up his beauty' by temporising with those 'minions of the moon' who claim to be 'men of good government, being governed, as the sea is, by [their] noble and chaste mistress' the Queen

(*1 Henry IV*, 1.2.175–7; 23–5). Thus, the political situation presented in play after play by Shakespeare is the incarceration experienced after 1588 by English Catholics, when 'a roaring tempest on the flood . . . scattered and disjoined' the 'whole armada of convicted sail' (*King John*, 3.4.1–3) and Elizabeth's hostages were left with the sensation that the cliffs of Dover confined them to 'a prison' with 'many confines, wards and dungeons' (*Hamlet*, 2.2.239; 241–2). Hence, in *King John* the rightful inheritor, Arthur, falls to his death when he attempts to leap from his prison wall dressed, as if to represent the exiles' fate, in a 'ship-boy's semblance' (*King John*, 4.3.4). And if *Venus and Adonis* ironises the Queen's tender mercies to her captives, it is *Richard III* which registers an awareness that, for a generation of Elizabeth's Catholic subjects, whether 'to suffer / The slings and arrows' of 'outrageous fortune', or 'to take arms against a sea of troubles' – to cut a way through the narrow seas for rescuers to free them from their sufferings, 'And, by opposing, end them' – was, as Hamlet says, *the* great question of the age (*Hamlet*, 3.1.58–62):

> The causes of their troubles would not change unless somebody made an effort to change them. They had no access to Parliament; rebellion, in view of the condition and outlook of the Catholic gentry, could never be more than a weak auxiliary; they were therefore forced back on foreign intervention, which might range from verbal good offices to a declaration of war, but must involve in the last resort the threat of force. They concluded that [the situation] demanded intervention of this kind and the negotiation that would procure it; and deduced from the failure of earlier attempts that they could not afford to leave this to *émigré* gentlemen but must do it for themselves.[29]

When Hamlet poses what he calls *the question* – and the one that dominated the minds of Elizabethan recusants – of whether to suffer under an 'outrageous' system, or take up arms in suicidal resistance – it is revealing that he imagines this gesture as a Canute-like defiance of those waves governed by the Queen. For most of Shakespeare's life the problem of a 'blessed conscience' was indeed presented to English Catholics in terms of the sea, in the form of the infamous 'Bloody Question' first put to Campion in 1581: 'If the Pope or any other do invade this realm, which part would you take?'[30] What is so notable, then, in view of Hamlet's – and Campion's – fatal question, is how crucial to Shakespeare's representation of English history is the possibility of invasion from overseas. To some recent critics, this preoccupation with the ocean, and John of Gaunt's foreboding for 'this precious stone set in the silver sea' (*Richard II*, 2.1.46), combines Shakespeare's own paranoid 'fear of Jesuit infiltrators penetrating every national orifice', with his excitement over 'women raped'; but the difficulty with this reading is its assumption that the dramatist must have shared the phobias of 'a Protestant country obsessed with the threat of papal takeover'. The new historicist idea that in

Shakespeare 'the enemy is always without'[31] cannot quite accommodate the fact, therefore, that in scene after scene, starting with *Richard III*, it is an exile or invader from the offstage, unseen space who promises respite from the enemy within, and that even Gaunt's eulogy to England as 'This other Eden' (42) enlists the audience, as Phyllis Rackin admits, 'on the side of the rebels who set sail from France'.[32] But research on his Catholic affiliations underlines how Shakespeare's sense of a world elsewhere was more complex than that of any Tudor imperialist. For it was, of course, their pragmatic calculation that 'Not all the water in the rough rude sea / Can wash the balm from an anointed king' (3.2.50–1) that actually determined the stance of Elizabethan Catholics towards the prospects of a maritime invasion; and if Shakespeare articulated this 'split heart', he was doing no more than even a Jesuit like Southwell, who answered the burning question of whether Catholics would take up arms against their troubles, by swearing that they would 'be broached on their country's swords' before they would bring rebellion from abroad.[33] So, considering just how suicidal the 'Bloody Question' was deliberately designed to be, what is remarkable is how close Shakespeare came to endorsing the thought of the outside as an extreme solution on his stage. As Richard Simpson observed in 1874, far from being panic-striken by the thought of 'foreign penetration', Shakespeare seems to have amplified the ambivalence of his Catholic contemporaries towards the possibility of salvation from a world elsewhere, 'and it is only wonderful that allusions so plain should have been tolerated':

> All the changes [by Shakespeare to historical sources] seem made with a view to the controversy on the title to the Crown. This was the standing trouble of Elizabeth's reign. Her own title was controverted, first because she was illegitimate, next because she was excommunicate. And all the parties – those who opposed her, those who maintained her, those who advocated the succession of the Scottish King, or Arbella Stuart, or the Spanish Infanta, or Derby, or Huntingdon, or Essex – all appealed to foreign intervention . . . Foreign arbitration was no strange idea in Elizabethan politics. The English Queen helped the French. She assisted the Netherlanders. She interfered in Scotland, imprisoned the Queen, and finally beheaded her. She set up James I against his mother, Francis of Valois and Antonio of Portugal against Philip of Spain, and supported Henry of Navarre as heir and king of France. The example of their own government taught the English to intrigue with foreign princes . . . And amidst these seething anxieties, before the youthful heirs of the very families on whom the foreigner counted, Shakespeare made the example more apposite and the allusions more telling, by altering history.[34]

Students of Elizabethan culture have become familiar with the idea that 'Catholicism was the enemy against which Protestant nationalism defined itself', as Alison Shell observes in her revisionist study, 'but absent from their discussions has been even a consciousness of the other side: how English Catholics' experience of diaspora, combined with the necessity to re-evangelise a nation from overseas, shaped their ideas of nationhood'.[35] And nowhere has this blindness been more limiting than in the assumption that to be Catholic in Tudor England was necessarily to be unpatriotic. In fact, the Catholic response to Protestant nationalism 'was not that religion was more important than patriotism, but that Catholics were the only ones who had the country's interests at heart'.[36] Thus, Gaunt's lament belongs to a resistance genre that identifies England with 'the sepulcher, in stubborn Jewry' (2.1.55), or, as Catholic *émigrés* sang, 'Jerusalem my happy home'.[37] This is a providentialism in which Jerusalem signifies 'Weeping England' and crusaders are equated not with imperialists but with pilgrims in exile. Such are the connotations of Margaret's hope 'To meet with joy in sweet Jerusalem' (*Richard Duke of York* [*3 Henry VI*], 5.5.8); and King Henry's discovery, just as he tells Hal to 'lead out many to the Holy Land', that the heaven to which he goes, 'supposed the Holy Land', is the Jerusalem Chamber at Westminster (*2 Henry IV*, 4.3.338; 362–8). So, the crusaders' 'holy purpose to Jerusalem' (*1 Henry IV*, 1.1.102) becomes, in this discourse, code for the 'Enterprise of England' – to rescue the 'Jews' or recusants. As Shell explains, the 'parallel between English Catholics and conquered Jews' was perfect for articulating the divided loyalty of Elizabethan papists, since it had been because of Herod's tyranny (according to the historian Josephus, translated by the Catholic Thomas Lodge) that Jerusalem fell to Rome. Thus, responsibility for invasion could be blamed, as it is by Gaunt, on persecutors of the 'stubborn Jews' themselves (Shell, *Catholicism*, 137–40; 156–62; 174). 'Old Gaunt indeed' (*Richard II*, 2.1.74): the Duke of Lancaster's name itself denotes the split allegiance of those English nobles who acquiesced in an armada from their exile in Ghent. And with *King John* Shakespeare wrote an entire play on Gaunt's blackmail threat that England makes 'a shameful conquest of itself' (66) when it alienates its 'stubborn' dissidents, instead of enlisting them to fight the army of Rome:

> Do like mutines of Jerusalem:
> Be friends awhile and both conjointly bend
> Your sharpest deeds of malice

> (*King John*, 2.1.378–80)

Critics of *King John* point out that the patriotic prophecy that 'This England never did, nor never shall, / Lie at the proud foot of a conqueror' (5.7.112–13), is made by the character, Philip, a bastard son of the murdered crusader King Richard, whose own loyalties seem to be most confused and is based on an analogy with a city, Jerusalem, 'which, notoriously, lost its war', by failing to 'conjoin' its feuding 'mutines' against Rome. The Catholic providentialism which identifies England as 'the new object of crusading desire'

thus undercuts the superficial commitment of this play to the Protestant tradition that heroised King John for opposition to the Pope.[38] Likewise, the
emphasis on John's illegitimacy, excommunication and outlawry, all arguments levelled in *émigré* polemics against Elizabeth, undermines his defence
of royal supremacy. And though the author allows the king a blistering denunciation of indulgences, he pointedly tones down the anti-monastic bias of his
source, *The Troublesome Reign of King John*. These 'mixed polemical signals'
are usually interpreted as meant to 'call down a plague upon both Catholics
and Protestants' and in a recent reading Jeffrey Knapp proposes that its
'general ambivalence regarding England' secularises the play out of religion
altogether, away from 'attempts to organise Christendom in terms of some
old or new Holy Land' and towards an ideal of global fellowship. Knapp
views *King John* as a 'counter-crusading' work staged in recoil from 'the holy
wars in Palestine'. To American eyes, in other words, the motive of the play
has to be 'anxiety that Christian strife would open the door to Turkish invasion', an Islamophobia which led Shakespeare to empty Christian hostilities
of 'sectarian content' (Knapp, *Shakespeare's Tribe*, 100–12). In fact, it was
the Catholic party of massacre that put the crusades on the agenda, as a model
for reconquest of England (Bossy, 'Character', 49). What Knapp misses,
therefore, by taking 'Palestine' so literally, is the blackmail implicit in a text
which, as Honigmann perceives, gives to an 'Italian priest' (3.1.79), Cardinal
Pandulf, 'the only coherent authority in the play', which 'will ultimately claim
John' and the voice of 'uncompromising political and religious belief'. For the
final imperative of this play is not a 'westward longing' Atlanticism, but an
eastward call to Rome, and it is the Archbishop of Milan who truly 'moves
the play into a new realm' and a 'new kind of politics', with 'the destructive
fanaticism' of his *fatwa* against the King of England on behalf of 'the Church,
our Holy Mother' (*King John*, 3.1.67), in effect a dramatisation of the 1570
Bull of Pius V excommunicating Elizabeth:[39]

> Then by the lawful power that I have
> Thou shalt stand cursed and excommunicate;
> And blessèd shall he be that doth revolt
> From his allegiance to an heretic;
> And meritorious shall that hand be called,
> Canonizèd and worshipped as a saint,
> That takes away by any secret course
> Thy hateful life.

> (King John, 3.1.98–105)

'It cannot be denied that so many as should have obeyed that wicked
warrant', fumed Burghley, in his counterblast to the Bull, *The Execution of
Justice in England*, 'should have been in their hearts and consciences
secret traitors. And for to be indeed open traitors there wanted nothing but

opportunity . . . to assemble with arms and weapons.'[40] Yet as historians point out, if 'the great majority had only a vague knowledge of the Bull's contents', this was chiefly because the Holy See released the English from its injuctions in 1580.[41] So, it is highly suggestive that the Church itself took exception to their publication in *King John*, judging by cuts made by Father William Sankey, who censored the second Folio in 1649 for the English College in Valladolid. What is remarkable about this episode, of course, is that Shakespeare's *Works* were authorised for Jesuit students at all, considering how prescriptive reading was at the Society's schools. Thus, in 1656 staff at Valladolid would be criticised by even their own superiors for keeping boys in the dark about 'the theological questions of the day'.[42] But Sankey cut just twenty-four lines of *King John*, the effect of which was actually to tone down the scene of excommunication by excising all mention of regicide, including the report of how John was 'poisoned by a monk', 'a resolvèd villain' (5.6.24; 30). This is no surprise, as, following the assassination of Henry IV in 1610, the Society's General Aquaviva commanded Jesuits 'neither in public nor private so much as to suggest that anyone had a right to kill, or plot to kill a prince, even on grounds of tyranny'.[43] That the Father also struck out John's attack on the Pope's 'usurped authority' (3.1.86) is seen by some as proof, none the less, that 'Shakespeare was not a Catholic', whereas, as Gary Taylor counters, 'it proves only that like most English Catholics . . . he did not always agree with papal policies'.[44] 'When usurpers accuse others of usurpation', comments Honigmann, 'we are in a situation without landmarks for loyalty' (Honigmann, *King John*, 25). And that was also the view of Rome, which backtracked on its deposing power when over-zealous Catholics, such as William Allen, speculated that even the Pope might be deposed (Clancy, 'English Catholics', 119). Thus, far from from proving Anglican bias, what its Jesuit expurgation might go to show is that, by raising the threat of invasion so emphatically, *King John* was like Allen's *Admonition to the People of England* (which embarrassed Rome so much by urging subjects to rise up against Elizabeth, as a 'deprived, accursed, excommunicate heretic', that stocks of the book were destroyed) (*ibid.*, 122–3): more Catholic than the Pope.

Besides scissoring references to regicide in Shakespeare, Father Sankey underlined the passages he approved, such as Malcolm's cry of how 'our country sinks beneath the yoke . . . I think withal / There would be hands uplifted in my right, / And here from gracious England have I offer / Of goodly thousands' (*Macbeth*, 4.3.40; 42–5). Thus, with fifty years' hindsight, the Jesuits produced the text which, according to Thomas Clancy, most patriotic Catholics of the 1590s had desired: 'a work that would show the shortcomings of divine right and the dangers of a heretical prince', but which would put limits on royal power not 'from above, by papal supremacy', but 'from below, by popular sovereignty'. Their censor 'brought the discussion down to earth', that is to say, away from tyrannicide, towards the part the 'goodly thousands' should have 'in choosing from the candidates to the throne one who would protect their own religion'. This was, in fact, the 'natural' approach pushed by the Jesuit Robert Persons in his 1595 treatise, *A Conference About the Next Succession*, where the device of a symposium on the rival claimants dramatised the need for some similar 'means for the expression of popular feeling'. Unfortunately, 'there were no such institutions in England', Clancy admits (*ibid.*, 124; 126–7; 133). But in *King John*, the Catholic theory of popular sovereignty does, in fact, find its spokesman in the Bastard, who as the natural son of Richard Cordelion, inherits just those qualities of faith and valour which would later be carried to extremes by the true-hearted Cordelia. A 'lion's heart' wrapped in a player's hide, the Bastard is constructed as a gentry-figure in contrast both to the king, who treats Prince Arthur and his mother as Elizabeth did the Stuarts and the lords, who defect to France as exiles joined the 'league' (*King John*, 5.2.38) with Guise. His critical decision comes, therefore, as Honigmann notices, after John is poisoned and he has taken power, with 'sole claim to our respect and trust' (Honigmann, *King John*, 41), when news arrives that 'The lords are all comeback, / And brought Prince Henry'. His prayer to heaven at this reversal, to 'Withhold thine indignation . . . And tempt us not to bear above our power' (*King John*, 5.6.34–5; 38–9), defines exactly the 'loyalism' of England's Catholic gentry, which, Shell remarks, was 'not the same as loyalty' (Shell, *Catholicism*, 113). In the end, however, he submits to the succession, hoping that now the *émigrés* are 'come home again, / Come the three corners of the world in arms / And we shall shock them' (5.7.115–17). This would also be the hope of the gentry in 1603, when court Catholics likewise brought in a Protestant king. But the fact that the succession is conditional on the mutual tolerance of 'mended faiths' (75) makes it difficult to forget the sanction suspended over this reunion, which is the pledge to 'corner' the heretic island sworn by the Habsburg Archduke to 'the morsel of dead royalty' (4.3.144), Arthur, the legitimate prince:

> That to my home I will no more return
> Till . . . that pale, that white-faced shore,
> Whose foot spurns back the ocean's roaring tides
> And coops from other lands her islanders,
> Even till that England, hedgèd in with the main,
> That water wallèd bulwark, still secure
> And confident from foreign purposes,
> Even till that utmost corner of the west
> Salute thee for her king.
>
> (*King John*, 2.1.21–30)

Contrary to modern critics, who automatically assume he shared the inside/outside xenophobia of a later Protestant nationalism, Shakespeare structured his histories around the thought of the outside as a consummation devoutly wished, the escape from the 'water wallèd bulwark' of Dover cliffs. 'Walls, enclosures and facades serve to define both a *scene*', wrote the philosopher of space, Henri Lefebvre, 'and the *obscene* area to which everything that cannot happen on scene is referred: whatever is inadmissable thus has its own hidden space on the near or far side of that frontier'.[45] So, when we learn that 'Richmond is on the seas' (*Richard III*, 4.4.393), we register the proximity of this counter-space, beyond the horizon of Shakespeare's text, as a reserve which retains its subversive potential to the extent that it is never completely realised. If, for example, Imogen finds it difficult to reach Milford Haven to reunite with Posthumus in *Cymbeline*, despite having the place in view 'from the mountain-top' (3.6.5), that must be because the Welsh port had been identified as the most suitable landing-point for a papal army; a likelihood to which Shakespeare responds from the moment in *Richard III* when Richmond, 'with a mighty power landed at Milford' (4.4.464). What Imogen is told, when she asks 'how Wales was made so happy as / T'inherit such a haven', can never therefore be spoken in her play – because that is another story about Tudor politics, but the question is a reminder that the Pembrokeshire harbour is a gateway not only for those, such as her husband, bound innocently for Rome but for those Leaguers 'now in Gallia' from which, as a *loyal Roman* Briton, he detaches himself (*Cymbeline*, 2.4.18; 3.2.45). So, in *Richard III*, Milford Haven is the landfall for the 'valiant crew' of Tudor *émigrés* 'long kept in Bretagne' (4.5.12; 5.6.54) and their French hideaway, though it is never seen, polarises the history play with the politics of the Catholic resistance. On 'the extreme verge' of the text, Britanny with its choirs of 'singing birds', has the same violent terminal status here, therefore, as it does in *Richard II*, where it becomes the covert refuge of the banished Bolingbroke, who, far from serving 'long apprenticehood' on a grand tour of 'All the places that the eye of heaven visits' (1.3.256), as declared, dedicates himself at Port le Blanc to equipping 'eight tall ships' to carry three thousand commandos to Humberside (2.1.288). Waving 'his bonnet to an oysterwench', Bolingbroke embarks for his French redoubt in 1597 with precisely the treasonable political intention denied, a dozen years later, in the tear-jerking farewell of the loyal English 'Roman' Posthumus.

'Like the artillery from Flanders' fields heard in Kent during the war of 1914', writes John Bossy, it was 'the breaking waves of religious passion' from across the narrow seas that formed the ultimate background and determining factor of Elizabethan politics.[46] Likewise, in his study of Shakespearean art, Wolfgang Clemen noticed how leavetaking for the continent is vital to the sense of futurity that makes the histories different from other Elizabethan plays, for by 'combining retrospect with hopes and fears', departure of an exile like Bolingbroke suggests 'an inescapable line of development arises from the pressure of the past upon the future. Future is linked to past by workings of necessity, but also by planning and purposeful intention'.[47] Thus, with the collusion of its Duke, the Britanny of the histories becomes a base for guerrilla forces which glorify insurgency in their rolls of honour: Talbot, Oxford, Brandon, Pembroke, 'And many other of great names and worth' (*Richard III*, 4.5.13). As the roster of 'confederates' unfolds, it forms a roll-call, in fact, of the *fronde* of provincial 'peers, younger sons of gentry families and army officers' that mustered during the 1590s in hatred of the Cecils.[48] Dissolute, nostalgic and frustrated, this aristocratic clique has been described by Lawrence Stone as a duelling club of 'angry young men in a hurry, chafing at the infuriating grip on office retained by the Cecils . . . down-at-heel bankrupt swordsmen and unemployed officers who had seen better days and had little to lose by a desperate fling' (Stone, *Crisis*, 483; 486). Such, then, was England's 'nobility of the sword' and it drew its leadership, as Shakespeare shows, from his own region of the Borders and Wales. Names that recur in Richmond's rebel army are the Pembrokeshire Herberts and Worcestershire Blunts – both families linked to the writer – and when Bosworth Field turns on defection by 'Stanley's regiment' (5.5.13) a flag is flown for both Ferdinando and his cousin Sir William. For by the time Shakespeare awarded 'Stanley's regiment' the same pivotal role at Bosworth as it played at Deventer, the colonel's troop of papist veterans had been reinforced by 'diverse captains from the Earl of Essex' into a crack force, poised to cross the Channel.[49] Whatever Shakespeare knew of these expatriate plotters, their switch of loyalty was justified by Cardinal Allen in a notorious book, *Concerning the Yielding up of Daventry*, that appears to be quoted by the soldier in *Henry V*, who likewise enquires on behalf of 'those whom the matter touches in conscience, how they ought to carry themselves' and who is given the surname of Stanley's brother-in-arms, Roger Williams; himself an apologist, with his *Brief Discourses of War*, for 'poor gentlemen' of Catholic faith compelled by change of heart to cross to enemy lines:

> In these wars, and all others that may at any time fall for religion against heretics, or other infidels, every Catholic man is bound in conscience to inform himself for the justice of the cause, the which when it is doubtful or toucheth religion, as is said, he ought to employ his person and forces by direction of such as are virtuous.[50]

On the misty fields and beaches of Shakespeare's France the troubled faces of Elizabethan *émigrés* are almost visible. And Richard III's characterisation of the invaders as 'A sort of vagabonds, rascals and runaways, / A scum of Bretons' and its leader as a 'milksop . . . Long kept in Britanny' (5.6.46–7; 53–5) chimes with Burghley's 1591 Proclamation condemning the exiles as 'a multitude of dissolute young men, become Fugitives, Rebels and Traitors',[51] indoctrinated into French extremes. It confirms, that is to say, the analysis of historians that 'The most important factor influencing resistance by Elizabethan Catholics' was the *volte face* on polical terrorism by their French co-religionists when confronted by the succession of Navarre, they 'suddenly adopted ideas of resistance identical to those which their enemies, the Huguenots, had held' and founded the Catholic League. As Richard's curse suggests, in this period when the English dissidents congregated at Rouen and Rheims, 'What the League gave Elizabethan Catholic resistance was practical encouragement', as 'for the first time there were European Catholics in the same position as the English, who were reacting not with quietism, but by taking up ideas of resistance just as Calvinists were abandoning them'.[52] And crucial to the lesson exiles learned in France was the idea Richard scorns as 'but a word that cowards use, / Devised at first to keep the strong in awe' (5.6.39–40) and that Hamlet says 'makes cowards of us all' (*Hamlet*, 3.1.85): the 'conscience' that their tutors taught compelled them to 'patiently obey princes, under pain of eternal damnation' and yet to oppose those usurpers who came between those princes and God (Holmes, *Resistance*, 38). So, in *Richard III* the invaders can count on the belief that 'Every man's conscience is a thousand swords, / To fight against this guilty homicide' (5.2.17–18). 'Conscience' was a word, that is to say, which helped political Catholics to revive 'the time-honoured fiction of the evil counsellor' (Bossy, 'Character', 43) and maintain hostility to the government, even as they swore loyalty to the Queen. It was this 'split subject', torn between loyalty and League, or patriotism and treason, which was rehearsed in the polemic *Leicester's Commonwealth* of 1584, with its acid attack on the Queen's favourite, Robert Dudley, as a 'perfect potentate' of poisonings and plots (Holmes, *Resistance*, p. 133); and then by Persons in a torrent of books comparing Burghley and his son to Nero, Herod and, of course, the bogeyman Richard. It comes as no surprise then, that, when Henry Tudor inspires his army at Bosworth, he does so in the schizoid terms of Douai missionaries, when they preached that it was necessary to save the Queen from her ministers, by separating England from its own regime:

> Yet remember this:
> God and our good cause fight upon our side.
> The prayers of holy saints and wrongèd souls,
> Like high-reared bulwarks, stand before our forces.
> Richard except, those whom we fight against
> Had rather have us win than him they follow.

For what is he they follow? Truly, friends,
A bloody tyrant and a homicide;
One raised in blood, and one in blood established;
One that made means to come by what he hath,
And slaughtered those that were the means to help him;
A base, foul stone, made precious by the foil
Of England's chair, where he is falsely set;
One that hath ever been God's enemy.
Then if you fight against God's enemy,
God will, in justice, ward you as his soldiers.
If you do sweat to put a tyrant down,
You sleep in peace, the tyrant being slain;
If you do fight against your country's foes,
Your country's foison pays your pains the hire.
If you do fight in safeguard of your wives,
Your wives shall welcome home the conquerors.
If you do free your children from the sword,
Your children's children quites it in your age.
Then, in the name of God and all these rights,
Advance your standards! Draw your willing swords!

(5.6.193–218)

If Ferdinando wished to seize the Crown, his instructions were to reply to Rome that 'Your cousin the baker is well inclined and glad to hear from you and meaneth not to give over his pretence to the old bakehouse, but rather to put the same in suit when his ability shall serve'; which Cecil's agents had decoded as: 'by baker and bakehouse is understood my Lord Strange and the title they would have him pretend when Her Majesty dies' (Devlin, *Hamlet's Divinity*, 84). Shakespeare's histories, as Peter Thomson contends, seem to employ a similarly transparent code, in which medieval names stand for living personalities, since 'among the courtiers who watched these performances would have been many descendants of the Knights and Earls who made up the *dramatis personae*'. The indignation of Lord Cobham, 'that necessitated the change of name from Oldcastle to Falstaff', is well known, Thomson points out, but the question this leads to is, 'what contortions of self-censorship are hidden?' (Thompson, *Shakespeare's Professional Career*, 30). A possible answer is suggested by the list of Bolingbroke's party in *Richard II*, which includes the name, cut from the published text, of 'Thomas, son and heir to the Earl of Arundel' (2.1.281). In 1597 this might be deciphered as glancing at the martyred Philip Howard, Earl of Arundel and his crypto-papist son Thomas, whose London mansion was a headquarters for Catholic intrigue. That someone found this salute risky enough to push it out of sight raises the further question why Shakespeare came so near to advertising the schemes of Catholics who sponsored him, like the Hoghtons, whose ancestor escorted Bolingbroke to Europe.[53] The answer is critical to the dramatist's attitude to the politics of resistance. For from the day in 1597 when Raleigh reported Essex 'wonderful merry' that Robert Cecil had the 'conceit' that *Richard II* alluded to his plans, Shakespeare's history has been entangled in rumours that, like *Richard III*, it encodes the ambitions of those with most to gain from a rebellion, and that the Earl's 'great applause' at performances of the play were 'actions to confirm his intent' of treason.[54] Shakespeare, it is inferred, was far more implicated in the 1601 debacle than even the calamitous involvement of his patron, the Earl of Southampton, might imply, as Essex's brother was a son-in-law of his uncle Edward Arden. Certainly, one reason why any rebels, such as Robert Catesby, came from the Midlands was that Essex's 'promise of liberty of conscience' was irresistible to the gentry of such a Catholic region.[55] In fact, if the uprising could be painted by Attorney General Coke as a 'popish plot', that was because its ringleaders were indeed, we now learn, mainly 'Catholics, both converts recusants', fired by Essex's policy of religious toleration.[56] But it is expressly as a harbinger of reconciliation, rather than rebellion, that the Earl is welcomed home in the most indiscreet of all returns of history on the horizon of Shakespeare's stage:

> Were now the General of our gracious Empress –
> As in good time he may – from Ireland coming,
> Bringing rebellion broached on his sword,
> How many would the peaceful city quit
> To welcome him!

(Henry V, 5.0.30–4)

Of all topical irruptions into the Shakespearean text, Alan Sinfield observes, the 1599 allusion to Essex's impending return to England in *Henry V* is the least susceptible to the new historicist reduction of Elizabethan culture to a phobia about invasion, since the lines reveal a faultline in authority, at the instant when the challenger rivalled the Queen. For Sinfield, the indeterminacy of *Henry V* arises, in fact, from the instability of this moment, when dissidents such as Catholics belied the myth of English unity, as the state confronted the possibility that the ruler was no longer supreme. This is a reading that concludes, however, that the Essex threat is contained in the play, because Henry is identified with the Tudors; whereas it is more likely that he prefigures the Stuart claimant, James I, for whom the Earl was, the Chorus hints, an ambiguous and 'lower' representative (29). Shakespeare may have come closer to treason than cultural materialism allows.[57] The possibility that *Henry V* was written as the reveille for a coup links the text, that is to say, not only to the pro-Stanley project of *Richard III* but to the optimism of Catholics who saw the Scottish ruler as a peacemaker like Octavius and rallied around Essex, 'Like to the senators of th'antique Rome', as a means to 'fetch their conqu'ring Caesar in' (26; 28). Typical of these 'premature Jacobeans' was the Midland magnate Thomas Tresham, whose flattery of 'our gracious Empress' (30), mixed up with 'veiled expressions of passive disobedience', supplies a discursive context for the dramatist's tactical ambivalence, in the 'defensive resistance' of Shakespeare's recusant neighbours and friends.[58] Along with William Catesby, Tresham suffered years of imprisonment for hiding Campion; but in March 1603 it was this 'most affectionate servant of the glorious and blessed Queen of Scots' who hurried into Northampton to proclaim her son King of England, in face of jeering from the Puritan town.[59] His enthusiasm for James as a Catholic deliverer was shared by Southampton, who broke from gaol to secure the Tower for the new dynasty. And it seems also to have been briefly entertained by the poet himself, judging by the one euphoric text, a resounding coda to the histories, in which he trumpets his patron's new freedom; laughs at his own worries over the succession; insults the 'dull and speechless tribes' who mourn the passing of the Tudors; and even dares to dance upon the 'tyrants' . . . tombs':

> The mortal moon hath her eclipse endured,
> And the sad augurers mock their own presage;
> Incertainties now crown themselves assured,
> And peace proclaims olives of endless age.

(Sonnet 107, 5–8)

'Men must endure / Their going hence', moralises Edgar in *King Lear*, 'even as their coming hither' (5.2.9–10); but, as John Kerrigan glosses the Sonnet, relief at the final exit of Elizabeth and entry of James was tinged with anxiety, as Catholics 'feared the accession of a ruler even less sympathetic to religious liberty' than the Protestant Queen and 'anticipated an invasion from abroad' as a return to Civil War.[60] That foreboding had been hovering in *Julius Caesar*, where no sooner has Octavius landed than the plotters are made to ride 'like madmen through the gates of Rome' (3.2.258). The advent of a long-awaited Roman emperor might be followed, this play foretold, by the betrayal 'Octavius' confirmed, when he smirked, 'Na, na, we's not need the papists noo'.[61] So, if Shakespeare's texts had been shaped in the 1590s by the prospect of rescue from abroad, it may be telling that, as Clemen noted, *Hamlet* is the last play, until *The Tempest*, in which 'an unfulfilled past calls for future fulfilment' (Clemen, *Shakespeare's Dramatic Art*, p. 126). When the Prince of Denmark is 'set naked on [the] kingdom' (4.7.42–3) his suicide mission to avenge his father spells an end, therefore, to the thought of the outside as deliverance in these works. Jacobean

Shakespeare would be overcast, instead, by the disillusion of a decade when, in the words of Father Gerard, 'all hopes were foiled on which Catholics did build their comforts', while 'the King protested he would take it as an insult if anyone imagined he had entertained the slightest intention of tolerating their religion'.[62] As Antonia Fraser summarises it, the grim reality for Catholics was that 'By the time truth was known – that James did not intend to keep his promises – it was too late. Any hope from abroad vanished even before the death of Elizabeth . . . when the son of Mary Queen of Scots bamboozled two sets of Catholics: English recusants and foreign potentates, including the Pope' (Fraser, *Gunpowder Plot*, 287). Small wonder, then, that Shakespeare wrote no more plays, after 1601, with homecoming as a complete solution, devising instead a sequence in which the Puritan Malvolio exits to be revenged; Bertram returns only sullenly from Italy; the Greeks never sail home; Desdemona is killed on Cyprus; the restored Duke terrorises Vienna; Cordelia disembarks to be hanged; Malcolm's pledge to recall his friends is unfulfilled; Antony, Coriolanus and Timon all die in exile; and when a Roman army does finally invade Britain, even the persecuted subjects of King Cymbeline fight to defeat it. Rather than look for respite from a world elsewhere, the Shakespearean drama of the 1600s seems to stage, in fact, the predicament of a captive community, confined by coercive penal laws to the desperate remedies of an inner exile:

> No port is free; no place,
> That guard and most unusual vigilance,
> Does not attend my taking. Whiles I may 'scape,
> I will preserve myself; and am bethought
> To take the basest and most poorest shape
> That ever penury, in contempt of man,
> Brought near to beast . . .
>
> *(King Lear, 2.3.3–9)*

In *King Lear* 'all ports' are barred (2.1.79) and the claustrophobia of the histories is complete, as the resolution of the Elizabethan *émigré* – to 'shape his old course in a country new' (1.1.188) – succumbs to the stoic resignation of the Jacobean quietist – to 'sing like birds i'the cage' and so 'wear out, / In a walled prison, packs and sects of great ones / That ebb and flow by th'moon' (5.3.8–19). This 'religion of inaction' has been disparaged by Bossy as a 'gentleman's theology' of 'social convenience', which replaced the Jesuits' 'alarm spiritual' with the 'inertia' and contemplativeness of a revived Benedictine order (Bossy, 'Character', 56–7). Recently, however, historians have begun to interpret such passivity in face of persecution in the terms of which Lear speaks: as a war of attrition waged by Catholics in the faith that, as Southwell promised and Edgar affirms, 'Time goes by turns and chances change by course': 'When time shall serve . . . the right may thrive . . . Ripeness is all' (5.1.48; 5.2.2; 11).[63] Nothing could be further from this bitter consolation, in any case, than the idea that since 'Dover is the point of entry, the aperture through which domination can enter . . . Britain is the female body' in this text, which thus slavishly repeats some national myth of the white cliffs.[64] For it is by despairing of *rescue* from across the Channel that Edgar comes to typify Shakespeare's survivors, having 'escap'd the hunt' hidden 'in the happy hollow of a tree' and staked out in 'low farms / Poor pelting villages, sheep-cotes and mills' (2.3.17–18). Lear's hovel could be viewed, therefore, as symbolic of all those priest-holes and safe-houses that were vital to undercover operations of Elizabethan resistants. But if Edgar's disguise as 'Poor Tom' figures the 'secret lurking' of hunted priests,[65] Lear and his party seem aligned with Catholic peers like the Percys, whose madness, at the time of the play, was to continue to hope for deliverance from France. They retrace the folly, in particular, of the Earl of Northumberland, who in November 1605 gave tacit support to Catesby's plan to blow up king and Parliament, as a signal for the landing of Catholic troops in Kent, 'backed by 300 English cavalry expected to join once news of the invasion spread', which were intended to 'strike out rapidly from Dover and hold London at their mercy'.[66] Whether or not any fleet existed to carry over troops, this was, historians now confirm, 'one of the greatest challenges that early modern English state security ever faced' (Nicholls, *Investigation*, 218), but in Shakespeare's telling the campaign of reconquest is betrayed before it starts:

> KENT   Why the King of France is so suddenly gone back know you the reason?
> FIRST GENTLEMAN   Something he left imperfect in the state, which, since his coming forth, is thought of, which imports to the kingdom so much fear and danger, that his personal return was most required and necessary.
>
> (4.3.1–6)

The defection from Cordelia's side of her husband, the King of France, which recalls the desertion of Mary Stuart by her French family, may reflect the disillusion felt by the 1605 plotters towards foreign powers, when 'Stanley's regiment' once again failed to set sail and even 'the financial support formerly guaranteed to extremist Catholics in England remained nothing more than a promise unperformed' (Nicholls, 41). Intended for a court performance at Christmas immediately after the Gunpowder treason, however, the text of *King Lear* is literally broken by its divided loyalties. Thus, Albany seems to voice the patriotism of a majority of Catholics on hearing of the Plot, if historians are right, when he swears that though it 'bolds' the rightful claimants 'With others whom the rigor of our state / Forced to cry out', yet 'this business . . . touches us as France invades our land . . . Most just and heavy causes make oppose' (5.1.22–7). But the Duke's pledge of allegiance is so ambivalent that editors suspect textual corruption; and, in any case, Shakespeare's heirs evaded the 'Bloody Question' altogether, when the play was revised, by having all mention of a French invasion, including these lines, 'consistently eliminated'. The Oxford editor thinks it 'most implausible' that 'this business' at Dover was censored; but Greg may have been near the truth when he inferred that 'Shakespeare found himself in a patriotic dilemma' over a landing at the port by an *émigré* armada under French command, exactly like the invasion planned by his Warwickshire friends.[67] For if this was a case of self-censorship, the retraction would have been imperative if Dover did point, as the Quarto prints it, across the Channel to 'Douer' – or Douai.[68] So, though Gloucester's torturers repeat the question of 'Wherefore to Douai?' (3.7.52) with which the interrogators hammered English Catholics, Shakespeare, or his executors, flinched from the incriminating answer. The divided text of *King Lear*, with entire scenes suppressed, may be evidence, therefore, of the explosion which shattered Shakespeare's world in the autumn of 1605. But like the absence of the French, the pages lost from the Folio also testify to the void left in Shakespearean drama after the disaster of the Gunpowder Plot: namely, the collapse of any thought of outside aid beyond Dover cliff. Thus, in the end, as Simpson wrote, 'the moral of the dramatist amounts to this':

> He seems to say to the malcontents of his day – 'Whatever you think about the justice of your cause or the crimes of your opponents, whatever outrages you have to endure, whatever the merits of the losers or the demerits of the winners – despair of foreign intervention!' (Simpson, 'Politics', 406)

'These banished men . . . Are men endowed with worthy qualities', declares Valentine to his prisoner, the Duke, after the invasion which crowns what may have been Shakespeare's earliest play: 'Forgive them what they have committed here, / And let them be recalled from their exile' (*Two Gents*, 5.4.149; 51–2). The recurring dream of Shakespearean comedy, which was also the fantasy of England's *émigré* community, that 'every of this happy number / That hath endured shrewd days and nights' abroad, 'Shall share the good' of a 'returnèd fortune' (*As You Like It*, 5.4.161–3), is extinguished in *King Lear*, with the terse news that 'King Lear hath lost' and Cordelia's verdict on the 'Enterprise of England': 'We are not the first / Who with best meaning, have incurred the worst' (*King Lear*, 5.3.3–4). It is likely that Timon's cave beside the sea therefore symbolises both the ruin of the recusant gentry and the dead-end of their schemes of rehabilitation. In the wake of the Plot, Donna Hamilton agrees, the question of allegiance would be staged in *Cymbeline* as just such a choice between the cave and court: in the dilemma of Belarius – 'a sympathetic portrait of the English Catholic' – of whether to retreat 'higher to the mountains' of Wales, or submit, as he does, 'To the King's party' (4.4.8–9). At the time of the late plays there were many such 'absurd stories of kinsmen of the plotters, lurking amid the Welsh hills, at work on a plan of revenge' (Nicholls, *Investigation*, p. 219). But the theme of these tragi-comedies, acted as the Catholic Howards succeeded Cecil, is that 'The rarer action is / In virtue than in vengeance' (*Tempest*, 5.1.27–8) and their scenario of reunion in the exile's cell or chapel contrasts pointedly with the waste of the *émigré* generation, whose destiny had been to '*Exit, pursued by a bear*' (*Winter's Tale*, SD, 3.3.57). Shakespeare's stage direction gains resonance if the 'bloody-minded bear' was a symbol, as Nashe for one intended, for the Puritan Earl of Leicester who wore it as his crest. Then, the fate of the old lord would figure the nemesis of all those who fled, pursued by that 'savage blood-hunter', to European shores and never survived to see the spring which is romanced in these works: the Irish 'wild geese', for example, or the Lancashire mercenaries, who expired, after placing their daughters in the city's convents, at Antwerp, the Catholic haven that had indeed been founded by a ferryman named Antigonus.[69] 'A goodly city is this Antium', notes Coriolanus hopefully, of the 'enemy town' that seems another image of the Antwerp of the Archdukes (*Coriolanus*, 4.4.1; 24). But what is so dismaying about these destinations, or the Antioch to which Pericles sails, is how totally they disrupt Renaissance conventions of 'the borderlands and otherwheres of exile' as a ground of reconciliation.[70] For their frustration of all hope in 'a world elsewhere' (3.3.139) speaks of the actual continental experience of English Catholic exiles, who in the last analysis, as Shell concludes, 'came over only to die' (Shell, *Catholicism*, 172).

The battle of Bosworth takes place, in Shakespeare's rewriting, on All Souls' Day and it could be that *Richard III* was written for performance in 1593 on that day of the dead. The date is crucial in contextualising this defence of armed revolt. For that was the time when the Stanleys had most at risk. What happened that autumn doomed them, however, and has been a mystery ever since. For on 27 September another messenger arrived in Lancashire with a letter from Rome, again offering Ferdinando 'a hallowed Crown', if he could be 'persuaded to undertake the same'. This time, the message was carried by a neighbour named Richard Hesketh, who had fled abroad after slaying Thomas Hoghton of Hoghton Tower in 1589. Now he reappeared, just two days after old Derby died. Hesketh claimed to the end to be ignorant of the contents of the letter; but what we know is that it had been slipped to him at The White Hart in Islington, on 16 September. It was treated by the new earl, in any case, with extreme suspicion, for no sooner had he read it than he invited its carrier to London, where he had business with the Queen. Flattered, Hesketh rode along, but, when Ferdinando emerged from meeting Elizabeth, was arrested. Historians believe, of course, that Hesketh had been duped into a plot to trap Ferdinando, which Cecil planned to spring the moment Derby died. The new earl then acted, they infer, as befitted Shakespeare's patron and a connoisseur of drama, when he returned the letter to sender and called the Cecils' bluff. We may never know the truth, however, for Hesketh was hanged, protesting innocence, on 29 November and Ferdinando rode north in disgrace. Never again would Strange's Men perform at court in one of Shakespeare's plays. For, on 5 April, the Earl was suddenly taken ill, vomiting blood and pus, the symptom of arsenic poisoning. For ten days he writhed in agony, injected with mercury enemas that intensified his pain. On 16 April 1594 Ferdinando, for six months Earl of Derby and heir to the Tudors, died aged thirty-five, hoping, he is supposed to have said, 'to fly swiftly to Christ on the Eagle's Wings' (Bagley, *Earls of Derby*, p. 67). And Shakespeare, who also turned Tudor myth upon its makers, was left to consider the violence of the badge he wore as 'Jove's own page' (*As You Like It*, 1.3.118): a shepherd carried above a sea of troubles by the Roman bird of 'tyrant wing' (*Phoenix and Turtle*, 10).

Notes

1 P. M. Handover, *The Second Cecil: The Rise to Power of Sir Robert Cecil, First Earl of Salisbury, 1563–1604* (London: Eyre & Spottiswoode, 1959), xi, 1, 5, 15, 32, 34, 41, 55, 57, 60, 67, 86, 145, 166; Francis Bacon, 'Of Deformity', in *Essays*, ed. Michael Hawkins (London: Dent, 1973, rev. ed. 1992), 131–2; Dudley Carleton quoted in Daphne Du Maurier, *The Winding Stair: Francis Bacon, His Rise and Fall* (London: Gollancz, 1976), 77.

2 Quoted in B. N. De Luna, *Jonson's Romish Plot: A Study of 'Catiline' and Its Historical Context* (Oxford: Clarendon Press, 1967), 151.

3 Park Honan, *Shakespeare: A Life* (Oxford: University Press, 1999), 66.

4 Christopher Devlin, *Hamlet's Divinity and Other Essays* (London: Rupert Hart-Davis, 1963), 108; Edmund Spenser, 'Colin Clout's come home again', l, 437–40.

5 Scott McMillin, *The Elizabethan Theatre and 'The Book of Sir Thomas More'* (Ithaca: Cornell University Press, 1987), 57–8, 71–2.

6 Lawrence Stone, *The Crisis of the Aristocracy, 1558–1641* (Oxford: Clarendon Press, 1965), 573–4.

7 Thomas Nashe, 'Pierce Penniless', in *The Unfortunate Traveller and Other Works*, ed. J. B. Steane (Harmondsworth: Penguin, 1972), 142–5.

8 Robert Greene, 'Dedication' to *Ciceronis Amor, or Tully's Love* (1589), quoted in Thomas Heywood, *The Earls of Derby and the Verse Writers and Poets of the Sixteenth and Seventeenth Centuries* (Manchester: Chetham Society, 1853), 31.

9 George Peele, 'Polyhymnia', in David Horne (ed.) *The Life and Minor Works of George Peele* (New Haven: Yale University Press, 1952), 233.

10 Meredith Ann Skura, *Shakespeare the Actor and the Purposes of Playing* (Chicago: University of Chicago Press, 1993), 65.

11 Anne Barton, *Shakespeare and the Idea of the Play* (Harmondsworth: Penguin, 1967), 88; Stephen Greenblatt, 'Invisible Bullets: Renaissance Authority and Its Subversion, *Henry IV* and *Henry V*', in Richard Wilson and Richard Dutton (eds) *New Historicism and Renaissance Drama* (Harlow: Longman, 1992), 98.

12 Peter Thomson, *Shakespeare's Professional Career* (Cambridge: Cambridge University Press, 1992), 112–14.

13 E. K. Chambers, *William Shakespeare: A Study of Facts and Problems*, 2 vols (Oxford: Clarendon Press, 1930), I, 42.

14 Andrew Gurr, *Playgoing in Shakespeare's London* (Cambridge: Cambridge University Press, 1987), 50.

15 Martin Holmes, *Shakespeare and Burbage* (Chichester: Phillimore, 1978), 52–5; Thomson, *Shakespeare's Professional Career*, 106; Honan, *Shakespeare*, 142–3.

16 Alan Keen and Roger Lubbock, *The Annotator* (London: Putnam, 1954), 52–4.

17 E. A. J. Honigmann, *Shakespeare: The 'Lost Years'* (Manchester: Manchester University Press, 1985), 64.

18 See source notes to *Richard III*, (ed.) Anthony Hammond (London: Methuen, 1981), 369.

19 *Ibid.*, 367.

20 Barry Coward, *The Stanleys: Lords Stanley and Earls of Derby, 1385–1672* (Manchester: Chetham Society, 1983), 33; 371; 146–8.

21 Quoted in J. J. Bagley, *The Earls of Derby: 1485–1985* (London: Sidgwick & Jackson, 1985), 76.

22 Nashe, 'Pierce Penniless', 122–7; *Calendar of State Papers Domestic*, 69, 67; Da Luna, *Jonson's Romish Plot*, 211, n. 125. For the animal imagery see also D. C. Peck (ed.) *Leicester's Commonwealth* (Athens: Ohio University Press, 1985), 73; 77.

23 Da Luna, *Jonson's Romish Plot*, pp. 146–51; pp. 202–3; John Day, *The Isle of Gulls*, ed. G. B. Harrison (London: Shakespeare Society, 1936), sig. A2v, A4r, B1r; Handover, *The Second Cecil*, 244.

24 Thomas Dekker, Preface to *The Whore of Babylon*, in *The Dramatic Works of Thomas Dekker*, ed. Fredson Bowers (Cambridge: Cambridge University Press, 1955), II; Ben Jonson, *Catiline*, in Ben Jonson, *Works*, (eds) C. H. Herford and Percy and Evelyn Simpson (Oxford: Oxford University Press, 1925–52), IV, 4.2.158; Da Luna, *Jonson's Romish Plot*, 148.

25 Richard Dutton, *Mastering the Revels: The Regulation and Censorship of English Renaissance Drama* (Basingstoke: Macmillan, 1991), 103–7.

26 Nashe, 'Pierce Penniless', 122–4; and see the Dedications to 'The Unfortunate Traveller' and 'The Choice of Valentines', 251; 458.

27 Quoted in P. M. Handover, *Arbella Stuart: Royal Lady of Hardwick and Cousin to King James* (London: Eyre & Spottiswoode, 1957), 100.

28 For the repercussions of this abjuration of faith see Roland Mousnier, *The Assassination of Henry IV: The Tyrannicide Problem and the Consolidation of the French Absolute Monarchy in the Early Seventeenth Century*, trans. Joan Spencer (London: Faber & Faber, 1973), 109–16.

29 John Bossy, 'The Character of Elizabethan Catholicism', *Past and Present*, 21 (1962), 48–9.

30 See, in particular, Patrick McGrath, 'The Bloody Question Reconsidered', *Recusant History*, 20 (1991), 305–19.

31 Linda Woodbridge, *The Scythe of Saturn: Shakespeare and Magical Thinking* (Urbana: University of Illinois Press, 1994), 56–60.

32 Phyllis Rackin, *Stages of History: Shakespeare's English Chronicles* (London: Routledge, 1990), 123–4.

33 Robert Southwell, *An Humble Supplication to Her Majesty*, ed. R. C. Bald (Cambridge: Cambridge University Press, 1953), 11. See also Gillian E. Brennan, 'Papists and Patriotism in Elizabethan England', *Recusant History*, 19 (1988), 1–15.

34 Richard Simpson, 'The Politics of Shakespeare's Historical Plays', *The New Shakespeare Society's Transactions* (1874), 402–5.

35 Alison Shell, *Catholicism, Controversy and the English Literary Imagination, 1558–1660* (Cambridge: Cambridge University Press, 1999), 109.

36 Gillian Brennan, 'Papists and Patriotism in Elizabethan England', *Recusant History*, 19 (1988), 1–15, esp. p. 5.

37 Quoted in Shell, *Catholicism*, 195–6.

38 Jeffrey Knapp, *Shakespeare's Tribe: Church, Nation and Theater in Renaissance England* (Chicago: University Press, 2002), 100.

39 Ernst Honigmann (ed.) *King John* (Harmondsworth: Penguin, 1974), 24–6.

40 Quoted in Conyers Read, *Lord Burghley and Queen Elizabeth* (London: Jonathan Cape, 1960), 252.

41 Thomas Clancy, 'English Catholics and the Deposing Power, 1570–1640: I', *Recusant History*, 6 (1962), 115.

42 A. C. F. Beales, *Education Under Penalty: English Catholic Education from the Reformation to the Fall of James II* (London: Athlone Press, 1963), 155–6.

43 Thomas Clancy, 'English Catholics and the Papal Deposing Power, 1570–1640: II', *Recusant History*, 6 (1962), 219.

44 Gary Taylor, 'Forms of Opposition: Shakespeare and Middleton', *English Literary Renaissance*, 24 (1994), 303–4. See Roland Mushat Frye, *Shakespeare and Christian Doctrine* (Princeton: Princeton University Press, 1963), 282–8.

45 Henri Lefebvre, *The Production of Space*, trans. Donald Nicholson-Smith (Oxford: Blackwell, 1991), 36.

46 John Bossy, *Under the Molehill: An Elizabethan Spy Story* (New Haven: Yale University Press, 2001), 4.

47 Wolfgang Clemen, *Shakespeare's Dramatic Art* (London: Methuen, 1972), 127–33.

48 Mervyn James, 'At a Crossroads of the Political Culture: The Essex Revolt, 1601', *Society, Politics and Culture: Studies in Early Modern England* (Cambridge: Cambridge University Press, 1986), 424.

49 Albert Loomie, *The Spanish Elizabethans: English Exiles at the court of Philip II* (London: Burns & Oates, 1963), 147–57.

50 Chetham Society, vol. 25, p. 27; quoted *ibid.*, 142.

51 The Proclamation is printed as an appendix to Robert Southwell, *An Humble Supplication to Her Majesty*, ed. R. C. Bald (Cambridge: University Press, 1953), 60.

52 Peter Holmes, *Resistance and Compromise: The Political Thought of Elizabethan Catholics* (Cambridge: Cambridge University Press, 1982), 130–1.

53 This is based on Malone's conjecture and is adopted by the Norton (Oxford) edition and the *Riverside Shakespeare*, ed. G. Blakemore Evans (Boston: Houghton Mifflin, 1974). The Arden edition, ed. Peter Ure (London: Methuen, 1956), has 'The son of Richard Earl of Arundel'. For the story of Henry Hoghton's exile with Bolingbroke in Lithuania, where they enrolled together in the Teutonic knights, see George Miller, *Hoghton Tower: The History of the Manor, the Hereditary Lords and the Ancient Manor-house in Lancashire* (Preston: Guardian Press, 1948), 144–5.

54 Quoted in Evelyn Albright, 'Shakespeare's *Richard II* and the Essex Conspiracy', *PMLA*, 42 (1927), 698–701.

55 Carol Enos, *Shakespeare and the Catholic Religion* (Pittsburgh: Dorrance, 2000), 80–1; James, 'At a Crossroads', 426–7.

56 *Ibid.*, 435–6; and Robert Cecil quoted in H. Mutschmann and K. Wentersdorf, *Shakespeare and Catholicism* (New York: AMS, 1969), 123.

57 Jonathan Dollimore and Alan Sinfield, 'History and Ideology: The Instance of *Henry V*', in John Drakakis (ed.) *Alternative Shakespeares* (London: Methuen, 1985), 206–27; 217–20.

58 Sandeep Kaushik, 'Resistance, Loyalty and Recusant Politics: Sir Thomas Tresham and the Elizabethan State', *Midland History*, 21 (1996), 37–72, esp. pp. 63–4.

59 Sir Thomas Tresham, quoted, in *ibid.*, 61.

60 John Kerrigan (ed.) *The Sonnets and 'A Lover's Complaint'* (Harmondsworth: Penguin, 1986), 315.

61 James I quoted in Kenneth Fincham and Peter Lake, 'The Ecclesiastical Policy of James I', *Journal of British Studies*, 24 (1985), 184, n. 64.

62 Quoted in Antonia Fraser, *The Gunpowder Plot: Treason and Faith in 1605* (London: Weidenfeld & Nicolson, 1996), 89.

63 Robert Southwell, 'Times go by turns', in James H. McDonald and Nancy Pollard (eds) *The Poems of Robert Southwell, S. J.* (Oxford: Clarendon Press, 1967), 58; Kaushik, 'Resistance', pp. 63–4.

64 Graham Holderness, 'What Ish My Nation?': Shakespeare and National Identities', in Ivo Kamps (ed.) *Materialist Shakespeare: A History* (London: Verso, 1995), 224–5.

65 Stephen Greenblatt, *Shakespearean Negotiations: The Circulation of Social Energy in Renaissance England* (Oxford: Clarendon Press, 1988), 121; Peter Milward, *Shakespeare's Religious Background* (Chicago: Loyala University Press, 1973), 54; 72.

66 Mark Nicholls, *Investigating Gunpowder Plot* (Manchester: Manchester University Press, 1991), 7; and see A. H. Dodd, 'Spanish Treason, the Gunpowder Plot and the Catholic Refugees', *English Historical Review*, 53 (1938), 627–50.

67 Gary Taylor, '*King Lear* and Censorship', in Gary Taylor and Michael Warren (eds) *The Division of the Kingdoms: Shakespeare's Two Versions of 'King Lear'* (Oxford: Clarendon Press, 1983), 80; W. W. Greg, 'Time, Place and Politics in *King Lear*', in *Collected Papers*, ed. J. C. Maxwell (Oxford: Oxford University Press, 1966), 333. See also Madeleine Doran, *The Text of 'King Lear'* (Stanford: Stanford University Press, 1931), 73–6.

68 I am grateful to Gerard Kilroy, of Lancaster University, for drawing my attention to the Quarto spelling.

69 See Richard Simpson, 'The Political Use of the Stage in Shakespeare's Time', *The New Shakespeare Society's Transactions* (1874), 378. For the most informed account of the *émigré* Catholic community in Antwerp see Grainne Henry, *The Irish Military Community in Spanish Flanders, 1586–1621* (Dublin: Irish Academic Press, 1992), 53–7; 74–9; and for Antigonus as the legendary founder of Antwerp see Jervis Wegg, *Antwerp, 1477–1559* (London: Methuen, 1916), 1.

70 Randolph Starn, *Contrary Commonwealth: The Theme of Exile in Medieval and Renaissance Italy* (Berkeley: University of California Press, 1982), 7. See also A. Bartlett Giametti, *Exile and Change in Renaissance Literature* (New Haven: Yale University Press, 1984); and Dolora Wojciehowski, 'Petrarch's Temporal Exile and the Wounds of History', in James Whitlark and Wendell Aycock (eds) *The Literature of Emigration and Exile* (Lubbock: Texas Tech University Press, 1992), 11–21.

The commons will revolt: *Woodstock* after the Peasants' Revolt

Richard II without *Richard II*

What might early modern people have made of the reign of Richard II without Shakespeare's *Richard II*? Somewhat controversially, Blair Worden has proposed that when the Lord Chamberlain's Men put on 'the story of Henry IV being set forth in a play and in that play there being set forth the killing of the King upon the stage' for the Essex conspirators the day before their rising, this play was not Shakespeare's *Richard II*.[1] Worden's reading of Hayward does, however, lead him to envisage a play similar to Shakespeare's in its outlines, with 'the deposing and killing of Richard the obvious focus of the play' and both 'human tragedy' and 'martyrdom' readily available as angles for the prospective dramatist.

A simple unitary reading of what readers looked for in Richard is easy to complicate, for Essex was perhaps not the first 1590s courtier on the make to dwell on the king's significance. In the Salisbury manuscripts there is an invitation from Sir Edward Hoby to Robert Cecil of December 1595, 'where, as late as it shall please you, a gate for your supper shall be open and K. Richard present himself to your view'. Andrew Gurr points out that Hoby, the Constable of Quinborough Castle in Kent, had commissioned a series of portraits of his predecessors in the office, amongst whom were Richard II and Richard III.[2] The later Richard is, however, an unlikely candidate to entertain a man later to be linked in libels with the crookbacked monarch. Cecil was no Essex, though; if this *was* a private performance, it predates Shakespeare's play and Hayward's book.

The play and the book have obscured, however, other ways in which Richard's reign signified, particularly on the stage. We know of three other plays featuring him which are linked not by a focus on the tragic poet-king but on an event early in his reign: the 1381 Peasants' Revolt. The earliest, the anonymous *Jack Straw*, deals as its name suggests with the rising itself, was printed in 1594, and probably dates from the early 1590s. It was reprinted in 1604. The anonymous play now usually known as *Woodstock*, which is set in the aftermath of 1381, also had an afterlife; Macdonald P. Jackson's recent article on the play, which proposes a date at least a decade after its (until now) consensual dating to the 1590s, accepts that it was probably revived in the 1630s.[3] Finally, Simon Forman saw a 'Richard the 2' covering some of the events of 1381 at the Globe in 1611. The critical consensus on *Jack Straw* (though even with this widely maligned play such a notion is a dangerous one) is that it is clearly a hostile portrayal of the rising, presumably for an audience sympathetic to a 'tough on commons risings, tough on the causes of commons risings' reading.[4] But Forman's response in 1611 should give us pause. Did Shakespeare's company – understandably, in the light of its troubles a decade earlier – stage a 'Richard the 2' covering some of the events of the Peasants' Revolt on 30 April 1611 in order to show, the day before May Day, how civil disorder inevitably comes to a bad end? Or do Forman's comments on the death of Jack Straw at the hands of William Walworth, 'beware by this example of noble men and of their fair wordes', indicate a more complex staging, a more complex conception, of this founding moment of the English radical tradition?[5]

In this chapter I will argue, focusing on *Woodstock*, that mindfulness of the traditions of commons political action offers a new way of understanding popular historical consciousness, and, in addition, the mentalities of early modern audiences and writers. That there was a practical 'insurrectionary tradition' between the commons risings of the 1381 Peasants' Revolt and the mid-sixteenth-century 'camps' of Kett's rising, as well as a 'moral economy' governing smaller-scale actions until much later, is in itself uncontroversial.[6] However, recent work within literary studies on early modern English radicalism has often been focused on the mid-seventeenth century, challenging revisionism's downplaying of the role of culture, let alone ideology, in the transformations of the Civil War period.[7] The sheer newness of many of the cultural conditions at this time redefined English radicalism and in doing so helped to obscure elements of an earlier, residual, radical tradition. This tradition, and a range of commons political actions from local to national scale, was rooted in a quasi-autonomous plebeian critical or festive culture. Much recent work on this tradition within historical studies has focused on its rationality, mindful of the persistence of hostile representations of the commons-in-politics as crowd or mob.[8] This radical tradition, then, was a rational tradition, with a commitment to petitioning, formal written articulation of desired outcomes and self-limiting actions.[9] Yet, it possessed another and more utopian side, for the symbolic nature of some of its permitted actions encompassed inversion, parody, doubleness and travesty. This relationship between the carnivalesque and commons political action is of great significance for the history play.

One important element of the radical tradition was how it conceived its own history. Commons history, Anne Barton long ago noted in a discussion of the history play, is comic history. Historians, from the monks writing of 1381 to the sixteenth-century chroniclers, argued that the bad end of national-scale commons risings showed divine disapprobation. But the commons saw not defeat but modes and moments of empowerment. 'It was a merry world when we were yonder eating of mutton', recalled one of Kett's campmen in 1550.[10]

'Jack Straw', the probably fictional name of one of the leaders of the 1381 Peasants' Revolt, was a reference point for protestors throughout the fifteenth century.[11] The important point in popular memory seems to have been that the Peasants' Revolt provided a blueprint for commons political actions, including Utopian articulations, rather than actual reform of the polity.[12] The usefulness of 'tradition' in this context is that it encompasses a sense of the past outside, or in opposition to, the 'history' written by the victors, a 'nowhere' comprehensible to lettered and unlettered alike.

I wish to propose that working with tradition rather than 'history' offers a new perspective on connections between the 'pastness' of historical drama and a commons audience which has implications for our understanding of both. Unsurprisingly, when Tillyards walked the earth, tradition's place in legitimating political thoughts and actions lost out to a recognisably Brechtian view of political drama for radical critics. Margot Heinemann, for example, claimed that history plays in essence work no differently from other political plays, representing 'issues' and 'grievances', placing the audience 'in the position of weighing and judging the action' demystifying the 'mystery of state'. History, then, was a source of illustrative materials for oblique critique via analogy, accompanied by a cognitive shift regarding power and legitimacy.[13] Heinemann's work on *Woodstock* exemplifies this approach, fuelled by a reading of history which separates the pragmatic, politics based, issues and grievances, of what was to be a successful political rebellion against Charles I from the unsuccessful egalitarian and democratic social revolution coinciding with it. Indeed, she claims of the political plays of the pre-Civil War period that 'the aspirations and mentalities of the radical and democratic "second revolution" are articulated, if at all, in Utopian fables and wishful fantasies of a poor man's heaven, divine revenge on the rich, a world magically changed upside-down' (Heinemann, 'Political Drama', 204).[14]

The commons as public agents

Reading *Woodstock* through the radical tradition offers an opportunity to close Heinemann's separation between (successful) 'rational' and (unsuccessful) 'Utopian' commons politics. The first step in so doing is to recognise that the play-world is one in which the commons have already risen properly. In this sense the play should be considered as *Jack Straw II* rather than *The First Part of Richard the Second*. Indeed, the commons are on the verge of breaking *again* with the early modern pragmatic convention of the 'loyal rising' requiring some gentle or noble presence. As in Shakespeare's 2 *Henry VI*, the first we hear of the commons is from the leader of a court faction, Woodstock himself. But unlike the commons in Shakespeare's play, whom Salisbury defines in terms of favouring, fearing and honouring members of his own faction, the commons at the beginning of *Woodstock* have already sacked London (historically, some seven years previously, though the play elides this):

> WOODSTOCK   They tax the poor and I am scandaled for it
>   That by my fault those late oppressions rise
>   To set the commons in a mutiny
>   That London even itself was sacked by them.
>   And who did all these rank commotions point at?
>   Even at these two: Bagot here and Greene,
>   With false Tresilian whom your grace, we hear,
>   Hath made Chief Justice. Well, well, be it so:
>   Mischief on mischief sure will shortly flow.
>
>   (1.3.122–30)[15]

These commons are not angry but aimless stinging insects; they have got mad, and they have got even.[16] In the same scene, they are said to have rebelled, though they are not currently in 'open arms'. The discussion between Woodstock and his brothers registers the complexity of this State of affairs.

> WOODSTOCK   Speak, speak, what tidings, Cheney?
> CHENEY   Of war, my lord, and civil dissension.
>   The men of Kent and Essex do rebel.
> WOODSTOCK   I thought no less and always feared as much.
> CHENEY   The shrieves in post have sent unto your grace
>   That order may be ta'en to stay the commons,
>   For fear rebellion rise in open arms.
> WOODSTOCK   Now, headstrong Richard, shalt thou reap the fruit
>   Thy lewd licentious wilfulness hath sown.
>   I know not which way to bestow myself.
> YORK   There is no standing on delay, my lords.
>   These hot eruptions must have some redress
>   Or else in time they'll grow incurable.
> WOODSTOCK   The commons they rebel – and the King all careless.
>   Here's wrong on wrong to stir more mutiny.
>   Afore my God, I know not what to do.
> LANCASTER   Take open arms. Join with the vexed commons
>   And hale his minions from his wanton side.

Their heads cut off, the people satisfied.
WOODSTOCK   Not so, not so. Alack the day, good brother,
We may not so affright the tender prince.
We'll bear us nobly for the kingdom's safety
And the king's honour. Therefore list to me:
You, brother Gaunt and noble Arundel,
Shall undertake by threats, or fair entreaty,
To pacify the murmuring commons' rage;
And whiles you there employ your service hours
We presently will call a parliament
And have their deeds examined thoroughly,
Where, if by fair means we can win no favour,
Nor make King Richard leave their companies,
We'll thus resolve for our dear country's good
To right her wrongs or for it spend our bloods.

(1.3.231–63)

At the play's beginning, then, the country is in the grip of some kind of commons-led civil disorder, a disorder explicitly traced back to the doings of the king and his minions. Nothing of this is staged and its exact status is difficult to gauge, as can be seen by the shuttling between past, present and future in the descriptions of it. A linear trawl through the play offers the following examples: 'The commons murmur 'gainst the dissolute king' (1.1.157), 'those late oppressions rise / To set the commons in a mutiny' (1.3.123–4), 'the men of Kent and Essex do rebel' (1.3. 233), 'It must be done with greater policy / For fear the people rise in mutiny' (2.1.45–6), 'Thy wronged kingdom's in a mutiny' (2.2.43), 'the ragged commons . . . / . . . should grow mutinous about these blanks' (3.1.103–4), 'Let each man hie him to his several home / Before the people rise in mutiny, / And, in the mildest part of lenity, / Seek to restrain them from rebellion' (3.2.91–4), 'The commons will rebel without all question' (3.2.110), 'the fire / Those blanks have made' (3.2.236–7). This clearly is not 'rebellion' as usually understood. But awareness of the radical tradition of commons action allows us to see it as something more than mere atmospheric filler until the action intensifies with the kidnapping and murder of Woodstock; politically powerful commoners impose themselves on the mental world of the court. Indeed, the sacking of London during 1381 functions rather as the murder of Woodstock does in Shakespeare's *Richard II*; the play-worlds of both begin in the aftermath of a catastrophic event and the mental world of its characters should not be understood without reference to it.

Woodstock looks a much more conventional work if this context is missed. For example, William C. Carroll considers that the play rejects 'peasant rebellion' while eventually condoning 'aristocratic rebellion'.[17] Characterising the unstable state of the commons as 'rebellion', which thus must be 'suppressed', smooths out the play's more complex delineation of commons agency in the play's first half. It also simplifies the agency of both commons and nobles in the play's fifth act, when York and Lancaster rise up 'in open arms' against Richard with 'the gentlemen and commons of the realm' who 'break their allegiance to their sovereign lord / And all revolt upon the barons' sides' (5.1.286–7, 289–90).[18]

These references to the collective agency, past and ongoing, of the commons militate against the notion that the play's interpretation of commons history ends with the representation of individual victims. For example, Alzada Tipton sees the non-presence of powerful commoners as a crucial indicator of the play's sympathy for them, or at least of 'their right to rebel against an exploitative prince'. Hence, the play avoids the (inevitably) stereotypical presentation of the rebellious commons 'and thus gives them dignity, moral credibility and even pathos' ('"The meanest man"', 125). Richard Helgerson, for whom the play 'takes its dramatic energy and interest from the representation of royal oppression' makes a similar point: 'The effects of Richard's misrule on his suffering subjects, Thomas of Woodstock most prominent among them, are what most engage our attention in *Woodstock* . . . How do they [the common people] take the disappearance of their chief defender, plain Thomas of Woodstock?'[19] The answer to Helgerson's last question is, as I have noted above, that they rise in armed rebellion, albeit offstage. This is not to say that victimhood is unimportant to a consideration of the commons in the play. As the critics quoted above agree, an important part of the play's impact lies in its staging of the oppression of the commons. As I will later argue, though, it is the ways in which the powerful appropriate the festive and inversive elements of commons politics that makes this oppression so egregious.

Commons reading the *Mirror* and the chronicles

The play's commons-centredness can clearly be seen by considering its relationship with one of the most important late-sixteenth-century reference points for reading the late medieval era – *A Mirror for Magistrates* (1559). The *Mirror*'s importance for the genesis of the history play and for Shakespeare's early histories is well known. Its early editions begin, as Hall's *Chronicle* does, with the reign of Richard II, who 'was for his evyll governaunce deposed from his seat and miserably murdred in prison'. Three major characters in *Woodstock* are given laments. *Woodstock*'s most recent editors claim that the *Mirror*, whilst not a direct source for the play, 'may be a significant influence on . . . the provision of a moral framework within which the dramatist organised his source material'.[20] This is most visible in the fall of Woodstock, who laments Fortune's inescapability in the *Mirror*'s third tragedy. But the other two characters with tragedies in the *Mirror* are depicted very differently in the play. The *Mirror*'s account of Richard's failings, in his own words, is blunt:

I am a Kyng that ruled all by lust,
That forced not of vertue, right, or lawe,
But always put false Flatterers most in trust,
Ensuing such as could my vices clawe:
By faythful counsayle passing not a strawe.
What pleasure pryckt, that thought I to be just.
I set my minde, to feede, to spoyle, to just,
Three meales a day could skarce content my mawe,
And all too augment my lecherous minde that must
To Venus pleasures always be in awe.[21]

Richard in *Woodstock* does have his *Mirror*ish moments, noting at the end of the fourth act that his wife's death is 'but chorus to some tragic scene / That shortly will confound our State and realm' (4.3.150–1). For the most part, however, this misruled lord is a lord of misrule, associated with inversion, excess and counter-intuitive novelty. When Richard removes his uncles from office, Woodstock responds with 'What transformations do mine eyes behold / As if the world were topsy-turvy turned' (2.2.142–3). The King's unfettered rule features excessive feasting ('Thirty fat oxen and three hundred sheep / Serve but one day's expense', according to Woodstock, 3.2.30–1), bizarre fashions ('They sit in council to devise strange fashions, / And suit themselves in wild and antic habits / Such as this kingdom never yet beheld', says Cheney to the Queen, 3.1.88–90) and a disguised masking, under cover of which he abducts Woodstock, which takes the form of the 'sports' of 'country gentlemen'. The mask is so far from being associated with the noble degree initially that, when Woodstock learns that his house is surrounded with armed soldiers, his response is 'Afore my God, the commons all are up then? / They will rebel against the king I fear me, / And flock to me to back their bold attempts' (4.2.161–3).[22]

Woodstock transforms its third *Mirror* character even more, for the very first tragedy in the volume is 'the fall of Robert Tresilian chiefe Justice of Englande' (Campbell, *Mirror*, 73). What *Woodstock* makes of Tresilian, however, is clearly the opposite of what the *Mirror* made of him; he is a Vice-like comic upstart. The play does not simply refuse the *Mirror*'s example; it directly challenges it, in what amounts to an assault on the 'tragedies of princes' genre. There are several possible explanations. One is made possible by Jackson's shifting of the play's date into the early seventeenth century. By then the *Mirror* would have been last century's news and ripe for ridicule, as indeed would Shakespeare's own *Richard II*, a play much more influenced by the *Mirror*'s first-person laments.[23] There is certainly scope for reading *Woodstock* as a proto-*Perkin Warbeck*, a play knowingly revisiting an unfashionable genre.

A critical perspective on the history play can be supplied by more than just shifts in theatrical trends, though. Remembering the radical tradition allows other readings too. Tresilian had led the judicial reprisals following 1381 and had tried and condemned John Ball, the radical preacher whose sermon opens the rising in *Jack Straw*. A commons-centred reading of history would have a bone to pick with Tresilian. It might be objected that this is far too close a reading of obscure historical details. This may be so; but it is not the only example of such close reading behind the play. In Holinshed, the primary source, Richard's actual apprehension of his uncle, as the play's editors, Corbin and Sedge, note, involves a simple deception. But the 'splendidly dramatic masque' is not an invention out of thin air, for Holinshed also reports that the deposed Richard's supporters planned to murder Henry IV under cover of a mask or mummery, or a joust – and, indeed, that the unintentional revelation of these plans by the Duke of Aumerle led directly to Richard's own murder.[24]

However hesitant Holinshed may have been over the kind of event at which the conspirators were to have pounced ('a maske or mummerie'), one text is absolutely clear. The *Mirror for Magistrates*, which cites Hall and Fabyan as sources, proposes as one of its early tragedies an account of this conspiracy:

> I would (quoth one of the company) gladly say sumwhat for king Richard. But his personage is so sore entangled as I thinke fewe benefices be at this day: for after his imprisonment, his brother and divers other made a maske, minding by Henries destruction to have restored him, which matter so runneth in this, that I doubt which ought to go / before. But seing no man is redy to say ought in their behalfe, I will geve who so listeth leasure to thinke theruppon and in the meane time to further your enterprise, I will in the kinges behalfe recount such part of his story as I thinke most necessary. (Campbell, *Mirror*, 110–11)

After Richard's tragedy, the conspirators are again mentioned as part of the introduction to Owen Glendower's tragedy: 'yet because their examples were not much to be noted for our purpose, we passed over all the Maskers (of whom King Richardes brother was chiefe) which were all slayne and put to death for theyr traitorous attempt'.[25] Richard's links with disguise and treachery were historical facts, cleverly woven into *Woodstock* and gesturing at his eventual downfall.

Appropriating the radical tradition

The commons-centredness of *Woodstock* thus can be discerned not merely in its sympathetic portrayal of commons as victims, but critical eye it casts on those misruling them, from Richard on down. At its simplest, this involves straight ridicule, as in the episode when the courtier attempts to explain his fashionable shoes, whose toes are joined to his knee with a chain, to Woodstock thus:

> For these two parts being in operation and quality different, as for example: the toe a disdainer or spurner; the knee a dutiful and most humble orator; this chain doth, as it were, so toeify the knee and so kneeify the toe that between both it makes a most methodical coherence or coherent method. (3.2.221–6)

Ridiculous visual excess, pointed up by the plainness of the courtier's inter-locutor, is accompanied by ridiculous chop-logic justification of a foolish costume, with a nice opportunity for physical and vocal comedy attempting to demonstrate toeifying and kneeifying. Here also is some sly mockery of the Elizabethan world picture's fondness for 'kind coherence', with the fable of the belly given a ridiculous spin; the shoe's chain works to unify toe and knee, just as the humble orator's rhetoric works to calm the disdainer or spurner.[26] In a further irony, Woodstock himself has said earlier in the scene that 'The commons will rebel without all question, / And, 'fore my God, I have no eloquence / To stay this uproar' (3.2.110–12). This skilled ridicule of an over-educated fashion victim presents no particular problems of inter-pretation.

There are more complex modes of representation, however, which aware-ness of the radical tradition can help explicate. It is a critical cliché that the carnivalesque representation of commons risings and in particular the use of comedy, is a representational strategy designed to discredit them.[27] I am unconvinced by the 'Lent good, Carnival bad' approach to commons in pol-itics and have argued elsewhere that as actual commons political actions fea-tured, in various degrees, elements conventionally located within the carnivalesque, showing commons actions as not completely 'serious' is not the devastating technique critics seem to think.

Representing the king, his court and the forces of law and order as carni-valesque, however, is another matter. This is not a case of simple inversion of a natural political order – that 'high' politics should be left to sober char-acters like Woodstock. Rather, from the point of view of the radical trad-ition, it marks Richard's and Tresilian's projects as not inversion but appropriation, for festivity and inversion are typical elements within the commons' political toolkit.

One key appropriation of the radical tradition is Richard's kidnapping of his uncle. Discussions of this tend to focus on Richard's visit as a 'masque', aided by modern editors' decisions over spelling (in the manuscript it is 'mask'). For example, Sandra Billington is much struck by the play's naming of the leader of the masque as 'Cynthia' given that name's common associa-tion with Queen Elizabeth, noting that 'the most extraordinary aspect of this political allegory is Cynthia presiding over the masque and, therefore, in microcosm, leading the corrupt court destroying good government' (Billington, *Mock Kings*, 229). G. K. Hunter contrasts Woodstock's 'attachment to the locality, to the nation and its traditions' with Richard's arresting him 'under cover of a neoclassical masque'.[28] Meredith Ann Skura classes Richard's disguising as an example of the 'revenge masque', where the typical outcome is death for either the 'players' or the onstage audience. In this case, *Woodstock* keeps company with Senecan moments such as Tamora's masque in *Titus Andronicus*.[29] These points however, distract from the ways in which Richard's 'masquing' is a 'masking', incorporating and subverting elements of festive customs, customs often amphibiously associated with social disorder and sometimes more significant political actions.[30] In particular, Richard's visit resembles mumming, a festive activity defined recently as 'going round the streets at Christmas after dark in a gang, dressed up in strange clothes and with your face concealed in some way, in order to enter other people's houses and play at dice with them'.[31] As Twycross and Carpenter note, mumming is not a communal activity, but a 'confrontation, between the masked and the unmasked'; they cite, alongside the preamble to the 1511 Act *Agaynst Disguysed Persons and Wearing of Visors* a plot in Beverley in 1537 'to beate and coil' political opponents under cover of a mumming (Twycross and Carpenter, *Masks*, 100).

Though Richard and his accomplices enter 'like Diana's knights, led in by four other knights in green, with horns about their necks and boar-spears in their hands' (4.2.124 SD), the context for their performance incorporates other elements associated with commons actions. One example is the attention the text gives to the noisiness of the murderous maskers. Cheney introduces them as 'country gentlemen', arriving at Woodstock's residence to 'proffer their sports this night to make you merry. / Their drums have called for entrance twice already' (4.2.85, 87–8). This emphasis on the noise made by the maskers continues through the stage direction's 'antic dance and music; then a great shout and winding o' horns' (4.2.101) and the 'drum afar off' at the moment Cheney reveals that the house is surrounded by soldiers (4.2.159 SD).[32] The noise itself signifies on more than the military level, as is indicated by the adverb in Richard's rather strained couplet on arresting his uncle, 'If for help he cry, / Drown all his words with drums confusedly' (4.2.170–1). In other words, the cacophony associated with Richard's escapade aligns it with one of the characteristic inversions of both popular protest and popular disciplinary actions, for, as Andy Wood explains, 'since order was synonymous with "quietness", inversive punishments were often attended by clamorous noise'.[33] Richard's challenge to right rule is thus not simply personal but structural; his actions not only invert and parody those of right rule but appropriate distinctively commons political modes.[34]

The central appropriation of the carnivalesque, however, is in the middle of the play. Tresilian, the Lord Chief Justice, has decided to extort money by taxing via the equivalent of a blank cheque – collecting signatures on blank charters. His servant Nimble immediately casts the project as appropriating the festive, with a reference to folk play or morris-dance: 'We will domineer over the vulgar like so many Saint Georges over the poor dragons. Come, sirs; we are like to have a flourishing commonwealth, i'faith!' (3.1.171–4). Once Nimble arrives in the country, he enlists Simon Ignorance, the baily of Dunstable and together they force some farmers to sign the blank charters before arresting them as 'privy whisperers'. A schoolmaster and his servant are likewise borne off for intentionally singing abusive songs, which the schoolmaster admits to the servant 'if they were well searched they're little better than libels; but the carriage of a thing is all, sir: I have covered them rarely' (3.3.166–8). But the scene ends with a remarkably original demonstration of the topsy-turvyness of the law:

> *Enter one a-whistling.*
> NIMBLE   Close again, Master Baily, here comes another whisperer I see by some – O villain, he whistles treason! I'll lay hold of him myself.
> WHISTLER   Out alas, what do ye mean, sir?
> NIMBLE   A rank traitor, Master Baily. Lay hold on him, for he has most erroneously and rebelliously whistled treason.
> WHISTLER   Whistled treason? Alas, sir, how can that be?
> NIMBLE   Very easily, sir. There's a piece of treason that flies up and down the country in the likeness of a ballad and this being the very tune of it, thou hast whistled treason.
> WHISTLER   Alas, sir, ye know I spake not a word.
> NIMBLE   That's all one; if any man whistle treason, 'tis as ill as speaking it.
> (3.3.233–45)

Like the scene with the courtier and the shoe, this is a comic routine, with the whistler feeding straight lines to the two comics. This is pointed up nicely by Ignorance's later demand, 'Who did set you a-work? Or who was the cause of your whistling? Or did any man say to you, "Go whistle"?' (3: 3, 254–6). 'Go whistle', of course, is proverbial for a futile quest and is used in that sense by the clown in *The Winter's Tale* (4.4.698). Whistling treason, however, is not as obviously absurd as some critics have thought, for there is some evidence from the seventeenth century that the phrase delineated political transgression. In 1679, one William Mandeville was indicted for seditious speech which included the words 'I dare not whistle treason, but I know what I think' (Wood, *Riot*, 178). Both John Taylor and Richard Baxter used the phrase during the seventeenth century, Taylor as early as 1621.[35]

Nimble and Ignorance's arresting the farmer or the schoolteacher earlier in the scene retained at least the appearance of legality in its charging with

privy whispering or libelling. But, as Garrett L. Sullivan notes, 'the project
of collecting information and signatures for Richard's survey is understood
as both undermining and exploiting rural social structures governing the
circulation of information' (Sullivan, *Drama of Landscape*, 75). Richard's
project strikes at basic commons modes of communicating, including its
political use of what the chroniclers of 1381 called 'dark riddles'. A
quarter-century ago, Steven Mullaney pointed out that the rhetorical device
of 'amphibology' was associated in Puttenham's *Arte* with commons radicalism and indeed that when 'amphibology surfaces in histories or on the
stage it is accorded a power that is generative rather than controlling or
restraining'.[36] Mullaney is less interested in political agency than in the
liminal ontological status of the 'traitor', 'athwart a line that sets off the
human from the demonic, the natural from the unnatural and the rational
from the enigmatic and obscure realm of unreason' (Mullaney, 'Lying Like
Truth', 32). Puttenham's text, however, is somewhat more grounded in a
reading of history. His examples of 'vicious speech . . . when we speak or
write doubtfully . . . that the sense may be taken two ways' include both
examples of grammatical ambiguity ('Thomas Taylor saw William Tyler
drunk') and prophecies, which 'turn them on which side ye will the matter
of them may be verified'. His exemplification of the effects of this is worth
quoting in full:

> Nevertheless, carrieth generally such force in the heads of fond people that by
> the comfort of those blind prophecies many insurrections and rebellions have
> been stirred up in this realm, as that of Jack Straw and Jack Cade, in Richard
> the Second's time and in our time by a seditious fellow in Norfolk calling
> himself Captain Ket and others in other places of the realm led altogether by
> certain prophetical rhymes, which might be construed two or three ways, as
> well as to that one whereunto the rebels applied it.[37]

Puttenham then goes on to offer the practical advice 'our maker shall therefore avoid all such ambiguous speeches, unless it be when he doth it for the
nonce and for some purpose' (Puttenham, *Arte*, 285). This avoidance is a
matter not simply of prudence – though the paranoid reaction of the government during crisis periods to suspect speech should not be forgotten – but
of delineating the 'maker' (and, we might add, the early modern 'politic'
intellectual) from the dispersed author-function of the commons.

But the third section of the Nimble/Ignorance scene takes the matter one
step further. Ignorance may sound like a stock stupid policeman, but he is
sending people off toward quartering and hanging, not so much a Dogberry
as a Reservoir Dogberry. The scene clearly demonstrates the inverted nature
of the legal process under Richard. Inversion, however, was the property of
the commons in politics; Richard's rule threatens centuries-old divisions

between high and popular politics. So *Woodstock* shows the attempted appropriation of the carnivalesque by the anti-commons faction; Woodstock himself is rather a Lenten figure, though characterised as charitable and aware of the reciprocal obligations involved in maintaining a great house. From the point of view of the radical tradition, this is wrong because it is appropriation. But it also means that the parodic function of commons disorder is disrupted. 'Normal' carnivalesque justice would parody a stable construct of 'real' justice, located elsewhere. The Lord Chief Justice, his officers and even to some extent the King are all situated in a parodic relationship to a norm of political behaviour embodied not only in the King's uncles, but also in the offstage and onstage commons, moderate and (so far as we can tell) nonviolent figures.

What, then, does mapping *Woodstock* on to our knowledge of the radical tradition allow us? It shows that the play offers a polity in which the commons are not only powerful, with a history of even greater power, but are justified in protesting and even taking part in armed revolt. At the same time, this political agency is dialogically placed in opposition to the disruptive, at times carnivalesque, agency of the King's party. The commons share with Richard's uncles a conception of relations between degrees within the polity, rather than simply assent to it. This mutual vision is in turn situated versus Richard's own boy-racer absolutism and the simple greed of his cronies.

But the clinching argument against Richard and his men is not that they are greedy, but that they attempt to disrupt and appropriate central forms of commons political life, especially the reservation of the carnivalesque to commons politics. The play shows Richard overturning a romantic-historical trope most famously identified by Anne Barton thirty years ago. Writing of the innovations of Shakespeare's *Henry V*, Barton notes its questioning the folk convention of the King, who adopts 'disguise as a caprice, for reasons that are fundamentally exploratory and quixotic'.[38] Barton identifies the convention particularly with plays set in the British past, where such romantic gestures are part of a merry world ethos. Typically, the disguised monarch personally engages with his subjects, whether to woo them or to meet with them in good fellowship. Extending Barton's insights, Richard Helgerson has recently suggested that 'in the more comical histories, good fellowship, including its lawless, anarchic, clownish and carnivalesque sides, seems an end in itself' and that for non-Shakespearean dramatists of history 'encourage their audiences to imagine themselves as members of a potentially disruptive community of good fellows'.[39] Remembering the radical tradition allows us to see that Richard's project is so transgressive because he seeks to appropriate the political forms of the merry world itself.

Notes

1 Blair Worden, 'Which Play Was Performed at the Globe Theatre on 7 February 1601?', *London Review of Books* (10 July 2003), 22.

2 Andrew Gurr, *The Shakespeare Company, 1594–1642* (Cambridge: Cambridge University Press, 2004), 179–80.

3 Macdonald P. Jackson, 'Shakespeare's *Richard II* and the Anonymous *Thomas of Woodstock*' in John Pitcher (ed.) *Medieval and Renaissance Drama in England Volume 14* (Cranbury, NJ: Associated University Presses, 2001), 22.

4 See the survey in my edition of *Jack Straw* (Lewiston and Lampeter: Edwin Mellen, 2002), 43–54 and my attempt to offer a more complex reading, 55–124.

5 E. K. Chambers, *William Shakespeare: A Study of Facts and Problems Volume 2* (Oxford: Clarendon Press, 1930; reissued 1988), 340.

6 For a useful survey of the former see Michael Bush's 'The Risings of the Commons in England, 1381–549', in Jeffrey Denton (ed.) *Orders and Hierarchies in Late Medieval and Renaissance Europe* (London: Macmillan, 1999), 109–25. For the classic exposition of the latter see E. P. Thompson's 1971 essay and 1991 reply to his critics in *Customs in Common* (Harmondsworth: Penguin, 1991). Andy Wood's *Riot, Rebellion and Popular Politics in Early Modern England* (London: Palgrave, 2002) is the indispensable starting point for students of early modern commons politics.

7 For useful contra-revisionist literary studies see Nick McDowell, *The English Radical Imagination: Culture, Religion and Revolution 1630–1660* (Oxford: Clarendon Press, 2003), and James Holstun, *Ehud's Dagger: Class Struggle in the English Revolution* (London: Verso, 2000).

8 Andrew Prescott's work on 1381 usefully points out the similarities between chronicle accounts of 1381 and tabloid newspaper stories about the British urban riots of 1981 in 'Writing About Rebellion: Using the Records of the Peasants' Revolt of 1381', *History Workshop Journal*, 45 (1988), 1–27.

9 Explication and defence of this vital point is central to Annabel Patterson's formidable body of work on representations of the early modern commons. See especially her *Reading Holinshed's Chronicles* (Chicago: University of Chicago Press, 1994) and her chapter on Shakespeare's Cade in *Shakespeare and the Popular Voice* (Oxford: Basil Blackwell, 1989).

10 Quoted in James Holstun's 'The Spider, the Fly and the Commonwealth: Merrie John Heywood and Agrarian Class Struggle', *English Literary History*, 71 (2004), 57–8.

11 I. W. M. Harvey, 'Was There Popular Politics in Fifteenth-century England?', in R. H. Britnell and A. J. Pollard (eds) *The McFarlane Legacy: Studies in Late Medieval Politics and* Society (Stroud: Alan Sutton, 1995), 168. Harvey comments on that same page that 'the success or otherwise of any of these uprisings would not seem to have been of much significance to those who looked back to them'.

12 For a patchy but suggestive list of appropriations from the seventeenth century onwards see Alastair Dunn, *The Peasants' Revolt: England's Failed Revolution of 1381* (Stroud: Tempus, 2004), 190–3.

13 For example, Heinemann's statement that 'dangers and disasters from earlier times could be seen as analogous to contemporary troubles which, given the censorship, could not have been presented directly': her account does not allow that such events might already have had meaning for their audience before the play. See 'Political Drama', in A. R. Braunmuller and Michael Hattaway (eds) *The Cambridge Companion to English Renaissance Drama* (Cambridge: Cambridge University Press, 1990).

14 More recent work on the play carries on in this vein. Alzada J. Tipton comments that 'the rebellion in *Woodstock* has its roots in some of the best-known theories of resistance that were part of Renaissance political dialogue'; Garrett A. Sullivan, Jr, sees it as an issues-oriented play which 'considers what would happen were the governance of the entire nation to be simultaneously modeled after that of the estate'. See Alzada J. Tipton, ' " The meanest man . . . shall be permitted freely to accuse": The Commoners in *Woodstock*', *Comparative Drama*, 32 (1998), 118, and Garrett A. Sullivan, Jr, *The Drama of Landscape: Land, Property and Social Relations on the Early Modern Stage* (Stanford: Stanford University Press, 1998), 57.

15 Quotations from the play are from the Revels Plays' *Thomas of Woodstock or King Richard the Second, Part One*, (eds) Peter Corbin and Douglas Sedge (Manchester: Manchester University Press, 2002), unless otherwise noted.

16 This is recognised shortly afterwards when Tresilian sees Richard's bright idea for a show trial and execution as a way out from under his uncles' authority as a dangerous provocation: 'It must be done with greater policy / For fear the people rise in mutiny' (2.1.45–6).

17 William C. Carroll, *Fat King, Lean Beggar: Representations of Poverty in the Age of Shakespeare* (Ithaca and London: Cornell University Press, 1996), 147.

18 These words are spoken by Lapoole in Calais, where he has just supervised Woodstock's murder, so the rising does not seem to be, in the performed action at least, a response to Woodstock's death, however much it might seem to be in the action of performance.

19 Richard Helgerson, 'Shakespeare and Contemporary Dramatists of History', in Richard Dutton and Jean E. Howard (eds) *A Companion to Shakespeare's Works, Volume II: The Histories* (Oxford: Blackwell, 2003), 37.

20 Corbin and Sedge, *Woodstock*, 10.

21 *A Mirror for Magistrates*, edited by Lily Bess Campbell (Cambridge: Cambridge University Press, 1938), 113.

22 Sandra Billington sees Richard's second crowning as a public demonstration that 'the topsy-turvy world is ruled over by the true-born mock king', in *Mock Kings in Medieval Society and Renaissance Drama* (Oxford: Clarendon Press, 1991), 224.

23 Jackson's new dating would also provide an intriguing link with Q4 of Shakespeare's *Richard II*, published in 1608 'with new additions'.

24 As noted by Inga-Stina Ewbank, 'These Pretty Devices: A Study of Masques in Plays', in *A Book of Masques in Honour of Allardyce Nicoll* (Cambridge: Cambridge University Press, 1967), 438; see *Holinshed's Chronicles of England, Scotland and Ireland Volume III* (London: for J. Johnson, *et al.*, 1801; reprinted New York: AMS Press, 1965), 3.

25 Campbell, *Mirror*, 119. Ian Lancashire notes the arrest in 1415 of Lollards accused of conspiring to kill Henry V at a court mumming in *Dramatic Texts and Records of Britain: A Chronological Topography to 1558* (Toronto and Buffalo: Toronto University Press, 1984).

26 Jackson's dating of the play makes possible a reading of the courtier's speech as a parodic travesty of the opening of *Coriolanus* (1607), a play with a very different view of the commons in politics. Here, Menenius' rhetoric is put in the mouth of Polonius.

27 A recent example is Simon Hunt's 1999 statement that 'the allegation that Cade is a carnivalesque figure serves, like his clownishness, to render ridiculous the rebellion with which he is associated', in ' "Leaving Out the Insurrection": Carnival Rebellion, English History Plays and a Hermeneutics of Advocacy', in Patricia Fumerton and Simon Hunt (eds) *Renaissance Culture and the Everyday* (Philadelphia: University of Pennsylvania Press, 1999), 303.

28 G. K. Hunter, *English Drama 1586–1642: The Age of Shakespeare* (Oxford: Clarendon Press, 1997), 207.

29 Meredith Ann Skura, *Shakespeare the Actor and the Purposes of Playing* (Chicago: Chicago University Press, 1993), 151.

30 Howkins and Merricks note that 'within popular protest in Britain, from at least the early modern period, we see strong ritual elements. These rituals . . . include many common forms, especially disguise/blacking of faces, wearing masks, different clothes (including cross dressing), processions and cacophony especially beating drums and blowing horns'. See ' "Wee be black as Hell": Ritual, Disguise and Rebellion', *Rural History*, 4, 1 (1993), 41.

31 Meg Twycross and Sarah Carpenter, *Masks and Masking in Medieval and Early Tudor England* (Aldershot: Ashgate, 2002), 83.

32 Though I quote here from the Revels edition, these stage directions are all present in the manuscript of the play. See Wilhelmina P. Frijlinck, *Richard II or Thomas of Woodstock* (Oxford: Malone Society Reprints, 1929), 72–4

33 Wood, *Riot*, 104. He is here referring primarily to popular shaming punishments, but chronicle accounts of commons political action also often refer to their disorderly noisiness. For example, Grafton's 1569 account of Richard's attempt to meet with the commons on the banks of the Thames during the Peasants' Revolt states that 'when they sawe the kings Barge comming, they began to showte and made suche a crie as if all the Devills in hell had bene among them'. Quoted from my edition of *The Life and Death of Jack Straw*, 222. Chris Humphrey makes the more general point that 'the principal characteristic of carnival-style festivities is a noisy interruption of everyday public life' in *The Politics of Carnival: Festive Misrule in Medieval England* (Manchester: Manchester University Press, 2001), 1.

34 And, as Garrett L. Sullivan notes, Woodstock's 'hospitality gets him killed'. Sullivan, *Drama of Landscape*, 89.

35 *Oxford English Dictionary* citation (where 'whistle' is supposed to mean 'whisper').

36 Steven Mullaney, 'Lying Like Truth: Riddle, Representation and Treason in Renaissance England', *English Literary History*, 47 (1980), 43.

37 George Puttenham, *The Arte of English Poesie* (1598), quoted from Brian Vickers (ed.) *English Renaissance Literary Criticism* (Oxford: Clarendon Press, 1999), 284–5.

38 Anne Barton, 'The King Disguised: Shakespeare's *Henry V* and the Comical History', in J. G. Price, (ed.) *The Triple Bond: Plays, Mainly Shakespearean, in Performance* (Philadelphia: Pennsylvania State University Press, 1975), 93.

39 Richard Helgerson, 'Shakespeare and Contemporary Dramatists of History', in Richard Dutton and Jean E. Howard (eds) *A Companion to Shakespeare's Works, Volume II: The Histories* (Oxford: Blackwell, 2003), 33.

National history to foreign calamity: *A Mirror for Magistrates* and early English tragedy

Some time in the later sixteenth century, the classical scholar and poet Gabriel Harvey acquired a copy of *The Posies* (1575), the miscellany collection of George Gascoigne's poetry, prose and drama, and, as he did with most of the books in his library, Harvey annotated this one with marginalia. In one note, on the title to *Jocasta*, he linked the play with two other mid-century works, *A Mirror for Magistrates* and *Gorboduc*, and in so doing pinpointed a line of influence that is the subject of this chapter, the *Mirror*'s on the tragedy of the 1560s. The title reads:

> IOCASTA: A Tragedie written in Greeke by *Euripides*, translated and digested into Acte by George Gascoygne, and Francis Kinwelmershe of Grayes Inne, and there by them presented, 1566.[1]

Above this, Harvey wrote:

> The Myrrour of Magistrates. The Tragoedy of Kyng Gorboduc: pennid by M. Thomas Sackvil, now Lord Buckhurst and M. Thomas Norton: as the same was shew'd before the Queenes Majesty at Whitehall, 1561. by the Gentlemen of the Inner Temple.[2]

Harvey appears confused here, running together the titles of the *Mirror for Magistrates* and *Gorboduc* in a way that suggests that they are the same work. The two are of course separate texts. The first is the multi-authored compilation of didactic poetry about the falls of English kings, lords and pretenders to power between the reigns of Richard II and Edward IV.[3] The second is Thomas Sackville and Thomas Norton's *Gorboduc*, one of the earliest examples of classical tragedy and historical drama in English. Harvey does not explain the link between the *Mirror/Gorboduc* and *Jocasta*, but even a glance at his note suggests one connection. They are tragedies associated with the Inns of Court. There, members of the law schools, most notably Sackville himself, read and added tragedies to the *Mirror* in the

1560s and there both *Gorboduc* and *Jocasta* were written and initially performed.[4] Harvey seems to have made this connection himself, noting that *Gorboduc* is 'by the Gentlemen of the Inner Temple', a comment that resembles the title of *Jocasta* by Gascoigne and Kinwelmersh 'of Grayes Inne'.

Yet he must have recognised other similarities as well. The three texts are alike in plot, each recounting tragedies from periods of Civil War. The *Mirror* covers the century of civil strife caused by the Wars of the Roses. *Gorboduc* replays an episode in ancient British history in which King Gorboduc divided the realm between his two sons, sparking a disastrous Civil War. And *Jocasta*, dramatising the story of Oedipus, likewise covers the conflict between the brothers Eteocles and Polynices for control of the Theban throne. The three are, moreover, similar in tone, admonishing those in power about the dangers of tyranny, ambition and pride. And, finally, they are comparable in elements of their production: all three were created through a process of shared writing and performance.[5]

The *Mirror*, *Gorboduc* and *Jocasta* make up a family of writings. More than that, the two dramas are the generic and political offspring of the earlier work. In the opening chorus of *Gorboduc*, we are told that the king a 'Mirror shall become to princes all / To learn to shun the cause of such a fall'. In *Jocasta*, the final chorus urges princes to take the king as a mirror, commanding that 'kings and princes in prosperitie' should 'example here, lo take by Oedipus'.[6] In the broadest terms, both plays are mirrors for magistrates.

The purpose of this chapter is to address one aspect of the political legacy of the *Mirror*. I have argued elsewhere that even as the *Mirror* speaks to power, it also presents a conversation about power, about the obligations and responsibilities of those who govern the realm.[7] As the following suggests, *Gorboduc*, *Jocasta* and indeed all of the tragedies of the 1560s show that *Mirror* helped to initiate a conversation in drama about the governance of the commonwealth. Almost immediately after it was published, writers at the Inns of Court, as well as at the universities and court, used the *Mirror* as a model to create their own representations of the falls of princes, and to produce a political discourse in the arena of drama about the rule and misrule of the state.

Gorboduc and *Jocasta* are two of the many tragedies produced over the 1560s, the decade when the genre first flourished in England. Not surprisingly, the *Mirror* had a significant impact on all of these plays. Such influence is suggested in the long list of works that depict the downfalls of men and women in positions of power and authority. Thomas Preston's *Cambises* (c. 1560) concerns the tyranny and eventual death of the ancient Persian king. Thomas Pickering's *Horestes* (1567–68) follows Orestes' revenge on his mother and her lover for the murder of his father, Agamemnon. And *Gismond of Salerne* (1567–68), by Robert Wilmot, Henry Noel, Christopher

Hatton and others, shows the tragic demise of a king who refuses to allow his daughter to marry.[8] In addition to those original works, a number of plays by Seneca, translated into English in this decade for the first time, present this plot as well. *Troas* (1559) illustrates the fall of Hecuba in the aftermath of the Trojan War. *Octavia* (1567), a play erroneously attributed to Seneca, depicts the downfall of another woman, Nero's first wife Octavia, whom the emperor divorced and murdered. *Thyestes* (1560) concerns the revenge of King Atreus on his hated brother. *Oedipus* (1563) depicts the fall of the Theban king, while *Agamemnon* (1566) dramatises the murder of that ruler. *Hercules Furens* (1561) and *Hercules Oetaeus* (1566) show two chilling episodes in the hero's life, his mistaken murder of his family and his own death at the hands of a jealous wife. *Medea* (1566) and *Hyppolytus* (1567) present still other stories about jealous and spurned women successfully revenging themselves on kings and princes.

Even more concretely, the influence of the *Mirror* is evident in those texts that, like *Gorboduc* and *Jocasta*, explicitly depict their protagonists as mirrors for the prince. Thus, in his translation of *Troas*, Jasper Heywood introduces a new passage describing Hecuba as a mirror: 'Hecuba that waileth now in care, / That was so late of high estate a Queene, / A mirour is, to teache you what you are / Your wavering welth, o princes, here is seen.' Likewise, Alexander Neville, in his translation of *Oedipus*, introduces a new chorus, presenting the main character as 'a mirrour meete. A patern playne, of Princes careful thrall'.[9] As such plays show, the *Mirror* appealed to early dramatists, who used the collection as a precedent and example for offering advice to magistrates on a number of issues, ranging from the dangers of autocracy, ambition and arrogance to the 'wavering welth' or instability of power generally.

The backgrounds of the writers and their audiences begin to explain such interest. For, more commonly than in earlier periods, the dramatic authors of the 1560s were very well-educated men who aimed to obtain positions in the government, as members of parliament, foreign ambassadors and secretaries.[10] Moreover, they composed their tragedies with the educated, urbane and sophisticated viewers and readers of the universities, law schools and court in mind.[11] It makes sense that people in such groups found literature on the rewards and dangers of power compelling. Their lives were directly and indirectly bound up with the successes and failures of those in power, the monarch and her counsellors and magistrates.

Even so, I would suggest that those who composed plays may have found one particular aspect of the *Mirror* useful and appealing, its use of history. In the work, historical events are more than a source of instructive counsel for leaders. Such episodes also allow the authors themselves and their readers to contemplate practical and theoretical aspects of governance. In the *Mirror*, in other words, history provides an opportunity for political contemplation and reflection and it was such an opportunity that the dramatists of the 1560s aimed to provide for themselves and their audiences as well.

In order to bring this particular aspect of the *Mirror* and its influence into focus, it is instructive to consider the one element of the collection that the dramatists neglected entirely: the subject matter, recent English history. For they never represent the Wars of the Roses, passing over those characters and events depicted in the *Mirror* and dramatising instead incidents from ancient British and world history, Greek mythology and continental literature. Why might they have ignored the *Mirror* as a source? The question may seem unrelated to the principal topic of this chapter. As we shall see, however, two obvious but weak responses to this query point to this idea: dramatists were drawn to the *Mirror* less for the specific content than the way such content functioned, inviting political discussion and deliberation.

To be sure, one way to explain the absence of English history is to propose that dramatists did not view such events as an appropriate subject for drama. After all, few plays at the time dealt with English events. Most popular history plays focused on biblical history and saints' lives and academic drama often addressed ancient history and mythology. With few precedents, the writers of the decade may have rejected or not considered the possibility of dramatising the English past. Nevertheless, some experimented with sources that went beyond established biblical and classical material: *Gorboduc* depicts ancient British history and *Gismond of Salerne* presents an episode from Boccaccio's *Decameron*.[12] A few writers, in other words, played with different kinds of sources, and this fact returns us to the question: why did they ignore those events depicted a popular book like the *Mirror for Magistrates*?

An alternative is that anxieties about censorship motivated them to avoid events represented in the *Mirror*. Shortly after coming to the throne, Elizabeth issued a proclamation on 'unlicensed interludes and plays, especially on religion or policy', which required official authorisation of all drama and 'permit[ted] none to be played wherein either matters of religion or of the governance of the estate of the commonweal should be handled or treated'.[13] One might suggest that playwrights shied away from representing the recent civil wars, since those contentious events obviously concerned matters of the 'governance of the estate of the commonweal'. Indeed, such worries may have been compounded by the fact that the privy council suppressed the *Mirror* when it first appeared in print (c. 1554) because some of the tragedies commented on political events too directly.[14] Be that as it may, several plays remark on contemporary affairs in obvious ways. Sackville and Norton's *Gorboduc* addresses one of the most hotly debated issues of the day, the succession question, doing so overtly enough that one observer at the original performance noted that 'many thinges were saied for the Succession to putt thinges in certenty'.[15] Moreover, critics have long argued that Pickering's *Horestes* alludes to the deposing of Mary, Queen of Scots, following the murder of Henry Darnley and her suspected affair with the Earl of Bothwell.[16] It is true that the distant settings in these works may have made such political commentary appear less direct and, hence, more acceptable to the authorities. For, alongside other conventions, such locales helped writers, as Annabel Patterson puts it, to 'encode [their] opinions so that nobody would be *required* to make an example of [them]'.[17] Still, on the whole, it seems unlikely that strong concerns about censorship prevented Sackville and Norton or Pickering from depicting English affairs. Why then, in the face of those concerns, would they still have written plays that comment on current events so directly?

A less obvious, but more intuitively plausible suggestion is that such writers were not interested in the specific period of English history represented in the *Mirror*, but liked the way that history functioned in the book: admonishing magistrates and facilitating political discussion. A look at the origin, content and form of the *Mirror* illustrates how historical events work in the collection itself.[18]

Written in the early 1550s, the *Mirror* was conceived as a continuation of Lydgate's *Fall of Princes* (c. 1431–39), itself a translation of Boccaccio's *De casibus virorum illustrium* (c. 1358). As the compiler and editor of the volume, William Baldwin, explains in the preface, the collection aimed 'to haue the storye contynewed from where as Bochas [Boccaccio] lefte, vnto this presente time, chiefly of such as Fortune had dalyed with in this ylande' (68). In the *Mirror*, Baldwin and his co-authors followed those earlier works both in content and style, presenting a series of tragedies about fallen figures from English history, who warn magistrates about the many dangers of rule. Even so, it is important to recognise that the authors deviated from the general layout and presentation of their sources in two important ways. First, they linked the tragedies together with a prose narrative, which recorded their conversations and activities as they worked on the poems themselves. Second, they presented the tragedies as first-person monologues, which were written and then performed by the co-authors themselves for the group. Such changes alter the emphasis and purpose of the poems in significant ways. For the prose frame, in essence, turns the *Mirror* into the record of a long conversation, in which the authors discuss, research and perform accounts of the falls of those in power. At the same time, the performed tragedies become a part of this conversation, appearing less as self-contained pieces on the falls of magistrates than as a collage of poems in which the authors offer and pick up on each other's arguments about the nature of governance.

One such conversation develops in the first few tragedies, a handful of poems on the reign of Richard II. As the *Mirror* opens, George Ferrers, one of the co-authors, offers a piece on Robert Tresilian, the lawyer and later chief justice to the king, aiming to 'warne all of [Tresilian's] authorytie and profession, to take heed of wrong judgementes, myscontruyng of lawes, or wrestyng the same to serve the princes turnes' (71). Ferrers then performs the tale, detailing how the lawyer deliberately interpreted laws to favour the monarch. While the king initially rewarded Tresilian for such biased legal decisions, the chief justice was later tried and hanged for his crimes. Thus, Ferrers concludes with this caution: guardians of the law should 'be sooth-fast in [their] sawes' and 'pronouce the lawes' with 'eyes shut & hands close' (80). Obviously, the tale provides moral admonition, but it does something else, allowing readers to speculate on an important issue: the extent to which fortune or chance controls the lives of those in power. Early on, Tresilian attributes his fall to mere chance, noting that 'unfrendly Fortune did traye [him] unto a trap' (73). Near the end of his tale, however, he tells us that his end is the direct result of predictable workings of justice: his death is the 'fyne of falshode, the stypende of corruption' (79). The tragedy, in essence, raises this question: are the lives of magistrates determined by fortune or predica-ble, if often providential justice? Over the next four tragedies, the authors consider and respond to this issue.

The two subsequent tales suggest that the answer is fortune. In the first, Richard Mortimer describes his elevation to heir apparent and eventual murder, speculating that fortune brought him down: 'Among the ryders of the rollyng wheele', he is one 'whose fatall threede false Fortune nedes would reele' (82). Likewise, the next tragedy, on the murder of Thomas of Woodstock, Duke of Gloucester, concentrates heavily on chance, contend-ing that 'Whan frowarde Fortune lyst for to frowne, / Maye in a moment tourne upsyde downe' (91).

Yet the next two focus on predicable, and divinely influenced justice. Thus in the tragedy of Lord Mowbray, Baldwin responds to the positions articu-lated by Mortimer and Gloucester, using the tale to illustrate the workings of providential justice. Describing Mowbray's career as a flattering counsel-lor, his banishment and his death, Baldwin ends: 'Note here the ende of pride, se Flateries fine, / Marke the reward of my enuy and false complaint' (109). The downfall is not the result of chance, but a just and predictable punishment for the offence of flattery. The next tragedy reinforces Baldwin's position. Here, Richard II links the loss of his Crown and eventual murder to his susceptibility to flattering counsel. The tragedy ends: 'Who wurketh his wil, & shunneth wisedomes sawes / In flateries clawes, & shames foule pawes shal light' (118). Unlike Mortimer and Woodstock, Richard II falls as a direct result of his actions.

   Critics have recognised the contradictory depictions of fortune and justice in the *Mirror*, with some arguing that the two ideas complement each other, and others suggesting that such inconsistency results from a larger cultural shift from the dominance of one idea to the other.[19] Yet there is another way to address the contradiction. Looked at in the context of the longer prose narrative, the poems do more than reflect static and opposing ideas; they emerge as contrasting positions in a larger discussion about governors and governance. It is worth noting in this regard that the authors of the *Mirror* continue their conversation about such issues in the prose sections. For example, following a later story about the Duke of Suffolk, Baldwin says that the peer deserved punishment: 'For though Fortune in many poyntes be injurius to Princes, yet in this and such lyke she is moost righteous: And only deserveth the name of a Goddes, whan she provideth meanes to punish & distroye Tyrantes' (170). Here, Baldwin reconciles the two positions voiced earlier, noting that Fortune sometimes serves to mete out God's justice. Even so, Baldwin's is not the last word; rather, over the course of the *Mirror*, the authors discuss and debate this topic, using the tragic histories to reflect on the relative power and agency of leaders.

   The *Mirror* raises other issues, concerning, for instance, the role of counsel in government, the problems of ambition and the justifiability of rebellion. Such conversations cannot be illustrated here in the detail they deserve, but the specifics of those discussions are less important than what they indicate about history in the *Mirror for Magistrates*. For the episodes help the authors to raise, develop, deliberate and respond to a number of questions concerning the rule and misrule of the state. Overall, history invites the authors and by extension readers too, to address and consider the nature of governance.

   As we saw earlier, the *Mirror* had a broad impact on the drama of the 1560s. A turn to what may be the earliest adaptation of the *Mirror* in dramatic form, Thomas Preston's *Cambises*, suggests especially the influence of the *Mirror*'s use of history. Robert Carl Johnson describes *Cambises* as 'first of all . . . in the *Mirror for Magistrates* tradition' and it is striking that intentionally or unintentionally it picks up on the subject of the very first tragedy in the *Mirror*, the tale of Tresilian's perversion of justice. For, in literature and art, King Cambises traditionally symbolises two contrasting ideas: impartial law and corrupt injustice.[20] Probably first presented at court in 1560, *Cambises* details events in the ancient Persian king's life, including his just execution of a corrupt judge, his gradual degeneration into a tyrant and his seemingly providential death by falling on his sword. Critics have observed that Preston uses this history to address a number of issues: the problems of princely pride and anger, humankind's inclination to act in evil ways, the tendency for a man's bad deeds to override our memory of his good ones and the links between tyranny and effeminacy.[21] Here, I look at

Cambises' transition from virtuous to tyrannical king in order to trace how the play employs the history to explore another central problem of governance: the extent to which counsel can constrain the will of the king.

Preston first raises the subject of counsel in the prologue, where he summarises the sage advice of three ancient counsellors, Agathon, Cicero and Seneca. Thus the prologue opens with a description of '*Agathon* he whose counsail wise, to princes wele extended' (1), noting that he offered three related observations for rulers: that, while the king rules over people, he should rule with law as well as with the humbling knowledge that he will not always have power. The prologue then describes Cicero: '*Tully* the wise' (8), who once noted that princes are themselves 'a plain and speaking law' (9). Finally, the prologue mentions 'the sage and witty *Seneca*', who shows that by 'the honest exercise of Kings, men wil insue the same' (11–12). Having described the observations and advice of the three counsellors, the prologue introduces Cambises, a king 'trained up, by trace of vertues lore', who later 'did clene forget his perfect race before' (19–20). Cambises' principal vice is that he fails to listen to counsel, often 'cleving more unto his will'. Thus he developed into a king who 'forwarning . . . did hate' and who 'think[s] that none could him dismay, ne none his facts could see' (21–3). As the prologue closes, we learn the play itself will illustrate these aspects of Cambises' personality: his 'crueltie we wil dilate and make the matter plain' (34).

The play 'make[s] the matter plain' by showing Cambises' change from virtuous ruler to cruel tyrant and indicating that this transition has much to do with his tendency to reject counsel. As the drama opens, the play introduces *Cambises* as a good king, who listens to the opinions of others. Thus, in the first scene, the king enters with an adviser, aptly named 'Counsel', who asks for leave 'his minde for to expresse' (46). Cambises agrees to hear Counsel's advice: the king is planning to leave to make war in another land and he, therefore, should appoint someone to rule in his absence. The king assents to the advice, naming the seemingly virtuous Sisamnes as governor in his stead. As the play continues, we see Cambises' virtue again, this time in his readiness to attend to the complaints of his people. Having completed his foreign wars, the king returns to Persia, only to hear Commons Cry rail against the corrupt rule of Sisamnes: 'We are undoon and thrown out of doore, / His damnable dealing dooth us so torment: / At his hand we can finde no releef nor succoure, / God graunt him grace for to repent' (361–4). The king solicitously encourages Commons Cry to 'keep nothing back, fear not thy tale to tel' (381). He then responds quickly to such complaints. After hearing the testimony of Trial and Proof, he executes Sisamnes, restoring order to the land. In the opening few scenes of the play, then, Cambises shows that he is a just king, who listens to the counsel of his advisers, heeds the concerns of his people and obeys established procedures of the law.

Soon, however, Cambises becomes a tyrant. The transition is evident in his sudden aversion to advice and complaint. Thus in the very next scene, the counsellor Praxaspes aims 'in freendly wise' to counsel the king about drinking, which 'infect[s]' Cambises with many 'great abuses' (479–82). To reinforce his point, Praxaspes cites the opinion of a group that Cambises had been disposed to hear before, his people: 'The *Persians* much doo praise your grace, but one thing discommend: / In that to Wine subject you be, wherin you doo offend'. He thus observes: 'My councel is to please their harts, from it you would refrain' (493–6). Far from heeding this advice, Cambises responds angrily with a vile plan: after having a few drinks, he will shoot an arrow at the son of Praxaspes and by his good aim prove that he is not a drunk. After quaffing several cups, the king hits the son accurately, remov- ing the heart of the bleeding son before the father's eyes. While showing that he handles his drink well, Cambises proves that he is a violent, autarchic ruler, who as the prologue tells us, 'clev[es] more unto his will' than he listens to the counsel of peers or the pleading of commoners.

The play illustrates the continued degeneration of Cambises in the next scene, in which he rejects a good counsellor and embraces a bad one. Here Smirdis, the king's brother, arrives at court. The play signals the potential of Smirdis as a good adviser. For he surrounds himself with trustworthy counsel- lors (tellingly named Diligence and Attendance) and he is wholeheartedly willing to serve the king, telling him that he is 'redy to fulfill: At all assayes my Prince and king, in that your grace me wil' (656–7). The king, however, fails to trust Smirdis' offer and instead listens to rumors spread by the duplicitous vice figure Ambidexter, who falsely accuses Smirdis of slander, of speaking in 'dispightful wise' (682) of the monarch. The king responds quickly and vio- lently, commanding the immediate death of his brother by Murder and Cruelty.

By this point, Cambises leaves off those actions that made him a virtuous king: a willingness to take counsel, an eagerness to listen to his people and an obedience to the law. Finally, the play extablishes the full extent of Cambises' tyranny in the next scene, where he orders his cousin, simply called 'Lady', into an incestuous marriage, a bond that the lady describes as 'a thing that natures course dooth utterly detest' and that 'would the God displease' (910–11). As Rebecca Bushnell rightly points out about this scene, the king's 'infatuation and marriage to his Lady, then, marks the apex of his tyrannical career', showing his desire entirely to master the will of another.[22] Indeed, when Cambises discovers that he cannot fully control the Lady, he has her murdered: soon after the marriage, she expresses dismay at the murder of Smirdis and in response, the king orders her death 'by *Cruels* swoord and *Murder* fel' (1049). Still, Cambises' tyranny does not continue for long. Soon after the murder of his queen, the king himself dies, fatally wounding himself in an accident in which he falls on his sword.

History in the play operates in much the same way as it does in the *Mirror*. Like some tales in the *Mirror*, Preston uses the story to call attention to the king's death as a deserved, providential punishment for his ill rule. Thus, one of the attending lords at the end of the play observes that the death is 'A just rewarde for his misdeeds, which God aboove hath wrought' and concludes: 'For certainly the life he led, was counted to be nought' (1187–8). Moreover, like the *Mirror*, the play emphasises the admonitory and cautionary power of the tale. Preston includes an epilogue, addressed to a 'gentle Audience' (1), the 'noble queen' and her counselors, praying that she may receive good counsel and 'be guided from trueth and defended from wrong' (21). Yet also, like the *Mirror*, as much as the play is a glass for governors, it also prompts one to speculate on the nature of tyranny and especially to explore the uncomfortable fact that, if the king is unwilling to listen to counsel, there is almost no way to guide or limit his will. Overall, like the authors of the *Mirror*, Preston uses history to admonish those who govern and additionally to raise and explore some central problems of monarchy in Cambises' day (and in his own).

Like Thomas Preston, other dramatists in the 1560s follow the example of the *Mirror*, using history to open up and explore aspects of politics and governance, for instance the role of counsel in promoting good rule and the general instability of power and authority. Thus, for instance, *Horestes*, as James Phillips has argued, searches the conditions in which it is permissible to depose a monarch. More broadly, the drama of the period probes two related issues, the succession question and Queen Elizabeth's marriage policy. Hence, as Marie Axton has shown, in plays at court and the Inns of Court, Elizabeth's subjects urged her to marry, bear an heir and settle the line to the throne. Tellingly, Axton observes that writers from the Inns of Court, such as Sackville, Norton and Gascoigne and Pickering 'used fictional or historical play situations much as they would use legal precedents', that is, to guide legal and political thinking in the present day. Even so, while their plays were often 'vigorously polemical', they also 'dealt with issues and situations' and not with specific events or people.[23] In other words, as we saw in the *Mirror*, dramatic history allowed authors to admonish those in power, but also to think through contemporary political issues, concerns, questions and debates.

By way of conclusion, we should notice that many of the tragedies of the period, such as *Jocasta* and *Gismond of Salerne*, as well as the translations of Seneca, are not histories in the way the *Mirror* is, describing episodes in the lives of real historical figures. Even so, all of the plays are 'histories' in the earliest sense of the word recorded by the *Oxford English Dictionary*: a 'relation of incidents . . . either true or imaginary', 'a narrative, tale, [or] story'. Thus Thomas Pickering's *Horestes* originally appeared in print with the title

'A new enterlude of vice conteninge the *historye* of Horestes' (my emphasis).[24] The play, in other words, follows events concerning Orestes, although it is not clear whether those events ever really occurred. Throughout their plays, the writers of the decade use history – narratives, tales and incidents – in order to explore questions concerning the governance of the realm. Indeed, in their appeal to foreign, mythological and fictional calamities, rather than to national history, the dramatists perhaps even enhanced the ability of their works to promote reflection and contemplation. For, as Jean Howard has recently observed: 'Part of the work of early modern tragedy is to desacralise kingship and evacuate dominant ideologies of their power.' For this purpose, foreign (and, I would add, imaginary) countries provided settings that were 'distant and close, strange and familiar', which allowed authors of tragedy 'to contemplate the undoing of greatness and the fragility of rule'.[25] In other words, tragedy and tragic history, conceived in the broadest terms, provided what might best be described as a rhetorical space to speculate on the nature of power. Certainly, such an observation raises a question about later historical plays, especially those written in a more celebratory, or even comic, mode, for instance Shakespeare's *Henry V* or Dekker's *The Shoemaker's Holiday*. Do such plays diverge from the tradition of historical writing in the *Mirror* and mid-Tudor tragedy, or continue this tradition in a new register? It is impossible to do more than raise this question here, but suffice it to say, for now, that the dramatists of the 1560s used tragic history to prompt contemplation and reflection on a wide range of issues concerning the responsibilities, obligations and dangers of monarchy and in the process helped to create a political discourse in the sphere of dramatic production about the governance of the state.

Notes

1 George Gascoigne, *The Posies* (London 1575; STC 11637), 69.
2 Quoted in G. W. Pigman's commentary on George Gascoigne, *A Hundreth Sundrie Flowers*, ed. G. W. Pigman III (Oxford: Oxford University Press, 2000), 516.
3 Compiled by William Baldwin, the first edition of the *Mirror* contains poems written by at least eight men, including Baldwin, George Ferrers, Thomas Chaloner and Thomas Phaer. Contributors to later editions include Thomas Churchyard, Thomas Sackville and John Dolman. On the authors of the *Mirror* see Lily B. Campbell, introduction, *The Mirror for Magistrates: Edited from Original Texts in the Huntington Library*, ed. Lily B. Campbell (1938; reprint, New York, Barnes and Noble, 1960), 3–60, esp. pp. 20–51. All further references to the *Mirror* are to this edition.
4 In the preface to his translation of *Thyestes*, Jasper Heywood suggests the popularity of the *Mirror* at the Inns of Court, stating that at law schools one hears 'a great report of Baldwin's worthy name / Whose mirror doth of magistrates proclaim eternal fame'. See Seneca, *Thyestes*, ed. Joost Daalder (London: Ernest

Benn, 1982), ll. 95–6. At least two members of the Inns contributed tragedies to an expanded edition of the *Mirror*, which appeared in 1563: Thomas Sackville included his 'Induction' and the tragedy of the Duke of Buckingham, while John Dolman contributed the tragedy of Lord Hastings.

5 As Harvey mentions, *Gorboduc* and *Jocasta* were played for audiences at the Inns of Court, yet the *Mirror* involves performance as well. Each author recites the tragedy he writes, taking on the character of an English king or lord and describing his downfall for the others in the group. For more on the role of performance in the work see Jim Ellis, 'Embodying Dislocation: *A Mirror for Magistrates* and Property Relations', *Renaissance Quarterly*, 53 (2000), 1032–52.

6 Thomas Sackville and Thomas Norton, *Gorboduc or Ferrex and Porrex*, ed. Irby B. Cauthen (Lincoln: University of Nebraska Press, 1971), 1.2.392–3. George Gascoigne and Francis Kinwelmersh, *Jocasta* in *A Hundreth Sundrie Flowers*, ed. Pigman III, 59–140, V. chorus. 1–2.

7 See Jessica Winston, '*A Mirror for Magistrates* and Public Political Discourse in Elizabethan England', *Studies in Philology*, 101, 4 (2004), 381–400.

8 The dates refer to the earliest recorded appearance of a play in performance or print.

9 Jasper Heywood, *The Sixt Tragedie of the Most Graue and Prudent Author Lucius, Anneus, Seneca, Entituled Troas, with Diuers and Sundrye Addicions to the Same* (London, 1559; STC 22227), sig. B3v. Alexander Neville, *The Lamentable Tragedie of Oedipvs Sonne of Laivs King of Thebes out of Seneca* (London, 1563; STC 22225), sig. D2v.

10 For instance, many of the writers mentioned above – Sackville, Norton, Gascoigne, Kinwelmersh, Preston, Pickering, Heywood, Neville, Noel, Wilmot and Hatton as well as others, such as the translators of Seneca, John Studley and Thomas Nuce – attended Oxford or Cambridge and usually one of the Inns of Court. Moreover, many of these authors, such as Norton, Kinwelmersh and Pickering, went on to hold a seat in Parliament and two of them, Sackville and Hatton, served in Parliament and, eventually, the Privy Council of the Queen.

11 For instance, Preston's *Cambises* was likely originally performed at court in 1560. Like *Gorboduc* and *Jocasta*, *Oedipus*, *Horestes* and *Gismond* were likely first performed at one of the Inns of Court. It is not clear that the translations of *Troas, Thyestes, Hercules Furens, Medea, Agamemnon, Hyppolytus, Hercules Oetaeus* and *Octavia* were ever performed. Even so, the prefaces and dedications to these works contain poems by and alluding to students, poets and translators at the universities and the Inns, a tendency that suggests that the authors produced their translations with readers from the schools in mind.

12 On the sources for *Gismond* see Giles Yardley Gamble, 'Institutional Drama: Elizabethan Tragedies at the Inns of Court' (Ph.D. Thesis: Stanford University, 1969), 197. Frederick Kiefer, 'Love and Fortune in Boccaccio's *Tancredi and Ghismonda* Story and in Wilmot's *Gismond of Salerne*', *Renaissance and Reformation*, 1 (1977), 36–45.

13 Paul L. Hughes and James F. Larkin, *Tudor Royal Proclamations*, 3 vols (New Haven: Yale University Press, 1969), 2, 115.

14 Although the reasons for the suppression of the *Mirror* are unknown today, critics tend to agree that it was the result of some kind of politically objectionable content. See Eveline Iris Feasey, 'The Licensing of the *Mirror for Magistrates*', *The Library*, 4th ser, 3 (1922), 177–93. Lily B. Campbell, 'Humphrey Duke of Gloucester and Elianor Cobham His Wife in the *Mirror for Magistrates*', *The Huntington Library Bulletin*, 5 (1934), 119–56 and 'The Suppressed Edition of *A Mirror for Magistrates*', *Huntington Library Bulletin*, 6 (1934), 1–16. Scott Campbell Lucas, 'The Suppressed Edition and the Creation of the Orthodox *Mirror for Magistrates*', *Renaissance Papers* (1994), 31–54.

15 BL MS 48023. For a discussion of this eye-witness account see Henry James and Greg Walker, 'The Politics of *Gorboduc*', *English Historical Review*, 110 (1995), 109–21. Norman Jones and Paul Whitfield White, '*Gorboduc* and Royal Marriage Politics: An Elizabethan Playgoer's Report of the Premiere Performance', *English Literary Renaissance*, 26 (1996), 3–16. Mike Pincombe, 'Robert Dudley, *Gorboduc* and "The Masque of Beauty and Desire": A Reconsideration of the Evidence for Political Intervention', *Parergon*, 20, 1 (January 2003), 19–44.

16 For some examples of such arguments see James E. Phillips, 'A Revaluation of *Horestes* (1567)', *Huntington Library Quarterly*, 18, 3 (1955), 227–44. David Bevington, *Tudor Drama and Politics* (Cambridge, Mass.: Harvard University Press, 1968), 150–3. Karen Robertson, 'The Body Natural of a Queen: Mary, James, *Horestes*', *Renaissance and Reformation*, 26, 1 (1990), 25–36. James Knapp argues against such a narrowly topical reading in: '*Horestes*: The Uses of Revenge', *English Literary History*, 40, 2 (1973), 205–20.

17 Patterson, *Censorship and Interpretation: The Conditions of Writing and Reading in Early Modern England* (Madison: University of Wisconsin Press, 1984), 11.

18 The next few paragraphs borrow from my essay '*A Mirror for Magistrates* and Public Political Discourse', esp. 387–95

19 Frederick Kiefer, 'Fortune and Providence in the *Mirror for Magistrates*', *Studies in Philology*, 74 (1977), 146–64. Paul Budra, 'The *Mirror for Magistrates* and the Shape of *De Casibus* Tragedy', *English Studies*, 69, 4 (August 1988), 303–12.

20 Robert Carl Johnson, introduction, *A Critical Edition of Thomas Preston's Cambises* (Salzburg: Institut für Englische Sprache und Literatur, 1975), 1–44, p. 1. All further references to *Cambises* are to line numbers in this edition. On representations of Cambises see Joel H. Kaplan, 'Reopening King Cambises' Vein', *Essays in Theatre*, 5, 2 (1987), 103–14. Eugene H. Hill, 'The First Elizabethan Tragedy: A Contextual Reading of *Cambises*', *Studies in Philology*, 89, 4 (1992), 403–33, esp. pp. 417–22.

21 See, respectively, Burton J. Fishman, 'Pride and Ire: Theatrical Iconography in Preston's *Cambises*', *SEL*, 16, 2 (1976), 201–11 and Karl P. Wentersdorf, 'The Allegorical Role of Vice in Preston's *Cambises*', *Modern Language Studies*, 11, 2 (1981), 54–69. Kaplan, 'Reopening King Cambises' Vein'; Rebecca Bushnell, 'Tyranny and Effeminacy in Early Modern England', in Mario D. Cesare (ed.) *Reconsidering the Renaissance: Papers for the Twenty-First Annual Conference* (Binghamton: Medieval and Renaissance Texts & Studies, 1992), 339–54.

22 Bushnell, 'Tyranny and Effeminacy', 346.
23 Axton, *The Queen's Two Bodies: Drama and the Elizabethan Succession* (London: Royal Historical Society, 1977), 3.
24 *Three Tudor Classical Interludes: Thersites, Jacke Jugeler, Horestes*, ed. Marie Axton (Cambridge: D. S. Brewer, 1982).
25 Jean Howard, 'Shakespeare, Geography and the Work of Genre on the Early Modern Stage', *Modern Language Quarterly*, 64, 3 (2003), 299–322, p. 322.

III

Identity and performance

Warlike women: 'reproofe to these degenerate effeminate dayes'?

Until fairly recently the women of the 'Histories' received very little attention: even feminist scholars who addressed gender issues in Shakespeare's plays tended to focus overwhelmingly on the 'Comedies' and 'Tragedies' in which female characters generally play larger, more significant roles. It was not until 1997, twenty-two years after the publication of Juliet Dusinberre's pioneering study *Shakespeare and the Nature of Women* (1975), that a significant step was made to redress the balance with Jean Howard and Phyllis Rackin's *Engendering a Nation*.[1] This excellent feminist reading, providing detailed analyses of the individual plays against a wealth of contextual information, is undoubtedly a major contribution to the field. Regrettably however, *Engendering a Nation* serves by and large to negate rather than promote the women in these plays, for the argument put forward is this: if we read the plays which were classified as 'Histories' in the First Folio in their order of production, women become increasingly contained within the domestic sphere and are finally erased from the political action altogether. In identifying a nascent ideology aimed at eroding female power, an ideology which certainly went from strength to strength from the seventeenth century until the early twentieth, we are left with a view of women pushed into the margins, rather than a celebration of the significant part played by numerous important and powerful female characters within these plays, most particularly in the first tetralogy.

In the brief space of this chapter I therefore propose to return these female characters to the centre of history's stage, to reopen the closet to which they were seemingly confined in *Henry V* (the last play in the second tetralogy) and identify them not as a 'monstrous regiment of women'[2] who had to be defeated and returned to servility (a misogynist view of female power not necessarily inherited from Shakespeare) but as important and influential historical examples whom Shakespeare chose to resurrect from the shadows of the Tudor history chronicles in order to make some very significant statements on the late sixteenth-century stage, not least in connection with gender roles.

I should like to begin with a brief consideration of the context from which the plays emerged. The words quoted in my title are those of Thomas Nashe, who famously defended historical drama in terms of gender and historical difference. Nashe argued that, in reviving our forefather's valiant acts, history plays might help to resurrect traditional values of honour and bravery and in so doing provide reproof to what he described as the 'degenerate, effeminate dayes' of the 1590s.

> Nay, what if I proove Playes to be no extreame, but a rare exercise of vertue? First, for the subject of them (for the most part) it is borrowed out of our English Chronicles, wherein our fore-fathers valiant actes (that have lyne long buried in rustie brasse and worme-eaten bookes) are revived, and they them selves raysed from the Grave of Oblivion, and brought to pleade their aged Honours in open presence: than which, what can bee a sharper reproofe, to these degenerate effeminate dayes of ours?[3]

Contrary to the popular view of the 'Histories' as 'mirrors' of an 'Elizabethan world picture',[4] Nashe claimed that these plays, which focus on medieval wars and struggles for power, would provide not a reflection of contemporary society but a contrasting picture to show up the comparative effeminacy of the period of production. But what was 'effeminate' about the period in which these plays were produced?

In the late sixteenth century the word 'effeminate' was sometimes used to convey more than merely 'womanish', the meaning perhaps most commonly implied today, particularly when attributed to a male person. According to the *Oxford English Dictionary*, 'effeminate' could also mean 'self-indulgent; delicate or over-refined' (A.1a), 'soft, voluptuous' (A.1d.) and in this latter sense it was also linked to being 'devoted to woman' (A.3). In Samuel Johnson's *Dictionary of the English Language* (1755) the word is similarly defined as 'soft to an unmanly degree, voluptuous, tender, luxurious' and Johnson provides an example from Bacon: 'the king, by his voluptuous life and mean marriage, became effeminate and less sensible to honour' (*History of Henry VII*). What is significant about these earlier connotations is the way 'effeminate' serves as a virtual antonym to military valour and honour, as revealed by an illustrative example in the *OED*, quoted from Barclay's *Argenis*, xxiii, 319: 'a soldier's death shall make amends for thy effeminate life'. These wider definitions – soft, voluptuous, luxurious, devoted to woman – are certainly appropriate to Nashe's usage.

In the period he was describing – the 1590s – a woman had held the supreme position of power in England for more than forty years (a lifetime for most Elizabethan playgoers) and Queen Elizabeth had indeed established quite a cult for woman worship, namely that of the Virgin Queen.[5] Additionally, in the second half of the sixteenth century England had enjoyed relative peace at home. This meant that the opportunities to display military strength were fewer and social promotion had come to depend increasingly upon diplomacy, learning and trade, rather than bravery on the battlefield.[6] In 1595 John Smithe noted with regret the decline of the military, remarking in his *Instructions, Observations and Orders Militarie*, that 'the discipline Militarie of our auncestors . . . is so forgotten and neglected amongst us . . . that . . . all is turned . . . to disorders and confusion'.[7] In his own nostalgia for traditional male heroism, Thomas Nashe further elaborates on those 'degenerate effeminate dayes', by highlighting the artificiality of the voluptuous, Elizabethan court, which centred on the star-spangled Virgin Queen. He described the Queen's courtiers as 'Peacockes . . . buckram giants . . . stuft with straw and letters . . . glittring Attendaunts on the true Diana',[8] identifying their showy, outward appearances and suggesting they had no substance, or shall we say muscle, beneath, only words and wadding, their purpose being merely decorative and servile.

At this point we must be careful not to confuse 'effeminacy' with elaborate fashions. That model of Tudor masculinity – Henry VIII – established an extremely excessive mode in male dress, so this in itself was not 'effeminate'. It is artifice – false outward showiness disguising an insubstantial or empty interior – which is regarded as effeminate in the early modern period, as illustrated by Joseph Swetnan's infamous description of woman as 'a painted shippe' who has 'nothing but ballace within her'.[9] In the mid seventeenth century Henry Peacham continued to point out that the wearing of gold and silver was a sign of courage in a true warrior, but effeminate in others: 'gold and silver, worn by martial men, addeth . . . courage and spirit unto them; but in others effeminacy, or a kinde of womanish vanity'.[10] In the history plays themselves we are provided with a direct comparison between the medieval warrior (perhaps even wearing silver armour, bronzed with blood) and an effeminate courtier, trimmed and perfumed and full of words. I am of course referring to Hotspur in *I Henry IV* (*The History of Henry the Fourth*) and the messenger he describes, sent from Henry's court after the battle on Holmedon plain. Hotspur is the epitome of the hotheaded warrior, an example of military masculinity in the extreme and he describes the snuff-taking courtier in marked contrast to himself, calling him a 'popinjay' (a pretty bird), being 'neat and trimly dressed' and 'perfumèd like a milliner', he also says that the messenger used 'lady terms', 'like a waiting gentlewoman' (1.3.28–49) – an effeminate Elizabethan courtier if ever there was one, anachronistically inset into the historical drama as a foil to offset the old-fashioned military man, still bloody and steaming from physical combat.[11]

Elizabethan London in the 1590s was 'effeminate' because the court centred on a powerful female monarch and the opportunities to demonstrate military prowess were greatly reduced owing to the relative peace enjoyed in England at this time. Interestingly, Shakespeare's *Richard III* addresses these very issues in the opening scene. It is not, however, the hero of the piece, Richmond, who laments the changing times but the arch demon, Richard of Gloucester, whose frightful appearance best suits the role of warrior. At the start of the play he points out that he is 'not shaped for sportive tricks / Nor made to court an amorous looking-glass' (1.1.14–15) and complains about this 'weak piping time of peace' (24) in which 'Our bruisèd arms [are] hung up for monuments' and 'stern alarums changed to merry meetings', 'dreadful marches to delightful measures' (6–8). Here, Richard might be echoing the words of Stephen Gosson, who in 1579 similarly lamented the loss of traditional manly pursuits for softer pleasures:

> the exercise that is nowe among us, is banqueting, playing, pyping and dauncing and all suche delightes as may win us to pleasure, or rock us to sleepe . . . Our wrestling at armes, is turned to wallowing in Ladies laps, our courage, to cowardice, our running to ryot, our Bowes to Bolles and our Dartes to Dishes.[12]

In *Richard III*, Shakespeare also makes Richard despise female rule. When Clarence brings news of his imminent arrest, we already know by Richard's own confession that he is behind his brother's demise, but what does the devil Richard suggest to Clarence by way of explanation? 'Why, this it is when men are ruled by women' (1.1.62) he claims and goes on to point the finger unjustly at Lady Grey – Edward's Queen. Of course, the readers and spectators know that Lady Grey is wrongly accused, that it is not a woman but a man who is to blame. And since it is the villain of the play who prefers war and male rule and in times of peace satisfies his taste for violence and aggression with espionage and murder, this play surely offers a critique of the nostalgic sentiments put forward by the likes of Thomas Nashe. Finally, at the end of *Richard III*, readers will recall that Richmond uses the power of disguise – the actor's 'effeminate' art – to trick his demonic rival and win the day.

Of the 'Histories' first performed in the 1590s, the events presented in *Richard III* come nearest in time to that so called 'effeminate' period of production, when peace, female rule, greater leisure and outward show were perhaps just beginning to affect the lives of women as well as men. According to the Swiss traveller Thomas Platter, England in the 1590s had become 'a woman's paradise'. He wrote in his diary that:

> the women-folk of England . . . have far more liberty than in other lands, and know just how to make good use of it, for they often stroll out or drive by coach in very gorgeous clothes, and the men must put up with such ways, and may

not punish them for it, indeed the good wives often beat their men . . . And there is a proverb about England, which runs, England is a woman's paradise.[13]

In the light of so many reports from the same period concerning the maltreatment of women at the hands of men, we must be cautious about the degree and extent to which Platter's observations can be trusted, but the fact that he recorded this appraisal cannot be completely dismissed. Furthermore, other writers were also observing the changed circumstances of women. For example, Gosson observed that women in olden times were far more physically active. In writing about the 'Manners of England in old time', this commentator pointed out that in the old days women enjoyed more 'manly' pursuits, that they surpassed Amazons in courage and that 'shooting, darting, running and wrestling' were enjoyed by both sexes.[14] Not surprisingly, the history plays include some very active women: Joan la Pucelle in *1 Henry VI*, the dowager Queen Eleanor in *King John* and Queen Margaret in *3 Henry VI* (*Richard Duke of York*) are amongst the women who lead armies and play their part in the physical action. Elizabeth I may have made something of a military performance at Tilbury in order to kindle the fighting spirit in her men before the Armada,[15] but the battlefield was not for this Queen; she even tried to keep her aristocratic men out of the line of fire.[16] Within this context, Shakespeare's plays may be less a backlash against female power and supremacy than an attempt to re-examine old-fashioned military heroism in a society in which attitudes to masculinity were evidently changing. None the less, in staging military heroism it is not only the valiant heroes but also those warlike heroines of the medieval past who, in Shakespeare's 'Histories', provide 'reproofe' to the 'effeminate dayes' of late Elizabethan England.

Returning to the plays themselves, let us now consider some of the important female characters whom Shakespeare resurrected and reconstructed for the Elizabethan stage, let us raise them again from the grave of oblivion to identify their courage and their fighting spirit and to hear how their sharp and witty tongues ring out loud, powerful and true against weak and inadequate men.

The only woman who fights in single combat in the 'Histories' is the unique Joan, La Pucelle, who in *1 Henry VI* brings the French Dauphin to his knees before taking on John Talbot, that mighty English warrior of renown, against whom she holds her own, setting his head spinning 'like a potter's wheel' (1.7.19). Interestingly, unlike Rosalind and Viola, heroines of the 'Comedies' who engage in sword play when disguised as men, this historic character fights as a woman. The many accusations of Pucelle's sexual promiscuity, which culminate in her own claim to be with child, draw further attention to her female body. And when the female Pucelle overcomes the male Dauphin we are surely invited to interpret this defeat as evidence of the Dauphin's weakness and effeminacy, not least since the English Talbot is not overcome by the French woman and therefore retains his manliness, manliness which is tested again when he is mocked as 'a seely dwarf' (2.3.21) by the fictitious Countess Auvergne. Pucelle's military prowess earns her the adjective 'masculine': Burgundy says 'Pray God she prove not masculine ere long' (2.1.22) in response to Bedford's interrogative remark that she can be both 'maid' and 'martial' (21) and, as Robin Hadlam-Wells observes, in Shakespeare's day 'masculine' was not interchangeable with 'manly' but used rather to signify martial or heroic qualities in man or in this exceptional case in woman.[17] Pucelle's martial prowess is set in contrast to the two other French women in this play – the Countess Auvergne and Margaret, daughter of Anjou, the King of Naples, women who are portrayed in more conventional female roles. Yet neither the Countess nor Margaret can be described as weak or suppliant since both challenge the superiority of the males with whom they are presented.

Margaret's appearance as the sharp and witty French seductress in *1 Henry VI* contrasts with the presentation of this historic character in *2* and *3 Henry VI* (*The First Part of the Contention of the Two Famous Houses of York and Lancaster* and *Richard Duke of York*). In these earlier productions Margaret is a strong, ambitious Queen, a female foil designed to offset her weak and effeminate husband. In *3 Henry VI* (*Richard Duke of York*) the contrast is carried to extreme. Shakespeare presents Henry VI as bookish and holy, qualities which better suit a member of the Reformation clergy than the leader of a country at war with France and, as the king is increasingly recognised as a failure to both wife and warring nation, Queen Margaret steps into her husband's shoes. Taking up the reins of power, she herself leads the King's army and confronts the enemy face to face on the battlefield. The qualities which Margaret embodies are described by her enemy, the Duke of York, as inappropriate to woman: 'How ill-beseeming is it in thy sex / To triumph like an Amazonian trull' (1.4.114–15) he says and famously labels her a 'tiger's heart wrapped in a woman's hide' (1.4.138). York argues that 'Women are soft, mild, pitiful, and flexible' (1.4.142), whereas his female opponent is 'stern, obdurate, flinty, rough, remorseless' (1.4.143), qualities which would be regarded as praiseworthy in the male warrior but are notably lacking in Henry VI. Thus Margaret's courage and her military prowess (or should we say 'masculine' qualities) on the one hand classify her as a brutal woman, whilst on the other they serve to highlight her husband's unmanly weakness.

Of course, not all the women who lead armies in Shakespeare's plays are as brutal as Margaret. In his later play, *King Lear* (classified in the First Folio amongst the 'Tragedies' rather than the 'Histories'), Cordelia is presented in marked contrast to her brutal sisters and yet she too plays a military role and leads an army across Shakespeare's stage. In *King John* the dowager Queen Eleanor is less brutal than Margaret, yet she too is active in both war and politics.

King John belongs neither to the first tetralogy of plays nor to the second. It stands alone among the 'Histories' in focusing on the so called '*Troublesome Reign*'[18] of this unpopular king. Although it is primarily an anti-Catholic play, masculine honour is also a key issue. The largest part in the play is given to a fictitious character – Philip Falconbridge, the Bastard – said to be the illegitimate son of Richard the Lionheart, a part devised largely to uphold masculine honour. Significantly however, it is Eleanor, John's mother, who first admires the physical fitness and military prowess in her grandson, who even shows off his well-turned limbs and flexes a muscle for the audience's pleasure and admiration. Eleanor is an advocate for military courage; she leads an army and her Bastard grandson into battle. There is no second place for this Dowager Queen, who describes herself as 'a soldier . . . bound to France' (1.1.150) and plays an active part in negotiations with the French over the English succession.

These plays were, of course, written for performance by an all-male company (evidence in itself of the institutional sexism current in Shakespeare's day); hence the paucity of female characters presented on stage was undoubtedly a practical consideration. However, one way of increasing the female element within the wider narrative is to include them in verbal accounts and figurative speech. In *King John*, in addition to the stage presence of the warlike Queen Eleanor, warrior women are vividly recalled within the language itself, verbally brought to the surface as a powerful reminder that, whilst the men are failing to protect their country and save 'mother England' from foreign occupation, brave English women are taking matters into their own hands. Towards the end of the play, the Bastard berates the English nobility with these words:

> You bloody Neros, ripping up the womb
> Of your dear mother England, blush for shame;
> For your own ladies and pale-visaged maids
> Like Amazons come tripping after drums;
> Their thimbles into armèd gauntlets change,
> Their needles to lances, and their gentle hearts
> To fierce and bloody inclination
>
> (5.2.152–8)

There can be no mistaking the message here; as Gosson pointed out, women of old time could and did fight and in this Elizabethan play female bravery is used to show up the sheer physical inadequacy of the men. Nero's notoriety was not only for the murder of women and children (in particular his own mother) but for his love of luxury and of course Nero ruled the Empire during the revolt in Britain in the first century AD led by that most famous English warrior-woman – Boudicca.

The impact of images of women conveyed via the language of the plays should not be underestimated. It has been argued that Shakespeare's audiences possessed a highly tuned 'image consciousness' inherited from their medieval ancestors,[19] so that spectators at the drama could readily construct offstage pictures in the mind's eye. Today, saturated in visual communications, we are perhaps in danger of minimising the importance of these descriptive passages. If the Bastard's speech in *King John* was visualised on screen, as is Ophelia's watery death in many film versions of *Hamlet*, the place of these warrior women would gain greater recognition. Similarly, in the second tetralogy, we are given another offstage image of female action on the battlefield, when Westmorland in *1 Henry IV* claims that Welsh women in Glyndŵr's army are said to have performed acts upon the corpses of English soldiers after the battle of Nesbit which are too terrible to be spoken of. In this example Westmorland leaves the details of the atrocity to the reader's or spectator's imagination, reporting that a thousand of Hereford's men were butchered:

> Upon whose dead corpse' there was such misuse,
> Such beastly shameless transformation,
> By those Welshwomen done as may not be
> Without much shame retold or spoken of.

(1.1.43–6)

What is established by this account is that Glyndŵr's forces certainly included women; we are not told whether they first killed the men in battle whom they subsequently mutilated, but the massacre is exacerbated by the fact that in these more masculine bygone days women were wielding knives to deprive the fallen warriors of their maleness if not their masculinity. Interestingly, since Westmorland's report does not spell out the full horror of this aftermath, perhaps the dramatist is sensitive to delicate, even 'effeminate' stomachs in the audience, not of course the Queen's, for she claimed to have 'the heart and stomach of a king'.[20]

In contrast to these women who are given a place on the battlefield, the 'Histories' also present strong female characters who exercise a more conventional female weapon – the woman's tongue. Constance, Eleanor's great rival in *King John*, is not a warrior in the military sense, but she certainly raises her voice to highlight false and inadequate masculinity and boldly criticises kings, courtiers, soldiers and social systems. Constance mocks the false heroism of Austria, she calls him 'coward' and says he is not fit to wear the lion's skin of bravery: 'Thou wear a lion's hide! Doff it, for shame, / And hang a calf's-skin on those recreant limbs' (3.1.54–5). She also identifies falsehood in King Philip, pointing to the lack of substance behind his royal exterior: 'You have beguiled me with a counterfeit / Resembling majesty, which being touched and tried / Proves valueless' (3.1.25–6). And she finally speaks out against the patriarchs and their failing system in words which cannot be dismissed lightly:

> O, that my tongue were in the thunder's mouth!
> Then with a passion would I shake the world,
> And rouse from sleep that fell anatomy,
> Which cannot hear a lady's feeble voice,
> Which scorns a modern invocation.
>
> (3.4.38–42)

Constance is very obviously a voice for women's rights and her decline into insanity casts her as the tragic heroine whose words are to be heeded, not mocked.

Constance's verbal performance in *King John* is reminiscent of the female roles in *Richard III*, for here women's tongues are likewise sharp and active. None of the women in this play takes up arms; momentarily in Act 1 Scene 2 Anne is given a sword and the opportunity to use it, but she fails to do so. None the less, instead of swords these women, whether Yorkist or Lancastrian, wage what Mowbray in *Richard II* describes as 'a woman's war, / The bitter clamour of . . . eager tongues' (1.1.48–9), voicing their venomous hatred of Richard, the evil protagonist, the man shaped for war not peace. Several times Richard is presented in verbal crossfire with women. In Act 1 Scene 2 Anne is the aggressor who first curses her evil seducer and labels him 'fiend' (1.2.34), 'Foul devil' (50), 'lump of foul deformity' (57), 'hedgehog' (102) and 'toad' (147). The angel Anne is, however, no match for the devil Richard, so two Queens of England continue the verbal onslaught. In the scene which follows Richard's seduction of Anne, Queen Elizabeth boldly defends herself from insult and points out Richard's 'interior hatred' (1.3.65) before the deposed Queen Margaret begins her own verbal attack. Margaret's appearance alone is evidently frightful: 'Which of you trembles not that looks on me?', she asks as she steps forward to show herself (1.3.160). As Margaret curses Richard her cruelty on the battlefield (earlier presented onstage in *3 Henry VI*) is recalled as a reminder of her prior military actions and at her exit Hastings describes the fear she instils, claiming: 'My hair doth stand on end to hear her curses' (302). A strong female presence is again clearly registered in Act 4 Scene 1 when four women share the stage (Queen Elizabeth, the Duchess of York, her niece and the Lady Anne) to lament Richard's progress and in Scene 4 of the same act Queen Elizabeth and the Duchess of

York are joined by Queen Margaret to bewail their losses and unite in a
chorus of cursing women. Margaret claims that her own words are 'sharp
and pierce' (4.4.125) like weapons, and when the Duchess of York urges
Elizabeth to join her 'And in the breath of bitter words . . . smother / My
damnèd son, that thy two sweet sons smothered' (4.4.133–4), she too equates
words with deadly actions. When the old Duchess delivers her 'most heavy
curse', that of a mother upon her own son, she describes it as a burden that
will 'tire [Richard] more / Than all the complete armour that [he] wears'
(189–90). Thus, when Richard finally falls in battle, the reader or spectator
is led to believe that the armoured warrior's inability to remount is due, at
least in part, to his mother's curse. In this, the last play of the first tetralogy,
the power of female speech is certainly a force to be reckoned with.

In the second tetralogy, female characters are indeed presented within
more domesticated situations, although it should be noted that courts and
castles are both political and domestic arenas. But whilst these women are
not seen on the battlefield, they are shown as self-willed and very far from
weak. In *Richard II*, as in *Richard III*, we see wives and mothers weeping on
stage and yet, before the Duchess of Gloucester makes her final exit in tears,
she does her utmost to make her brother-in-law shed blood on her behalf. In
this play Gaunt is the passive peacemaker whilst the Duchess harbours
bloody thoughts. The Duchess tries to prick Gaunt into 'heroic' action by
reminding him of the violence in his noble blood:

> Finds brotherhood in thee no sharper spur?
> Hath love in thy old blood no fire?
> . . .
>
> That which in mean men we entitle patience
> Is pale cold cowardice in noble breasts
>
> (1.2.9–10; 33–4)

She then goes on to give a graphic account of an imagined, brutal fight which
occurs only in her own imagination and in the vivid description she herself
constructs:

> O, set my husband's wrongs on Hereford's spear,
> That it may enter butcher Mowbray's breast!
> Or if misfortune miss the first career,
> Be Mowbray's sins so heavy in his bosom
> That they may break his foaming courser's back
> And throw the rider headlong in the lists,
> A caitiff, recreant to my cousin Hereford!
>
> (1.2.47–53)

The Duchess's lust for revenge in the form of physical combat aligns her with
the 'masculine' tradition; her values are certainly those of a bygone age

which Gaunt, in more 'effeminate' mode, rejects. In the same play Richard's Queen, who is also presented weeping in the central garden scene, is far from insignificant, particularly from the literary point of view, since it is she who is made custodian of Richard's sad tale: 'Tell thou the lamentable fall of me, / And send the hearers weeping to their beds' (5.1.44–5). But surely, the overall impression gleaned from this sad play is that war is disfiguring, a message vividly impregnated into the rich, figurative language itself, language threaded through with references to the female:

> He is come to open
> The purple testament of bleeding war;
> But ere the crown he looks for live in peace
> Ten thousand bloody crowns of mothers' sons
> Shall ill become the flower of England's face,
> Change the complexion of her maid-pale peace
> To scarlet indignation and bedew
> Her pastures' grass with faithful English blood.
>
> (3.3.92–9)

The significant role played by women may be less obvious in the plays of the second tetralogy, not least since 'our forefather's valiant actes' are performed by traditionally 'masculine' men – Bolingbroke, Hotspur, Douglas, Henry V – but women do continue to be presented, both onstage and off, as important and strong-willed.

Kate Percy, Hotspur's wife, in *1 Henry IV* is certainly no shrinking violet. At her first appearance Kate threatens her husband in language he best understands – that of physical violence – saying she will break his little finger if he will not tell her what is going on (2.4.78–86), a threat all the more significant in the light of the Welshwomen's reported actions. Later, at Glyndŵr's castle, Lady Mortimer is ready to follow her husband into battle: 'She'll be a soldier, too; she'll to the wars', explains her father (3.1.191), who goes on to describe her as 'self-willed' (194). In the same scene, Kate Percy disobeys her husband, refusing point blank to sing, irrespective of his request. Additionally, in the two parts of *Henry IV* and *Henry V* fictitious tavern scenes are inserted into the historical narrative which provide the opportunity for women to play a prominent part, not in battle but certainly in the rising world of trade and commerce.

It has to be acknowledged that in the last of the 'Histories' produced in the 1590s – *Henry V* – female characters have only a small part to play on stage. However, this should not be confused with female insignificance. If one thing is established by the deliberately convoluted second scene of this play, it is that Henry's claim to the French Crown is through the female line. Furthermore, at the end of the war with France, Isabel, the French Queen, plays her part in the marriage negotiations between her daughter and the

English King. As to the wooing scene, now made infamous by Howard and
Rackin's claim that 'Katherine is subjected to a symbolic rape when Henry
forces her to endure his kiss',[21] readers familiar with the Quarto edition of
this play will recognise in this version a greater willingness on the part of the
French Princess to enter into marriage with the English King. Compared
with the authoritative Folio edition Kate's part in the Quarto is longer and
Harry's much shorter, Kate speaks more English than French and she helps
Harry with his clumsy attempts to communicate his love by translating his
French words into English, producing overall an intermingling of tongues
and a more balanced wooing scene.[22] In the Folio version the play ends, none
the less, with a balanced couplet which unites man and woman, before the
Epilogue's final reminder of Henry VI's reign, returning the reader or spec-
tator to that earlier, popular play 'Which oft our stage hath shown'
(Epilogue, 13), in which a woman, Queen Margaret, took on the 'masculine'
role when an 'effeminate' king bowed out of the military action.

From these few examples I hope to have demonstrated that the women of
Shakespeare's 'Histories' have a central part to play, both in their own right
and in the reappraisal of traditional 'masculinity'. Furthermore, if we move
beyond *Henry V* to Shakespeare's later history plays written in the seventeenth century, we continue to find active, powerful and important women.
I have already brought Cordelia to the readers' attention, but the formidable
Cleopatra is not to be overlooked, she too leads a sea battle with the 'doting
mallard' (3.10.19), Antony, in tow. This powerful queen is certainly not to
be closeted and confined. Volumnia, the mother of Coriolanus, is another
mighty advocate for masculine values and we cannot leave unmentioned
Queen Katherine in *Henry VIII* (*All Is True*). One of the last plays in the
Shakespeare canon, *Henry VIII* has no warrior women, but the dramatist
creates in Katherine a paragon of female virtue.

In reality some women may have indeed been closeted and confined to the
domestic sphere over the centuries, but overall Shakespeare's 'Histories'
appear to negate rather than promote this situation, as one might expect
from a leading dramatist writing to please the men and women of those
'effeminate dayes' of female rule.

Notes

1   Jean E. Howard and Phyllis Rackin, *Engendering a Nation: A Feminist Account
     of Shakespeare's Histories* (London: Routledge, 1997).
2   From the title of John Knox's *The First Blast of the Trumpet against the
     Monstrous Regiment of Women* (London, 1558).
3   Thomas Nash, *Pierce Penilesse his Supplication to the Divell* (1592), (Menston:
     Scolar Press, 1969), 26.
4   *Mirrors of Elizabethan Policy* is the subtitle of Lily B. Campbell's study of the

history plays, *Shakespeare's Histories*, published in 1947, which endorses the view famously expressed by E. M. W. Tillyard in *The Elizabethan World Picture* (1943) and *Shakespeare's Histories* (1944).

5 On the Cult of the Virgin Queen see Helen Hacket, *Virgin Mother, Maiden Queen: Elizabeth I and the Cult of the Virgin Mary* (Basingstoke: Macmillan, 1995) and Frances Yates, *Astrea: the Imperial Theme in the Sixteenth Century* (London: Routledge and Kegan Paul, 1975).

6 See also Graham Holderness, *Shakespeare: The Histories* (London: Macmillan, 2000), 23–40.

7 Smithe quoted from Geoffrey Bullough, *Narrative and Dramatic Sources of Shakespeare*, vol. IV (London: Routledge and Kegan Paul, 1966), 431–2.

8 Nash, *Pierce Penilesse*, 39v.

9 Joseph Swetnam, *The Araignment of Lewd, Idle, Froward and Unconstant Women* (London, 1616), 3.

10 Henry Peacham, *The Worth of a Penny or a Caution to keep Money* (1641) (Dublin: Graham & Son, 1818), 33.

11 For a further discussion of masculinity in Shakespeare's plays see Holderness and Banks, 'Bravehearts: Images of Masculinity in Shakespeare's Plays', *Parergon*, 15, 1 (1997), 137–60.

12 Stephen Gosson, *The School of Abuse* (1579) (London: The Shakespeare Society, 1841), 24.

13 *Thomas Platter's Travels in England in 1599*, in Peter Razzell (ed.) *The Journals of Two Travellers in Elizabethan and Early Stuart England* (London: Caliban, 1995), 45–6.

14 Gosson, *School of Abuse*, 24.

15 The famous account of Elizabeth's appearance before her troops at Tilbury has been called into doubt by recent research. See Susan Frye, 'The Myth of Elizabeth I at Tilbury', *Sixteenth Century Journal*, 23, 1 (1992), 95–114.

16 Sir Philip Sidney was the only member of the English aristocracy to die from wounds received on the battlefield. At the start of the Netherlandish campaign, Elizabeth had sent a directive that young men of 'best birth' should be 'spared from all hazardous attempts'. See Anne Somerset, *Elizabeth I* (London: Weidenfeld & Nicolson, 1991), 423.

17 Robin Headlam Wells, *Shakespeare on Masculinity* (Cambridge: Cambridge University Press, 2000), 7.

18 A play entitled *The Troublesome Reign of King John* was published anonymously in 1591 and is regarded by some scholars as a source for Shakespeare's own play thought to have been written four or five years later in 1595–96.

19 See also Maurice Charney, *Shakespeare's Roman Plays* (Cambridge, Mass.: Harvard University Press, 1961), 197–8.

20 Frye, 'The Myth of Elizabeth I at Tilbury', 98.

21 Howard and Rackin, *Engendering a Nation*, 214–15.

22 For a further analysis of the Q and F versions of *Henry V* see my chapter '*Henry V* Tudor or Jacobean?', in Mike Pincombe (ed.) *The Anatomy of Tudor Literature* (Aldershot: Ashgate, 2001), 174–88.

Of tygers' hearts and players' hides

Noticing the monster

The play the First Folio styles *The third Part of Henry the Sixt* generated the earliest surviving notice of Shakespeare in performance, a review by Robert Greene, writing in *A Groats-worth of Witte*. Greene's narrative finds the author's faintly disguised alter ego, the impoverished university man, Roberto, consulting a Player whose ostentatious clothes have caused the poor scholar to mistake him for a 'substantial' person of quality. Roberto is casting about, wondering how he might find employment. 'Why easily', answers the lofty Player. 'For men of my profession get by schollers their whole living.' 'How meane you to use mee?' asks Roberto. 'Why sir, in making playes, for which you shall be well paied, if you will take the paines', answers the Player. So Roberto is hired, becomes 'famozed for an Arch-playmaking poet' and prospers: 'his purse, like the sea, sometime sweld, anon like the same sea fell to a low ebbe; yet seldom he wanted, his labours were so well esteemed'. Alas, however, this story is a moral tale that ends, narratively, with Roberto's ruin, and biographically, with Greene's direct address to 'his Quondam acquaintance' outside the narrative. He writes 'To those Gentlemen . . . that spend their wits in making Plaies' to instruct them, 'by my misery . . . be warned':

> For unto none of you (like me) sought those burrs to cleave – those Puppits (I mean) that speak from our mouths, those Antics garnished in our colours. Is it not strange that I, to whom they all have been beholding; is it not like that you, to whom they all have been beholding, shall . . . be both at once of them forsaken? Yes, trust them not: for there is an upstart Crow, beautified with our feathers, that with his *Tygers heart wrapt in a Players hide* supposes he is as well able to bombast out a blank verse as the best of you: and being an absolute *Johannes fac totum* is in his owne conceit the only Shakescene in a country.[1]

Greene's wretched tone is explained by the date. On 19 February 1592, when Lord Strange's Men, led by Edward Alleyn, opened at Henslowe's newly enlarged and refurbished Rose, the company launched the season with a play by Robert Greene, *Friar Bacon*. It took a respectable 17s 3d as Henslowe's share of the receipts that day but nothing like the amount Henslowe might have expected on such a gala occasion; thereafter, *Friar Bacon* played only twice more in the seventeen-week run. More gallingly, perhaps, Greene's *Looking Glass for London* took a disappointing £2 15s for Henslowe on Easter Monday, normally one of the most lucrative days in the playhouse, and played only once more that season, taking £1 9s on 8 June. By contrast, the play Henslowe entered in his *Diary* as a 'ne' (new?) play, 'harey the vj', on '3 of marche' 1592 earned him £3 16s 8d – a cracking sum that suggests the playhouse was packed to the gunnels.[2] A 'ne' play often took £3 – because it was 'ne'. What was astonishing about 'harey the vj' was that the company played it another fourteen times that season, and on several of those dates it took the kind of money expected of a premiere. This play seems to have been a runaway hit. Was 'harey the vj' Shakespeare's? I believe so. Was it Shakespeare's *'third Part'*? Scholars are still debating, but certainly the play we now know as *Part Three* was the play Robert Greene had on his embittered mind later that summer as he wrote *A Groats-worth of Witte*. His pamphlet was entered on the Stationers' Register on 20 September. He died later that same month – destitute.

Obviously, Greene's satire was aimed at Shakespeare. His 'Tygers heart wrapt in a Players hide' parodies a line that comes four scenes into *3 Henry VI*, at the death of Richard, Duke of York. Captured by Queen Margaret, made to stand upon a molehill (whose dizzying elevation locates his aspirations by mocking them) and to wear a paper crown, York endures her scorn. He 'wrought at mountains with outstretchèd arms,' Margaret scoffs, 'Yet parted but the shadow with his hand', 1.4.68–9). When he is cynically invited to make his 'orisons' in preparation for death, however, he instead defies his tormentors to pay back scorn for scorn:

> She-wolf of France, but worse than wolves of France,
> Whose tongue more poisons than the adder's tooth –
> How ill-beseeming is it in thy sex
> To triumph like an Amazonian trull
> Upon their woes whom Fortune captivates!
> . . .
> O tiger's heart wrapped in a woman's hide!
>
> (1.4.112–16; 138)

Greene remembers that line in his *Groats-worth of Witte* and expects that his cognoscenti readership, 'those Gentlemen' playwrights, his 'Quondam acquaintance', will remember it too. For the barb of satire to stick, the target it's aimed at must be recognised.

Thus Greene, resenting it, testifies to the power of the theatrical moment that etched itself upon his unwilling spectatorship and memory, to the extent even of inserting itself into his own writerly performance space. But more than the bare testimony, it interests me that the part he noticed, found notorious and made 'fame-ous' by his own remembering and recapitulating, was Margaret. Inarguably, 1.4 is shocking. More than humiliating York, Margaret needs to punish him and proceeds with a series of rhetorical questions: 'What – was it you that would be England's king? / Was't you that revelled in our Parliament?' (71–2). Then her questions, as she begins to count York's children: 'Where are your mess of sons to back you now?': 'wanton Edward', 'lusty George', 'that valiant crook-back prodigy, / Dickie your boy' (74–7)? These, of course, are York's warrior sons, fair game in the fluctuating battle-tides of civil war. But now Margaret's inventory starts counting the noncombatant children, the schoolboy son of York: 'Or with the rest where is your darling, Rutland?' she asks. And she directs York's suddenly alert attention to atrocity – 'Look, York' – as she pulls its evidence into the father's view:

> I stained this napkin with the blood
> That valiant Clifford with his rapier's point
> Made issue from the bosom of thy boy.

She offers her trophy as consolation:

> And if thine eyes can water for his death
> I give thee this to dry thy cheeks withal.

$$(79–83)$$

York answers her monstrous courtesy with his own rhetorical question, prompted by his monster-making apostrophe, 'O tiger's heart wrapped in a woman's hide!':

> How couldst thou drain the life-blood of the child
> To bid the father wipe his eyes withal,
> And yet be seen to bear a woman's face?
> Women are soft, mild, pitiful and flexible –
> Thou stern, obdurate, flinty, rough, remorseless.
> . . .
> That face of his the hungry cannibals
> Would not have touched, would not have stained with blood –
> But you are more inhuman, more inexorable,
> O, ten times more than tigers of Hyrcania.

$$(139–43; 153–6)$$

The three parts of *Henry VI* offer any number of similarly appalling spectacles; *Part Three* alone (if we imagine perhaps only this instalment of an eventual *Henry VI* trilogy existing at this date, the two further parts written later, as prequels) stages the York boys' savaging of Warwick, their awful slaughter of the Prince of Wales, 'Dickie's' torture and murder of King Henry, all of them scenes as sensational, as triumphalist, as raw and ugly in their savagery as Margaret baiting York. But all of them are also scenes among men. Male violence, it seems, is natural, therefore unmemorable. But Greene *remembers* Margaret. And remembering her, he conducts an interesting transfer across the chain of metaphors he recruits to his own purposes. Where York in his speech makes Margaret monstrous, Greene in his citation makes Margaret Shakespeare. He crafts his analogy to associate the tiger with the crow, the woman with the player, a move that rhetorically slides the woman's monstrous violation of gender off on to the player, troping other violence done upon the order of things. That is, Greene's metaphors simultaneously degrade Shakespeare to a woman and cast him as an aspiring 'upstart', a 'wannabe' university man. In Greene's flexible analogies, women turning into cannibals suggest players – 'Puppits', 'Antics' – turning into playwrights. All of them are flesh eaters. But players, Greene thinks, should use their mouths only to mouth words the scholars write; not to cannibalise them.

Staging the tiger

If Greene's notice turns out to be as much about performance theory as performance practice, it nevertheless documents the *force* of a role's early modern performance. Margaret is Phaedra, Medea, Progne and Hecuba (as Shakespeare read them in Ovid's *Metamorphoses*) rolled into one. Where 'bookish' Henry is a part that explores political anxieties via the problem of the weak king, Margaret is a part saturated with male anxieties about the domestic. He is the king who 'inherits the role of Caesar and would prefer to be Christ': he has no interest in factional backbiting and political backstabbing because, 'haunted by the enduring presence of the apparently past and seemingly departed',[3] his perspective outreaches the merely topical. By contrast, she is the queen of the here and now who anatomises male anxieties by playing out (English) men's worst fantasies, not least because the symbolic space assigned to the female domestic body in *Henry VI* is literally occupied by a stranger, a foreigner, an upstart, a French 'other'. So one role asks: 'What is a king?' Is he human, or divine? What is his power? The other asks: 'What is a woman?' Celestial? Bestial? Rational? Hysterical? What is her power? Erotic? Demonic? Political? What is her 'nature': 'soft, mild, pitiful and flexible' – or not? Is savagery in the woman against nature? Or does savagery confirm her nature, even constitute it?

These were questions that came live again when, having lain mostly dormant for 350 years, the *Henry VI* plays were rediscovered for the postwar English stage, first by Sir Barry Jackson at the Birmingham Rep (1951–53), then adapted by Peter Hall and John Barton at the Royal Shakespeare Company (1963).[4] Since then, in both adapted and unadapted versions, the *Henry VI* cycle in Britain has become virtually the exclusive property of the RSC, with productions in 1977 (directed by Terry Hands), 1988 (Adrian Noble), 1994 (Katie Mitchell) and 2000 (Michael Boyd). The period of this rediscovery has meant, for Margaret, that her recovery has coincided with the mobilisation of the postwar women's movement and the sexual revolution it incited – in 'Annus Mirabilis', we remember, Philip Larkin dated 1963 very precisely in Britain as 'the year when / Sexual intercourse began'. Even before women in Britain had worked out a language to theorise themselves as 'female eunuchs', Shakespeare's Margaret on the stage was role-playing issues women recognised, issues consistent with their growing awareness of their political exclusion, their bewilderment, grievance and frustration with social inequalities and sexual discrimination. Margaret anticipated contemporary stereotypes:[5] in youth, a sex object men imagine using to lever themselves into positions of power; in age, a dried-up harridan, a bitch or goddess, a dominatrix, York's 'Amazonian trull'; in-between, in scene after scene, a lone woman surrounded by men, excluded from real, official power and excluded, too, from the homosocial bonds (Henry/Gloucester, Talbot/John, York/York's boys) that mean so much more in these plays than marriage or motherhood. So Margaret experiments with alternative access to power. Plotting substitutes for politics, sexual coaxing for rhetorical persuasion, cattiness for authority: excluded from government, she meddles instead.

Moments selected from across the RSC's productions briefly demonstrate these observations. Shakespeare scripts Margaret's first entrance near the end of *Part One* as an object lesson in objectification. Arrested, as she wanders across a battlefield by, Suffolk who makes her his 'prisoner', a word he loads with sexual innuendo, she is wooed in a language of courtly dalliance, Suffolk only tardily remembering that he already has a wife. So he decides to make her *Henry's* wife – but keep her as a paramour and pawn: thus, 'Margaret shall now be queen and rule the King; / But I will rule both her, the King and realm' (*1 Henry VI*, 5.7.107–8). Euphemism masks the scene's latent violence: 'She is a woman, therefore to be won' (5.5.35) echoes the rapist in *Titus Andronicus* (2.1.83). And erotic objectification marks its end: Margaret is the 'wonder' who will 'bereave' King Henry 'of his wits' (5.5.151). In 1963, Peggy Ashcroft made Margaret an arch adolescent and the scene a flirtation choreographed as a *pas de deux*. In 1977, Helen Mirren's sexual scent and sexual appetite were more powerful: where Ashcroft danced rings around Suffolk, Mirren's body language – a whole alphabet of desire shuddering through the curves of her breasts, hips and thighs – showed her entertaining fantasies of capture by this suave Englishman. In 1988, Penny Downie played the explicit sexual danger in the scene: her Margaret, muffled in a filthy cloak, was a battlefield scavenger on the point of being killed for a looter when, pulling back her hood, Suffolk suddenly thought of other ways to die. In 2000, in a staging that owed not a little to postmodern pastiche, Fiona Bell parodied Margaret's objectification. Materialising Suffolk's fantasies as he spoke her praises to the King and giving those fantasies 'local habitation' as they took shape in Henry's mind, she descended from the flies in figure-hugging red velvet, posed inside a gold picture frame. In none of these readings was Margaret contained by Suffolk's metaphors – 'fairest beauty', 'nature's miracle'. That he'd miscalculated should have been clear from Ashcroft's haughty reply, when he offered to make her queen, that 'a queen in bondage' was 'more vile' than 'a slave in base servility': 'For princes should be free (5.5.2; 10; 67–9).' Or from Downie's sharp interruption of the gush of Suffolk's promises to make her Henry's queen, give her a sceptre and a Crown, 'If thou wilt condescend to be my –' 'What?' So prompting Suffolk to correct himself: '*His* love' (76–7). Or from Mirren's dismissing as toys the fascinating sex games she played with such assurance. The kiss Suffolk took, pretending it a 'loving token' for the King, she instantly gave – 'That for thyself'. But dismissed, with a bright, uninterpretable smile, what Suffolk was over-endowing with suggestiveness. Suffolk's kiss was meaningless: for she would 'not so presume' to 'send such peevish tokens to a king' (141–2).

In all these actors' readings of the role, Margaret wanted what England's brawling barons wanted: power. A stunning moment in Ashcroft's performance located her exclusion from male power. Entering the Council chamber for the first time as Henry's bride and England's Queen, Margaret took a place at the Council table as if she belonged there. Filing in behind her, Henry's peers refused to sit. Finally Gloucester, ostentatiously ignoring her, broke the charged silence to direct a loaded question to the King, 'Is it your will / Her highness should attend on our proceedings?' (*Wars*, Scene 19). It *was* the King's will – but it was not the Council's liking. This French woman, whose accent coded her as always foreign, affronted English manliness. Every time she opened her mouth they heard an echo of their loss of empire. But as Mirren and Downie played her, Margaret also wanted Henry's love. Mirren staked everything in *Part Two* on finally winning the competition with Gloucester for her husband's love – and she surely held all the aces, once Gloucester was dead. In 3.2 she was like Nora dancing the tarantella in the doll's house. But the performance didn't work. Re-citing the whole dazzling history of their odd love affair in an unabashed seduction speech before the whole court, Margaret still could not penetrate the blankness shrouding Henry's eyes. Her dead rival triumphed. Men mattered to men more than women did.

By the time Margaret in each of these productions arrived on the molehill to face York, she was a woman looking for revenge, a wife who had divorced herself from her irresolute husband's bed, a mother who had taken responsibility for ensuring her disinherited son's birthright, a militant in armour who led the Lancastrian troops from the front. Humiliated, mocked, betrayed, enraged, ignored, Margaret wanted a redistribution of power, and she got it. But the sexual equality she achieved with York was an equality of savagery. Ashcroft's Margaret had grown not just into an 'Amazonian trull' but an Aeschylean harpy. The 'napkin' she slapped across York's face, taunting him with Rutland's death as he involuntarily howled 'No!', was heavy with Rutland's still-wet blood, and the paper crown she jammed down on his head was the toy Rutland had been romping with when Clifford ambushed him. The gesture Downie's Margaret made wiping York's face with his son's blood recalled young Talbot smearing his father's face with blood in *Part One*, and her gaze was both horrified and fascinated when the napkin, thrown back in her face, fell open on her lap, spreading a stain of blood across her womb. Skewering York with stab wounds to the neck, Downie's Margaret pinioned him – and waited while he drowned in his own blood, making the same gurgling noises the Clerk of Chatham made when Cade's laughing rebels strangled him in *Part Two*. For Mirren's Margaret, killing York was a voluptuous act, a kind of necrophilia. Her hatred was silken, so wiping York's face was an intimacy, a perverse caress; kneeling, they were close enough to kiss, but when York suddenly sprang forward, grabbing her, forcing her down under him, spreading her legs, his climax a curse, Clifford moved to complete the perverse sexual action, thrusting into him from behind. And Margaret, almost parodying phallic superiority, reached for a weapon, pushed it slowly into York and, as he fell into her lap, arched her body in orgasmic ecstasy before rolling out from under him, disgusted, exhausted, to order with brutal indifference, 'Off with his head and set it on York gates' (2.1.180).

Having these productions in view over the past forty years, any women who cared to read a contemporary, politicised parallel text against the Shakespeare-driven performance might have seen in Margaret their own history historicised. 'Madam . . . these are no women's matters' (*Wars*, Scene 19) settled not just Margaret's place in the early modern patriarchal system; it anticipated theirs in a system that persisted. Savaged by York for her savagery ('O tiger's heart wrapped in a woman's hide! / How couldst thou drain the life-blood of the child . . .?'), Margaret exposed the hypocrisy of men making unnatural to women the violence they themselves had naturalised to England. York's appalled utterance wanted to identify women 'naturally' with softness, mildness, pity; and through that identification, to express an essential truth – Margaret the wild contrastive – anchoring (but only just) the social order in an England that was free-falling into chaos. But York's essentialism sounded like male fantasising – a vast denial that worked polit-ically as sexual discrimination, loading on to women the imperative to occupy the emotional spaces men disdained, to care for culture, for the future, for the children the men were single-mindedly intent on destroying. And who was fooled by this agenda?

Significantly, if the Margaret whom Shakespeare scripted anticipated female stereotyping (and even provided a language to conduct it), she like-wise interrogated it and gave contemporary women a language for interro-gating the cultural valuation of women they themselves were negotiating, if not violently subverting, in their own lives. Margaret had a comeback to Suffolk when he wanted to make her his doxy: 'What?' (*1 Henry VI*, 5.5.77). A comeback to Gloucester when he wanted to erase her by infantilising the King, keeping him bound to a protectorship he had outgrown: 'What . . .?' (*The First Part of the Contention* [*2 Henry VI*], 1.3.50). A comeback to York when he usurped her son's throne: 'What . . .? What . . .?' (*3 Henry VI*, 1.4.71; 88). And all those comebacks registered her scepticism – more, her incredulity – of the 'natural' order, an opposition that was demonised as impudence. To various degrees, then, Margaret in postwar productions in England could be read simultaneously as an icon of radical feminism or an argument for reactionary conservatism and the status quo. Fusing, as in Katie Mitchell's production, ideas ancient and modern, she could offer a space for exploring alternatives – and imagining their consequences.[6] In Mitchell, who used a painting nearly contemporary with the history Shakespeare stages in the *Henry VI*s as her production image, Margaret ani-mated and tested the narrative space Brueghel opened up to 'Mad Meg', a.k.a., 'Dulle Griet'. In the painting, Brueghel poses the almost cartoon-figure of the embattled, clown-booted warrior woman on the lip of a medieval hell-mouth as an illustration of the proverb, 'She could plunder in front of hell and return unscathed'. Was the proverb true? Was such plunder the kind of work women aspired to? Going to war, Mitchell's Margaret looked like Dulle Griet – except that her face was hidden behind a gold mask. How did spectators read that production choice? As an effacement of gender? Did that mean that, far from coming back unscathed, the woman who plundered at the gates of hell had better be a man?

Killing the quean

York on the molehill might rail against the 'tiger's heart', but his rage cannot penetrate the 'woman's hide'. The audacious Margaret who breaks every code and outfaces every threat of retribution – a kind of Tamburlaine in skirts – survives the Wars of the Roses, survives the fall of Lancaster, the Cade rebellion, the slaughter of Edward, the murder of Henry; survives into *Richard III* where, like Alecto, she distributes discord and, like Nemesis, presides as vengeance descends upon the House of York. The violence men want to commit upon Margaret, to punish the upstart virago, is stymied. But I want to go on to argue that the male rage denied in one place is satisfied elsewhere in the *Henry VI* trilogy, in the capture and killing of Joan la Pucelle, whose exit from the story shadows Margaret's entrance into it. If Margaret in the productions I have cited has offered spectators a space for observing some kinds of feminist manoeuvres – a sort of shadowboxing Kate Minola from *The Taming of the Shrew* – and to see stereotypes of womanliness produced, inhabited, exploded and recuperated, Joan la Pucelle from *Part One* has, over the same forty years since 1963, borne the brunt of misogynist backlash.

From her first entrance in *1 Henry VI* (1.3), Joan is an oxymoron nicely framed by the contradictory language of male desire. For the French, the virgin la Pucelle is 'A holy maid' (1.3.30); for the English, a 'puzel', a harlot and witch (1.6.85). In the French camp, the 'spirit of deep prophecy' is claimed for her (1.3.34) and divine election, 'God's mother . . . in a vision' appearing to the shepherd girl and telling her to leave her 'base vocation' and 'free' her 'country from calamity' (57–8; 59–60). As a sign of her appointment, Joan has been made an object of light: 'black and swart before', she has been 'infused' by 'those clear rays' that have marked her with divine whiteness (63–4). Joan passes two tests, first identifying the Dauphin then beating him in the trial by combat. Both are acts read as miracles. And as early as 1.8 the Dauphin is making plans to canonise her:

> when she is dead,
> Her ashes in an urn more precious
> Than the rich-jewelled coffer of Darius,
> Transported shall be at high festivals
> Before the kings and queens of France.
> No longer on Saint Denis will we cry,
> But Joan la Pucelle shall be France's saint.

$$(1.8.23–9)$$

But equally in the French camp, the same language that figures la Pucelle a 'wonder' is used to eroticise and degrade her. 'Subdued' by the warrior woman, the Dauphin instantly, 'impatiently', burns with 'desire' to serve her as her 'prostrate thrall', and his courtiers looking on from the sidelines start to snigger, their lewd jokes collapsing worship into profanation: he 'shrives this woman to her smock'; 'women are shrewd tempters with their tongues' (1.3.88; 87; 96; 98; 120). When rumours of her enter the English camp, the transvestite 'woman clad in armour' is immediately figured not just as a monster but a demon, the 'Devil or devil's dam', 'a witch' who 'by fear, not force . . . conquers as she lists'

(1.7.3; 5; 6; 21–2). In Talbot's brand of essentialism, mobilised here to over-compensate for England's martial failure, politics is always sexual politics. There is no way for a woman to act (as patriot or freedom fighter, for example) except sexually, and, by definition, any action marks her as sexual transgressor, therefore impudent and demonised, a monster. Thus, power in a woman has one single source, darkness, with two names, sexuality and witchcraft. So, among the English generals and their allies, Joan is smutty gossip. But their jokes fail to hide their anxieties about one who dresses as a man, fights like a man and defeats them as a better man than they are, who may 'prove . . . masculine' in ways their sarcasm can't anticipate:

> BURGUNDY   But what's that 'Pucelle' whom they term so pure?
> TALBOT   A maid, they say.
> BEDFORD   A maid? And be so martial?
> BURGUNDY   Pray God she prove not masculine ere long.
>   If underneath the standard of the French
>   She carry armour as she hath begun –
> TALBOT   Well, let them practise and converse with spirits.
>   God is our fortress . . .

>   (2.1.20–6)

Part One keeps these competing fictions of Joan, the saintly virgin, the witch-whore, in play until Act 5. Lifting the siege of Orleans, raiding Rouen, parleying with Burgundy, persuading him to capitulate to the Dauphin, Joan is France's handmaid and hero – but, disconcertingly, her actions are inscribed in language that troubles their interpretation. Her words 'enchant', and Burgundy is 'bewitched' by the business her maidenly body performs upon him. Troublingly for the English, 'fortress God' fails: so what does that say about la Pucelle? Talbot, 'parked and bounded in a pale' like deer, dies 'Mazed with a yelping kennel of French curs' (4.2.45; 47). And Joan stands over the corpse, deadeningly realistic about this 'great Alcides' whom the English would apotheosise: 'Stinking and flyblown' Talbot 'lies here at our feet' (4.7.60; 76). It's a critical moment. When the idealised heroic body is set against the actual frail material body, hyperbole fails. What is fame if the body starts immediately to decompose? Momentarily, the stage picture freezes. Then Joan steps into the gap between fantasy and form that she has just observed, taking Talbot's place in the hero-worshipping, hero-toppling project of the play.

She, too, like her alter ego Talbot, arrives at the point when she is abandoned, when she is as exposed as Talbot was in 4.2. In 5.3, 'The Regent conquers and the Frenchmen fly'. Alone onstage la Pucelle finally declares herself and her masters, summoning her 'spirits' and 'speedy helpers', those 'substitutes / Under the lordly monarch of the north' who are to 'aid me in this enterprise!' The Folio stage directions indicate 'Thunder', then 'Enter Fiends'

(5–7; SD, 4; SD, 7). So the 'holy maid' was Satan's whore, after all! How convenient for English historiography and a new world order whose architects, York and Warwick, have provided no space for idealists like Talbot and Joan. Now, her fiends 'walk and speak not'; 'They hang their heads' when Joan promises her 'body shall / Pay recompense' for a French victory (SD, 12; SD, 17; 18–19). But it's not enough. 'Cannot my body nor blood-sacrifice / Entreat you to your wonted furtherance?' 'They shake their heads.' Then 'take my soul – my body, soul and all', she urges. But 'They depart' (20–3). And York enters. 'Damsel of France,' he observes with devastating understatement, 'I think I have you fast' (5.4.1). In 5.6, he orders, 'Bring forth that sorceress condemned to burn' (1). Her humiliation is to be faced with a man York produces as her father, a rustic Dogberry, who claims her as 'a collop of my flesh' (18), no mystic maid – but la Pucelle repudiates him and his base decrepitude. Not just a witch, then, but a thankless child instantly metamorphosed whore, she calls down upon herself the patriarchal curse: 'Dost thou deny thy father, cursèd drab? / O burn her, burn her! Hanging is too good' (32–3). So the English oblige him.

I am interested in how postwar productions have staged the killing of Joan, but first need to locate the killing inside the context of individual performances. In 1963, in the heavily adapted *Wars of the Roses*, Janet Suzman was a boyish crop-haired warrior-maid with a dirty face who entered 1.2 in chain mail, found the French playing war games instead of planning tactics and kicked the chessboard into the air, sending the fake kings and queens flying. In 1977, in a full-text trilogy, Charlotte Cornwell was a spring-heeled peasant Joan in a rough, low-belted tunic over leggings and sheep-skin boots, her flaming red hair evidently cut round a porringer – making her, uncannily, a double of the infantile King Henry. In 1988, Julia Ford (in another severely cut adaptation) was a waif, a little Orphan Annie Joan with punk hair, but wearing 'grown-up' clothes, a medieval-style tabard with a *fleur de lys* on the front, inscribing her with the official insignia of France. In 2000, Fiona Bell played a Joan in skirts: no child, but a formidable woman whose voice marked her as 'other', Bell's muscular Scottish accent dinning the ears of the dispirited French.

For Suzman, Cornwell and Ford, the hand-to-hand combat with the Dauphin was a test that put the woman on top. They were assured fighters who wielded the sword with real power in the wrist – only Cornwell resorting to comic business, stomping on the Dauphin's toe to get the edge over him. Ford was astonishingly tough, later beating the bullish Talbot to his knees as he visibly quailed, and all of these Joans got out from under the Dauphin's desire to remake his personal defeat as sexual conquest: they rode *his* prostrate body, hip to hip, before springing away from the invitation implied in 'I burn with thy desire' (1.2.87) with broad laughter (Cornwell) or icy severity (Suzman). All of them, too, were swaggeringly triumphalist in their successes, Suzman straddling the gates of Rouen and kicking her heels at the enemy, Cornwell grinning from ear to ear and mimicking Talbot's furious speech, Ford at the centre of the massed, glittering French, a tiny Titan. Suzman and Cornwell played the capitulation scene with Burgundy as a seduction scene, Suzman moving with a rocking motion as if she were hypnotising him; Cornwell standing on tiptoe, speaking into his ear an insistent temptation. For Ford, however, 3.3 marked the beginning of Joan's humiliation. She had fled Rouen in her smock – her feet, arms and legs bare – and in this near stripped state she had to take on the massively produced, fully equipped, padded, armed, helmeted Burgundy, her nakedness not empowering but exposing her, in flesh, an abject.

In Boyd's production, Fiona Bell was directed to make something very different of these early scenes. In her long, belted peasant dress, she came before the Dauphin as a woman, but ambiguously so: her severely short red-gold hair made her face powerfully masculine. But she was on the point of losing the trial by combat when three silent figures, beautiful women clothed neck to ankle in sensuous blood-red, filed on to the stage, their movements eerily synchronised, taking up a position behind Joan, a line of 'seconds'. Now, as la Pucelle swung her sword, these 'spirits' (as the prompt book named them) mimed her action – or were they directing it? Whichever, Joan's sword took power from the parallel play. As though made impotent by witchcraft, the Dauphin fell back until the weapon was at his throat. He was on his knees, she kneeling, braced, when he slowly pushed her on to her back, straddled her and began to 'caress P's body', as the prompt book records, his 'hand' moving up her skirts 'toward crotch' (prompt book) as he uttered the lines about burning with desire. She stopped the hand – and pulling back, the Dauphin gave her a chaste kiss on the forehead. But from the flies, a single white feather floated to the ground. It would take another six hours of playing time in this *Henry VI* trilogy to unpack the symbolism suggested in this first, then repeated, fall of feathers. For now, it felt as if somewhere above the mortal space of England and its history, angels were being murdered.

Bell's la Pucelle was established from the first as one of the fiends. Her three familiars went everywhere with her. The massive metal doors that barricaded one end of the playing space – and came to represent the gates of hell – opened to release these always silent, always impassive figures when Joan attacked Talbot. Later, from the balcony, they let 'drop silk for French' (prompt book) to use as scaling ropes to enter Rouen, but filed out to leave the space to Joan who appeared there, taunting maimed Bedford, 'What will you do, . . . run a-tilt at death without an arm?' (3.5.11) before exultantly producing his severed member, holding it aloft, a bloody trophy. Preparing to work on Burgundy, la Pucelle traced the same talismanic circle on the ground with her sword's tip that she had used to figure England's glory 'like a circle in the water' in 1.2, stabbing it to signal 'Henry's death' (112; 115). Now, she made not just a circle on the ground but one in the air, as if summoning malign spirits from every point of the metaphysical compass. Duly, they entered with Burgundy, took up their places behind Joan and mirrored all her actions, weirdly echoing the word 'relent'. As unsettling as the mirror play was, the acoustics of Joan's scenes were even more unsettling. That accent that marked her strange branded her more menacingly. Every time she opened her Scots mouth the English heard her as a witch.

Demonising Joan, Boyd's production made explicit what Shakespeare's script withholds and earlier productions juggled – until 5.3. Suzman's Joan, summoning 'ye charming spells and periapts . . . cull'd / Out of the powerful regions under earth' grew increasingly desperate as, facing into the dark auditorium, she made no spirits appear, even when she drew her sword blade across her open palm, offering her blood, then, smearing blood across her breasts, gave them her prostrate body. Still, even when she was abandoned of all power and York ambushed her, he had to fight to disarm her. And to silence her curses he had to kick her hard in the stomach. Unconscious, she fell, doubled over a lance and was dragged off by York's thugs. In 1977, York materialised behind Cornwall's Joan from palpable darkness like the fiend her fruitless prayers couldn't raise. As she knelt, hands outstretched clutching at air and straws, York delicately drew his white silk scarf from around his neck, looped it around her grimacing mouth then suddenly yanked tight, gagging her with a do-it-yourself scold's bridle and dragging her off by the 'reins'. In 1989, la Pucelle's capture was even uglier. Routed by the combined forces of York and Somerset, the French fled yet again. This time, the Dauphin turned on la Pucelle. He shoved her, lifting her off her feet and she fell among the corpses still piled there from the slaughter of the Talbots and their army. Abandoned by her own side, she turned to the spirits, spells and periapts and as the incantation formed in her lines, around her, the dead began uncannily to stir. But she had not enough power to breathe life back into her project. Horribly, they sank again. And now she was suddenly trapped by York's troops, the stink of male violence sharpening to gang rape: clearly, they were in the mood for testing the credentials of the 'holy maid'.

In her final scene, ordered to make her appearance to be taunted as the 'sorceress condemn'd to burn', Suzman entered transformed by her captivity. For the first time in this production, she was dressed like a woman – in a smock, like a penitent, with a bill around her neck that cited her crimes. But the refashioned Joan was both a joke and an insult. The men stood around drinking, amused. When she claimed to be 'A virgin . . . / Chaste and immaculate, whose maiden blood' would 'cry for vengeance at the gates of heaven', Somerset's considerate order was for 'barrels of pitch' to be piled 'upon the fatal stake' so that 'her torture may be shortened' (51–3; 57–8). Suddenly terrified, la Pucelle lost all composure, weeping, scrabbling on the ground trying to embrace her captors' knees, finally crying, 'I am with child' (62). But the men merely mocked on, York and Warwick both enjoying this sport of witch-baiting that would end in blood. Joan wearied of it first. 'Lead me hence', she demanded. Then, eerily calm, turned on her captors to 'leave my curse' (86), a pronouncement that doomed England to darkness, England's posterity to 'wretched years', the land to be 'a nourish of salt tears' and 'none but women left to wail the dead' (1.1.48; 50; 51). The curse bit hard, rankling York, who threw his drink in her face but still looked rattled when, dragged away to the stake, Joan let out a soul-shattering scream. For Cornwell, too, this final scene was about humiliation, the woman's rising hysteria put against the men's leisurely game-playing. York stood sniffing a white rose, keeping upwind of the stinking peasant who claimed Joan as his daughter. When all her subterfuge failed, this Joan was ready for the stake. Breaking free, she spun a wild circle, aiming slaps at the faces of her captors, tainting them with a polluting touch. York leapt out of range – but felt her mark upon him.

In 1988, la Pucelle's capture and execution scenes were cut into one, the rape the men wanted, denied, to be replaced by a ritual humiliation that registered French defeat as national spectacle but also put the death of Joan on stage, in full view. Stripped of her French accoutrements, Joan's satanism was violently recuperated inside the sacred and her body made a surface for English nationalism's graffiti: soldiers painted a red George Cross on her white smock, then bound her to a scaling ladder and hoisted her aloft as faggots were piled around this makeshift stake – and lit. The men carried flaming torches – the director, Adrian Noble, reputedly wanted a 'real' burning but settled for symbolism – bathing the scene in red light. Beneath the pyre, York's men jeered and joked and fed their faces as the 'virgin's' flesh went up in smoke. Carnival collided with another kind of carnal consumption, and the scene's nationalist triumphalism was spectacularly secured when gender hegemony was restored, the French defeated and the woman satisfactorily punished. Joan's body hung sagging from the stake in view while all these matters were concluded.

When Fiona Bell's spirits deserted her in Act 5, they retreated to remote corners of the auditorium to observe her plead and rip off her wrist bands to display underneath her witch tokens, then impassively processed through the metal gates that closed behind them. La Pucelle pursued them, banging her ineffectual sword on the metal. Weirdly, the racket was transformed to knocking, the English, outside, eager to come on, York at their head. Like la Pucelle, he had cropped hair, and they faced each other as twins. Then he threw her to the ground, tied her hands and dragged her to her feet to be taken away to

death. But she somehow managed to grab him around the neck and kiss him –
they fell, he recoiling in disgust as soldiers swarmed to pin her down.

This Joan, too, was executed in full view of spectators, the English army
dragging her to the 'stake', a ladder hoisted over an abyss that opened under
her feet as trap doors in the stage-floor swung wide, giving a vision of hell
below England's brittle surface. Suspended, each time she struggled la
Pucelle made her torture sickeningly terrifying, the ladder juddering and
lurching over the pit. Pleading her belly – 'I am with child' (65) – momentarily paused the proceedings, until York jumped on to the bottom rung of
the ladder, pressing himself into her as if tempted by her sexual power. Then,
to test her contradictory claims – the 'holy maid with child?' (65) – he drew
his dagger at knee height, pointed it upwards, slowly thrust it up under her
skirt, withdrew it and inspected the blood on its tip. Was the blood from the
penetrated hymen, proving what he'd (now ironically) spoiled? Or did the
blood flow from an abortion? York inserted his hand up between her legs,
sarcastically observing 'and yet forsooth she is a virgin pure' (83), before
dragging his hand away, showing a fistful of blood. Whatever she was
before, now she was York's whore. As smoke enveloped la Pucelle, the ladder
slowly descended into the pit, the hell-mouth swung shut and a storm of red
feathers rained down to cover the sealed ground. But even then, the metal
stage doors were swinging open – and in a stunning *coup de théâtre* Joan
walked back on the stage. Only now she was dressed in blood-red crushed
velvet, like Joan's fiends and she was reincarnated as Margaret of Anjou. As
la Pucelle's substitute or double, Bell's Margaret would complete on a battlefield outside Wakefield the action York thought he'd ended here, only
then, their roles would be reversed. The Amazonian warrior, her 'tiger's heart
wrapped in a woman's hide', would be the one figuratively dancing around
the bonfire and York would be tied to the stake, hung up to the jeering view.
There would be a qualitative difference in how the parallel deaths would register. For all that they mocked him, York in agony, sweating blood, would
be tragic; Joan, womb-ripped, was only sensationally, horrifically grotesque.

Inventing the theatrical future

Writing Margaret savaging York, writing the 'Tygers heart wrapt in a Players
hide', Shakespeare was inventing a new kind of role for the English stage, a
role whose sources lay certainly not in 'real' history but probably in
Shakespeare's schoolboy reading of Ovid where fury-ous women (like
Hecuba in *Metamorphoses XIII*, Progne in *Book VI* and Dido in *Heroïdes
XIII*) regularly – and 'naturally' – plan and perform extravagant acts of vio-
lence upon men who have abused, violated or betrayed them. In Margaret,
Shakespeare 'naturalised' to English history the kind of 'barbarian' atrocity

he would write for the gothic Queen Tamora in *Titus Andronicus* – a play that premiered in the same playhouse where *Henry VI* was first performed and with the same company, almost exactly two years later (Foakes and Rickert, *Henslowe's Diary*, 21 (f. 8v)). Writing a radical performance text that put female violence squarely (and in Robert Greene's case, notoriously) in view, Shakespeare simultaneously wrote a 'conservative' language of patriarchal reaction that condemns violence as 'unnatural' to women, that de-natures women, degrading them to animals. Setting Margaret's performance against York's interpretation of that performance, Shakespeare can have it both ways: his stage can play both the status quo and the subversion of the status quo. York's simultaneous fascination with and revulsion for Margaret, however, is nicely prophetic of the subsequent performance of the women's roles in the *Henry VIs*. The new female prototype, the ambitious woman who operates – in the jargon of 1970s feminism – 'in a man's world' – must count the costs of her aspiration. Joan, significantly, is the role in performance in *Henry VI* that has figured these issues most sensationally. Again, attached to her is both the radical and the reactionary – and the suspicion might be hard to dismiss, in the spectator watching the *Henry VIs* today (as in Michael Boyd's productions), that la Pucelle grounds contemporary culture's new-model misogyny, that she offers a culturally sanctioned space to play out the complicated manoeuvres that first celebrate then punish the 'uppity' woman. But if killing Joan reinstates misogyny, doubling Joan with Margaret, as Boyd directed, rethinks the satisfactions of that reactionary move.

Notes

1 *A Groats-worth of Witte*, entered on the Stationers' Register 20 September 1592 (Arber, II, 620), sig. F1r.
2 See R. A. Foakes and R. T. Rickert, *Henslowe's Diary* (Cambridge: Cambridge University Press, 1968), 16–19, ff. 7, 7v, 8.
3 Ralph Williams, RSC programme note, 'This England: Henry VI'.
4 All references to 1963 are to John Barton and Peter Hall, *The Wars of the Roses* (London: BBC, 1970). For an account of the trilogy's life onstage between 1592 and 2001 see Stuart Hampton-Reeves and Carol Chillington Rutter, *Shakespeare in Performance: The* Henry VI *Plays* (Manchester: Manchester University Press, 2006).
5 Reviewing Michael Boyd's *Henry VI* cycle in 2000 Susannah Clapp in *The Observer Review* (17 December 2000) described 'the plays as treasure-troves that have been raided for archetypes by subsequent generations'.
6 For a brilliant reading of Mitchell's production see Barbara Hodgdon, 'Making It New: Katie Mitchell Refashions Shakespeare-History', in Marianne Novy (ed.) *Transforming Shakespeare: Contemporary Women's Re-Visions in Literature and Performance* (New York: St Martin's, 1999), 13–33.

Mapping Shakespeare's Britain

Late one evening, a farmer in Eastern Europe suddenly heard a knock at the door. Outside were overcoated officials from Russia and Poland. They explained that they were redrawing the boundary line, the border between the two countries and the line went straight through the man's farm. 'You have a perfectly free choice', they explained, 'No pressure at all. You can either be in Poland or in Russia but we need an immediate answer.' 'That's easy: I'd like to be in Poland.' 'That's fine, no problem but, just out of curiosity, why did you pick Poland?' 'Oh, the winters are better there.'

History is written in the drawing of national borders and borderlines are a visible manifestation of the politics of map-making, what Shakespeare contemptuously calls in *Troilus and Cressida* 'mapp'ry' (1.2.205),[1] a word so rare *OED* can offer only this example before 1840. Whether they are straight lines that divide countries along lines of latitude or longitude or complex lines following the course of a river, the line is the central feature of human intervention in the political acts of cartography, a manifestation visible on the landscape only through the accompaniment of such symbolic acts, the barbed wire and border posts, the barriers and human presences that enunciate the language of nation as limited space and a nation's own sense of perimeter. On the map the habit of colouring for empires also demonstrates possession, the ownership of territory far removed from the nation at the heart of its colonialism.

National histories are defined through geographies, not the whole earth analysis that is the true province of geography but the partial mappings and explorations, the study of regionality that made up the new early modern discipline of chorography, not only the delineation on the map but also the description, the analytic account both of the landscape and the history of human interventions on that landscape, in towns and castles, villages and battlegrounds, the whole course of human activity which is indivisible from that delineation.[2] As William Cuningham defined it in 1559, as the word 'chorography' makes its entrance into English usage, in his book *The Cosmographical Glasse*, there is already the beginnings of a definition of chorography as a discipline separable from geography,

> For lyke as Cosmographie describeth the worlde, Geographie th'earth: in lyke sorte Chorographie, sheweth the partes of th'earth, divided in them selves. And severally describeth, the portes, Rivers, Havens, Fluddes, Hilles, Mountaynes, Cities, Villages, Buildinges, Fortresses, Walles, yea and every particular thing, in that parte conteined. (6–7)

In Cunningham's sequence he moves from the natural to the human, from rivers, havens and floods to cities, villages and buildings. As I shall return to much later, the history of early modern English cartography to some extent recapitulates that sequence as the subsequent remappings, from Saxton to Norden to Speed, make increasingly prominent the human over the natural and the local over the regional. Yet the natural is not impermeable to the human:

> See how this river comes me cranking in,
> And cuts me from the best of all my land,
> A huge half-moon, a monstrous cantle, out.
> I'll have the current in this place dammed up,
> And here the smug and silver Trent shall run,
> In a new channel fair and evenly.

(1 Henry IV, 3.1.95–100)

In the politics of maps we are of course aware of the two crucial examples in Shakespeare, the map of England being divided up and redivided here in Hotspur's irritation in *1 Henry IV* and the map of Britain being divided up in *King Lear*. Hotspur's refusal to accept the map as an account of the new political division will instead require a future new survey, of the kind that had been undertaken for the counties of England by Christopher Saxton between 1574 and 1579, so that the map can in future accurately represent the retrenched river. The local chorography would then reflect both the moved Trent and the political consequences of possession that would have caused the winding river to be even. The new survey would have recorded the history of division, mapping as a marking of history as well as geography.

It is immediately striking how comparatively infrequently maps appear on the early modern stage. Alan Dessen and Leslie Thomson, in their *Dictionary of Stage Directions in English Drama: 1580–1642* (Cambridge, 1999), list only two, neither of them the examples from Shakespeare since, such is the nature of their work, there is no stage direction to refer to the maps and hence they cannot be indexed. The later example is in Middleton's *Anything for a Quiet Life* (performed around 1621) where, as Knavesby tries to persuade the Cressinghams to buy land in Clangibbon in Ireland, a map of the estates is produced for Sir Francis to consider: 'What's this, Marsh ground?' 'No, these are Boggs, but a little Cost will drain them.'[3] The map here is an example of by far the commonest form of early modern mapping, the delineation of an estate to mark out ownership, the map's extents equivalent to the limits of possession.

Dessen and Thomson's earlier example is the map that is brought on for the dying Tamburlaine to consider in Marlowe's play, a map across which he can chart his past and lament the absence of the future: 'Here I began to martch towards *Persea*' but also 'And shall I die and this unconquered?'[4] Tamburlaine's map here is written over with his biography, just as, in Part One, he proposed to redefine both the outline form of contemporary maps and their contents:

> I will confute those blind Geographers
> That make a triple region in the world,
> Excluding Regions which I mean to trace,
> And with this pen reduce them to a Map,
> Calling the Provinces, Citties and townes
> After my name and thine *Zenocrate*:

> (4.4.81–6)

The conventional triple pattern of the early form of universal maps, what are called T-O maps (that is, a world map centred on Jerusalem and divided into three regions, Europe, Africa and Asia), is insufficient for Tamburlaine's ambition and his sense of the geography of the world: there are regions that lie beyond the geographers' records, their construction of knowledge and he will draw these spaces beyond the three continents and subject them – the word 'reduce' comprises both possibilities – and, most significantly, rename them, leaving a different kind of recording of his geographical presence in the transformation of place-names, that activity of which, in the context of Ireland, Brian Friel has written so brilliantly in his play *Translations* (1981).

But it is remarkable that there are no more examples of maps on stage. Being suspicious of Dessen and Thomson's methodology I have checked the occurrences of the word 'map' and its cognates on the Literature online database for the period 1580–1620 and can find only two more occurrences that are as firmly unequivocal as these two and the two in Shakespeare. One I mention here: the anonymous play *The Puritan* was performed by the St Paul's boys company in 1606 and, since the 1607 quarto announced that it was written by 'W. S.', it found itself added to the Shakespeare canon among the apocryphal plays included in the 1664 second issue of the Third Folio. At one moment in its frenetic action, George Pyeboard tries to occupy the Serjeants who come to arrest him with maps that are clearly present onstage but Serjeant Puttock is sceptical: 'these Mappes are prittie painted things, but

I could nere fancie 'em yet, mee thinkes they're too busie and full of Circles and Conjurations, they say all the world's in one of them, but I could nere find the Counter in the Poultrie'.[5] Puttock cannot find the one place that is most significant for him, the debtors' prison where he takes those he arrests. He cannot, that is, locate his own world on the map, cannot find himself in relation to the 'Circles and Conjurations', the quasi-magical forms of representations out of which maps are constructed. Raven, the other Serjeant, isn't surprised: 'how could you finde it? For you know it stands behind the houses.' Dogson, their yeoman, elaborates this sense in which the map ought to replicate the physical reality it signifies: 'Masse, that's true, then we must looke ath' back-side fort; Sfoote here's nothing, all's bare.' Turning the map over shows only the absence of its marks. But Puttock, though he finds maps overcrowded and busy, would still prefer them to be busier with a different kind of blurring between the real and the representational: 'I should love these Maps out a crye now, if wee could see men peepe out of doore in em, oh wee might have em in a morning to our Breake-fast so finely and nere knocke our heeles to the ground a whole day for em.' If work could be accomplished within the reality of the map rather than of that to which the map alludes, life would be easier for the workers.

Those missing markings, the absence of the people to whom the human geography of mapping alludes, are gaps that Puttock regrets. Their presence is of course at the same time a dense signifier of human histories, since few maps show only or primarily a non-human landscape, the ones in Michael Drayton's *Poly-Olbion* (1612) with their emphases on rivers and other natural features and representations of what are in effect the *genii loci*, the spirits of each place, being a marked exception. But, just as throughout the early modern period the making of maps was itself an assertion of a moment of history and the charting of histories, especially histories of ownership, so in *King Lear*, the play with which I shall be primarily concerned for its mapping of a particular concept of Britain, the map in the first scene functions powerfully in relation to histories of mapping as well as histories of ownership. In a brilliant passage in his autobiography, Ingmar Bergman describes *King Lear* as itself a continent:

> We equipped expeditions which with varying skill and success mapped a few heaths, a river, a few shores, a mountain, forests. All the countries of the world equipped expeditions; sometimes we came across one another on our wanderings and established in despair that what was an inland lake yesterday had turned into a mountain today. We drew our maps, commented and described, but nothing fitted.[6]

In this vision of a metamorphic landscape, Bergman marks the impossibility of mapping. Within the play itself the landscape has a certain stability but the action's remapping still hovers at the outermost edge of the possible.

My aim is to place that mapping of Britain at the opening of *King Lear* in a set of contexts, a series of adjacencies that function for me as ways of reading the map, a way of using context as thickening of meaning that also functions as a paradigm of this map in multiple histories, an early modern one and *King Lear*'s history. I shall move on to consider the map in stage and film versions of the play and the map in connection with Elizabethan and Jacobean mapping of England. I want, though, first to try to bring a group of other dramatic or performative works into relationship with *King Lear*, to create for a moment a different kind of density of dramatic presence from that which the play is usually given, to surround the play with other images of Britain.

The first three are plays that have centrally to do with the division of Britain. I mention briefly here a fourth but will not pursue it: *Gorboduc*, a play that, for all its interest in the consequence of the division of the kingdom, seems to me not to be particularly active in London by 1606. There had been no edition of *Gorboduc* since 1590[7] and no sign of a continuing performance presence in England, though there was an important performance in the Great Hall of Dublin Castle in September 1601 before Mountjoy, the Lord Deputy of Ireland, who had perhaps chosen the play to define his position in relation to the rebellion by O'Neill, the Earl of Tyrone and the imminent arrival of an invading Spanish force in Kinsale[8]. Of my three two are tied up with that company that has such a probably crucial presence in Shakespeare's life, the Queen's Men. Since Scott McMillin and Sally-Beth MacLean's brilliant and measured study, certainly the most outstanding exploration of an early modern theatre company we yet have, the case for Shakespeare's close knowledge of the Queen's Men's repertory seems to me conclusive.[9] Whether he joined them as an actor after the death of William Knell in Thame in 1587 does not matter. What is significant is his evident connection with their repertory, including, of course, the unpronounceable *King Leir*.[10]

One other play that may have been in the Queen's Men's repertory, the first of my three contextual plays, is *Locrine*, published in 1595, without a specific link to the Queen's Men on its title-page, by Thomas Creede, who published a number of other Queen's Men's plays. Though McMillin and MacLean are typically careful in seeing no more than a possible case for its inclusion,[11] its links with *Selimus* strengthen the connection. More significant is Katherine Duncan-Jones's recent advocacy of the identity of the W.S. named on this title-page, like *The Puritan*, for *Locrine* is 'Newly set foorth, overseene and corrected' by W. S. The play's author might well have been Charles Tilney who was helped out for the dumb shows by Sir George Buc, later Master of the Revels, according to a manuscript note in Buc's hand on a copy.[12] As Duncan-Jones puts it, 'there is no good reason to doubt that [Shakespeare] was indeed the "overseer" of the text'.[13] I would not go so far but I do not find it remotely improbable that Shakespeare knew the play.

Of course the action of *Locrine* is not the *Lear* narrative but its status as a triumphantly British drama, a narrative of national success for a nation that had once existed and would not begin to exist again until after James's accession in 1603, is intriguing. There are comparatively few Elizabethan plays on *British*, rather than English, history (and not much of a rash of them after 1603): we can add to *Gorboduc*, *King Leir* and *Locrine* little else beyond the multi-authored Gray's Inn play *The Misfortunes of Arthur* (1587). *The Misfortunes of Arthur*, by the way, has a number of fascinating resonances with *King Lear* – though I should emphasise that I am not arguing for it as source, simply as a kind of dramatic context: its cast includes the Duke of Cornwall, the King of Albanie and Arthur 'King of great Brytain'[14] as well as a great battle at Dover between Arthur and Mordred who is assisted by foreign princes and British earls (compare the French forces of Cordelia with the Earl of Kent) to whom Mordred offers a division of the kingdom with one to receive 'all Brytish lands that lie / Betweene the floud of Humber and the *Scottes*', one to have 'The *Albane* Crowne' and one 'The *Cornish* Dukedome' (2.4.21–2, 33, 40). It is striking then that all four of these British history plays concern the division of the kingdom. It was, in effect, impossible to think dramatically of British history without also thinking of the mapping of division.

In the case of *Locrine* the play is an account of the first division of Britain, the turning of Brutus' united land into a divided one, a necessary and pragmatic response both to Brutus' imminent death and to the presence of the three sons, Locrine, Albanact and Camber. Brutus' is not a full-scale division of the kingdom into thirds; Locrine is to be 'a captain to thy brethren', given 'the regal Crown' while Camber is given 'the South for thy dominion' and Albanact, 'thy father's only joy, / Youngest in years, but not the youngest in mind', is told 'Take thou the North for thy dominion'.[15] Is it over-fanciful to hear in those words to Albanact some kind of pre-echo of Lear's words to Cordelia? Perhaps, but I also note that the division is, in Locrine's case, as with Lear's daughters, bound up with marriage, as Brutus arranges his son's marriage to the 'peerless Guendoline' (1.2.197). I also note at this point that there is no description offered by Brutus of the country that is being divided up, except for his comment that Albanact's northern share is 'A country full of hills and raggèd rocks, / Replenishèd with fierce untamèd beasts', a moment of chorography whose significance is less regional than individual, the country matching the individual's temperament: it is a country 'correspondent to thy martial thoughts' (1.2.208–10). These two lines are conventional and therefore reasonably similar to – though I do not want to argue an influence on – the only two lines of description in Lear's division: 'With shadowy forests and with champaigns riched, / With plenteous rivers and wide-skirted meads' (1.1.64–5).

Brutus's division is rational, a strategy for controlling the kingdom with, as it were, a president and two vice-presidents, that fails only when, after Albanact's death, Locrine falls in love with his murderer's widow. Brutus in, for example, Holinshed creates three distinct nations, effectively named after his sons: Albania (Scotland), Cambria (Wales) and Loegria (England).[16] But the author of *Locrine* denies the completeness of this separation, instead both allowing the putative ruler of England a triumphant control over the others and relocating the geography of the drawing of the line: Camber rules the south, not the west and Albanact's land is not explicitly coterminous with Scotland. The map is redrawn to accord with a hierarchical structure that early modern historiography had not anticipated. There is no hint of a critique of the division in the play – nor indeed is there in Holinshed's *Chronicles* – only of Locrine's irrational sexual desire. There is also no map.

But the second case that I want to place alongside *King Lear* is, similarly to but far more troubling than the division in *Locrine*, supremely rational. *Thomas of Woodstock*, also often known as *Richard II Part One*, is mostly familiar as a supposed source for Shakespeare's *Richard II*, narrating the events preceding Shakespeare's action. As such it seems to belong to an earlier date and an earlier period of Shakespeare's work. But recent work by Mac Jackson has produced a startlingly later redating for the play.[17] Jackson's investigation of vocabulary and of verse forms, among other characteristics, completely undermines the conventional claim for the play as coming from 1592–93. Instead Jackson's thoroughly convincing arguments place it some ten years later, in the first decade of the seventeenth century and therefore written as a deliberate prequel to Shakespeare's *Richard II* and not a source.

The division of the kingdom in *Woodstock* is a terrifying scene. Tresilian reads the conditions: the four recipients 'all jointly here stand bound to pay your majesty, or your deputy, wherever you remain, seven thousand pounds a month for this your kingdom'.[18] The legal document defines the handing over of the kingdom, its leasing out, in terms that might well have infuriated Shakespeare's Gaunt. But when the king turns to the details of the division what is most striking is the extraordinary weight of detail that it attracts. This time there is a map (another that Dessen and Thomson cannot list). Richard asks for it: 'Reach me the map' (4.1.220) – again and perhaps only driven by my major concern, I find a possible pre-echo of *King Lear* ('Give me the map there, F 1.1.37), though how many ways are there for a king to demand a map? He then moves on to the division: 'we may allot their portions and part the realm amongst them equally. / You four shall here by us divide yourselves into the nine-and-thirty shires and counties of my kingdom parted thus: – / (Come stand by me and mark those shires assigned ye)' (4.1.220–5). But as the five crowd round the map with four eagerly watching what they will receive, Richard does not simply mark lines and speak of them; instead he lists the thirty-nine shires and counties he is handing over. 'Bagot, thy lot betwixt the Thames and sea thus lies: Kent, Surrey, Sussex, Hampshire, Berkshire, Wiltshire, Dorsetshire, Somersetshire, Devonshire, Cornwall, those parts are thine / As amply, Bagot, as the Crown is mine' (226–30). Bushy receives Wales 'together with our counties of Gloster, Wo'ster, Hereford, Shropshire, Staffordshire and Cheshire: there's thy lot' (234–5); Scroope's land goes 'From Trent to Tweed' and includes 'All Yorkshire, Derbyshire, Lancashire, Cumberland, Westmoreland and Northumberland' (238–40). Mockingly, Richard turns last to Greene, by this point looking a little peeved, 'Now my Greene, what have I left for thee?' (242)

> I kept thee last to make thy part the greatest.
> See here sweet Greene: –
> Those shires are thine, even from the Thames to Trent:
> Thou here shalt lie, I' the middle of my land.

This erotics of this division is then completed by Greene's list, an extraordinary detailing of the remaining sixteen shires in one single run: 'Thou hast London, Middlesex, / Essex, Suffolk, Norfolk, Cambridgeshire, / Hertfordshire, Bedfordshire, Buckinghamshire, / Oxfordshire, Northamptonshire, / Rutlandshire, Leicestershire, Warwickshire, Huntingdonshire; / And Lincolnshire – there's your portion sir' (252–7).

In a fine article, 'The Scene of Cartography in *King Lear*', an article that has provoked a great deal of my thinking in this chapter, John Gillies has rightly commented on the parallels here between Greene and Cordelia, both placed structurally last, both especially favoured (Greene alone is identified as Richard's 'minion'), each given the richest piece of land.[19] But I am less happy with Gillies's assumption that the map must be a hand-prop simply because of 'the sheer exhaustiveness of the geographical detail in the dialogue' (113). Gillies finds something excessive about the passage where I find it powerful as a litany of space, a counting of the shires, an indexing of Richard's England that will be fully Richard's no more.

Shakespeare, if he did indeed know *Thomas of Woodstock*, must have seen it only a few years before writing *King Lear* (or seen a manuscript like the only version that survives). Its method of creating the account – or more properly the accounting – of the nation is a conscious and inimitable creation of the kinds of chorographical sequence that marked Elizabethan cartography and chorography. These projects can be seen first in Christopher Saxton's maps, engraved between 1574 and 1579 and brought together into a single volume atlas in 1579, 'the earliest uniform national atlas produced by any country',[20] and a twenty-sheet wall map in 1583; secondly in Camden's *Britannia*, first published in Latin in 1586 (going through six editions by 1607) and published in English in 1610 in Philemon Holland's translation, the 1607 Latin and 1610 English edition carrying maps based on Saxton and John Norden, drawn by William Kip, the inclusion of which Camden has planned as early as 1589;[21] thirdly, the two parts of *Speculum Britanniae* covering Middlesex and Hertfordshire, the only completed segments of John Norden's project to be published, in 1593 and 1598 respectively, containing maps and extensive accompanying listings; and finally, a few years later, in John Speed's superb 1611 volume *The Theatre of the Empire of Great Britaine*. All are part of the growing mass of Jacobean chorography. Camden's *Britannia* was first published in Latin in 1586 with the subtitle identifying it as *chorographica descriptio* while Holland's 1610 translation as *Britain, or A chorographicall description of the most flourishing kingdomes, England, Scotland and Ireland and the ilands adioyning, out of the depth of antiquitie*, brings the regionalism to the fore. These projects – Saxton, Camden, Norden and Speed – provide the chorological context for *King Lear* and I shall return to them later.

Shakespeare would rightly and inevitably chose a radically different method from *Thomas of Woodstock* in *King Lear*, a massive refusal of such detailing. In *1 Henry IV*, the lines are clear if not on the stage then at least to anyone with a rudimentary knowledge of English geography:

> The Archdeacon hath divided it
> Into three limits very equally.
> England from Trent and Severn hitherto
> By south and east is to my part assigned;
> All westward – Wales beyond the Severn shore
> And all the fertile land within that bound –
> To Owain Glyndwr; and, dear coz, to you
> The remnant lying northward lying off from Trent.

(3.1.69–76)

It has a precision mid-way between the deliberate exhaustiveness of the scene in *Thomas of Woodstock* and the equally deliberate imprecision of *King Lear*, 'Of all these bounds even from this line to this . . . this ample third . . . A third more opulent' (1.1.63, 80, 86). *Thomas of Woodstock*, as a development of Shakespeare's method in *1 Henry IV*, marked the limit of that approach. In moving from a known England with its counties which had been the subject of such exhaustive, popular and prestigious study as in Camden's and others' work to a Britain that belonged to ahistorical past connected with but discontinuous from the present growing political reality of Great Britain – something that, for instance, would constitute Elizabethan cartographers' representations of particular kinds of national and local histories in their maps – Shakespeare shapes a vagueness that would pose its especial problems to directors having to show this map.

My third play in this group is, of course, *The True Chronicle History of King Leir and His Three Daughters*, first published in 1605. In a recent scholarly study, Richard Knowles has persuasively argued that the detailed evidence for Shakespeare's use of this source play shows that he was using the edition of 1605 and that there is no conclusive evidence for its influence on his earlier work derived from whatever contact he may have had with it in the Queen's Men's repertory. Shakespeare's choice to organise the opening of his play in marked contrast to *King Leir* had been prompted by reading an old play newly published.[22] It is worth remembering the action of the opening sequence in the play. It begins with the funeral of Lear's queen, that figure so typically suppressed in Shakespeare's version of the narrative. None of the daughters is married. Leir is thoughtfully and wisely advised by his sensible counsellors to marry his daughters to 'some of your neighbour Kings, / Bordring within the bounds of Albion, / By whose united friendship, this our State / May be protected 'gainst all forrayne hate',[23] a sense of the potential unity of the geographical unit of the island, Albion, set against the foreign threat of continental Europe. The love-test here is explicitly a stratagem, explained by Leir to his counsellors, to ensure that pressure can be put on Cordella, who, annoyingly, 'vowes / No liking to a Monarch, unless love allowes' even though 'She is solicited by divers Peeres' (61–3); the love-test will make her agree to be matched 'with a King of Brittany' (91), the word used here not to indicate a part of France but as a form of Britain that will rhyme with 'policy'. Gonorill will marry the *King* of Cornwall, Ragan the *King* of Cambria – and I note, incidentally, that the status of the suitors is, as the noble advised, of equal rank with Leir himself. Cordella's intended husband is the King of Hibernia, the Irish King, not self-evidently a monarch within the island but clearly conceived of as being within a concept of Albion as Britain. Significantly there is no sign of Scotland in the play. Given the westward bias of the two husbands of the elder sisters, it is significant too that the division is not predetermined; as Leir announces,

> My Kingdome I do equally devide.
> Princes, draw lots and take your chaunce as falles.
>
> > *Then they draw lots.*
>
> These I resigne as freely unto you,
> As earst by true succession they were mine.
> And here I do freely dispossesse my selfe,
> And make you two my true adopted heyres:
> My selfe will sojorne with my sonne of Cornwall,

[Confusingly in view of Shakespeare's play, this means he will be staying
   with Gonorill.]
And take me to my prayers and my beades.
I know, my daughter *Ragan* will be sorry,
Because I do not spend my dayes with her:
Would I were able to be with both at once;
They are the kindest Gyrles in Christendome.

(549–60)

Cornwall and Cambria had anticipated getting equal shares, halves, in a conversation earlier, each getting 'The moity of halfe his Regiment' (441), with
the same ambiguity about whether a moiety is a half which Shakespeare so
cunningly pursues in the opening lines of his play 'neither can make choice
of either's moiety' (1.1.6). The arbitrary nature of the division here and the
movement of the action eventually towards France mean that the division
can stay unmapped, unlocated, dis-placed.

   Cumulatively, the texts I have been looking at figure the dramatic possibilities of a divided Britain as Elizabethan dramatists, including Shakespeare
himself, had explored the topos by the time *King Lear* was being written.
But the second group of works I want to place briefly beside *King Lear* is a
new and particular kind of outcropping of British performance after 1603
within the context of a newly emerging Jacobean Britain. Britain itself – or
more properly, given the particular forms of representation, herself –
appeared in Dekker's *The Magnificent Entertainment*, the performances at
James's coronation procession through London on 15 March 1604. At the
first of the seven gates of the spectacle, set up at Fenchurch, the design, not
by Dekker but by Ben Jonson, showed at the top a figure Dekker called
simply '*The Brittayne Monarchy*'[24] but which Jonson describes more fully.
The theme of the first gate was London itself and was dominated by
'Monarchia Britannica' because London was '*camera regia*', the king's
chamber. Jonson quotes Camden's *Britannia* here: London is 'the epitome of
the whole of Britain, the seat of the British Empire and of the kingdoms'.[25]
Britain, 'a woman, richly attyr'd', with the two crowns of England and
Scotland above her throne and with 'her hayre' symbolically 'bound into
foure severall points, descending from her crownes', becomes visible here, a
Britain not yet Great but one whose position is unequivocal.

   Something similar in making Britain present in spectacle was the major
part of the pageant for the new Lord Mayor written by Anthony Munday
and put on by the Merchant-Taylors Company on 29 October 1605, *The
Triumphes of Re-United Britannia*. If, as is of course quite possibly the case,
Shakespeare had never come across the play *Locrine*, let alone rewritten it,
he could have seen the events of that division of the kingdom dramatised in
Munday's pageant where Britannia, 'a fayre and beautifull Nymph', tells

Brutus that 'his conquest of her virgine honour . . . she reckons to be the very best of her fortunes.'[26] The children who perform the pageant narrate the history in the characters of Brutus, the three kingdoms he created, his three sons, Troia Nova (London, the city founded by Brutus) and the three great rivers, Thames, Severn and Humber, the last two being, as Munday's preface identifies, the initial boundaries between the three kingdoms, before 'the limits of Loegria were enlarged' and the Tweed and the Solway became 'the principal boundes betweene us and *Scotland*'.[27]

The links and parallels, stopping far short of influence, between *King Lear* and Munday's pageant were well explored by Richard Dutton in an article in 1986.[28] Dutton points to the allusive nature of Munday's pageant, its assumptions of spectator knowledge of the early history of Britain and, in particular, to the leap of Gogmagog, a member of the indigenous population of 'uncivill, monstrous huge men of stature, tearmed Giants'; Gogmagog was thrown off a cliff by Brutus's counsellor Corineus, the father of Guendoline in *Locrine*, a leap 'at a place beside *Dover*' as a result of which '*Brute* gave unto *Corineus* a part of his lande, which according to his name, was and yet is unto this day, called *Cornwall*'.[29] The complex etymologies of place, like the naming of Britain itself on which Camden and others spend so much space, here link across the different narratives that lie behind *King Lear*: Cornwall, Corineus and a fall from a cliff near Dover.

For Dutton the significance of Dover lies not only in its presence in the Gloucester narrative but also in its placing as 'one of the three supposed "corners" of Britain',[30] a space alluded to by Munday's placing his figures on 'a Mount triangular, as the Island of *Britayne* it selfe is described to bee',[31] and which in Holinshed and Camden (and many others) are located at the tip of Cornwall, at Dover and at Caithness in Scotland. As Dutton notes, 'Shakespeare had invoked all three 'corners' of that triangle in his play, in the names of the characters', since he includes both Cornwall and Albany, from Holinshed, but, Dutton goes on,

> it was Shakespeare's own decision to make Lear's staunchest advisor the Earl of Kent and to concentrate so much of the action . . . near Dover. His is the only version of the Lear story to project the action so clearly against the tradi- tional symbol of the three-cornered island.[32]

Though Dutton does not discuss it, the three-cornered island will be divided into three in *King Lear*, which was performed before the person who is the true focus of Munday's pageant, James.[33] I do not want to consider the much-examined significance of the Boxing Day performance of *King Lear* before King James,[34] except to emphasise the possible presence there of two of the three dukes James had created, the only three dukes in Britain, the Dukes of Cornwall and Albany. As Andrew Gurr has recently reminded us, there were no dukes in England after Elizabeth had executed the Duke of Norfolk in 1571. The most senior rank was earl. But James had made Prince Henry Duke of Cornwall in 1605 and Henry's younger brother had been Duke of Albany since 1601, a fact which, as Gurr suggests, must have 'prompt[ed] a *frisson* at the very outset of the performance':[35] 'I had thought the King had more affected the Duke of Albany than Cornwall' (1.1.1–2).

This balance of king and dukes, strikingly unlike the status of the equivalent characters in *King Leir*, seems to me to matter. More than anyone has noted, *King Lear* is a play concerned about the status relationship of king to dukes, a relationship in part mirrored by the relationship of the *King* of France and the *Duke* of Burgundy, a figure whose historic equivalents were in continual conflict with the Kings of France, until Burgundy was annexed on the death of Charles the Bold in 1477, conflicts which were intensified not least by problems over marriages, as the rulers of Burgundy fought to maintain the independence of their territory which extended north across the Netherlands, making it as geographically proximate to Cordelia's share as France was.

The moment of this performance, as the title-page of the quarto stated, on 'S. Stephans *night*',[36] that is, 26 December 1606, is the culmination of the play's accumulation of its own histories but its subsequent histories rethink its mappings. From the contexts of division and the early modern mapping of Britain, I want to turn to the play's performance histories, to see how the map has figured in particular productions. I suggested earlier that the map poses a problem for directors. I want to note four of their solutions, examining them for their mapping of the symbolic geography of each production's views of the play's politics.[37] In Michael Elliott's television version (1983), with Olivier as Lear, a massive map, backed by hides, is unrolled across the floor of the space in front of the king. Little in the theatre is ever new: Jackie Bratton notes the same thing being done in 1923 in a production in Florence.[38] Before speaking, Goneril responds to a gesture from Lear and throws herself prostrate on the map, kissing it, saluting, as it were, the sign of nation. Regan, later, kneels before her father and, just as she is about to kiss his hand, kisses the map first, with a smile shared with her father, displaying herself as a daughter who has learned from her sister's example. This repeated emphasis on the map's potency makes it a symbol in some respects stronger than the Crown itself: when this Lear confirms the redivision in two, 'This coronet' (1.1.139)[39] is his own Crown, not Cordelia's and he throws it on to the map where it rolls across it with no respect for the boundaries Lear has drawn. But it is the drawing of the boundaries themselves that intrigues for, by the use of an overhead shot, Elliott makes clear who gets what: Olivier's sword marks the north for Goneril and the west for Regan, leaving for Cordelia a vast tract of England, even bigger than Greene's share in *Thomas of Woodstock*.

Unlike the very visible map in this version, the map in Peter Brook's 1971 film is only slowly revealed, a section uncovered as Goneril is given her share and then a third more when Regan has spoken. The map is not here a two-dimensional representation but a relief model that physicalises the presence of the kingdom as landscape, moving from symbolic geography to something much more representational, as if the hills and rivers that had been seen on Christopher Saxton's Tudor maps have taken on a three-dimensional form more adequately to show the share of which 'With shadowy forests and with champaigns riched, / With plenteous rivers and wide-skirted meads, / We make thee lady' (1.1.64–6). The division has been made with strings and pins, the three shares of this pie-chart coming from a geographic centre, that imaginary mid-point of Britain (though, unlike Elliott's emphatic representation of the islands, nothing about Brook's map clearly shows that it is Britain that is being divided). Lear re-marks the division after the rejection of Cordelia, uprooting two pins and bisecting Cordelia's share, leaving the strings dangling over the relief's edge, the wedge that Cordelia's third had driven on one side of the land between the moieties of Cornwall and Albany now removed.

That the play is anxious about the potential rivalry between Albany and Cornwall is clear: Curan asks Edmond, 'Have you heard of no likely wars towards twixt the Dukes of Cornwall and Albany?' (2.1.10–11) and Kent tells the Gentleman of the 'division, / Although as yet the face of it is covered / With mutual cunning, 'twixt Albany and Cornwall' (3.1.10–12). In Adrian Noble's Royal Shakespeare Company production in 1994, the map, on paper, spread across the entire stage-floor, later being ripped apart as the production continued, so that the events were played out across the divided kingdom, just as Kenneth Branagh's Renaissance Theatre Company's production in 1990 had been played across a stage-floor covered with red rubber fragments, initially arranged within a template of the outline of Britain (and through which Lear's stick could mark division) but scattered across the stage as the actors moved through it in the course of the rest of the play. But when Noble's Fool, gagged, drew the lines of the shares across the stage-floor with a paintbrush, it became clear (especially if one was not seated in the stalls) that the division had a political aim, deliberately making Cordelia's share the one that prevented any contact at all between Albany and Cornwall, a means of separation of the dangerous elements. The use by Anthony Ward, Noble's designer, of the stage-floor map may owe something to Branagh's production but it may also have been influenced by Chris Dyer's set for Cicely Berry's brilliant production at The Other Place in 1988, one of the finest, least-known and certainly least-studied recent productions of *King Lear*. Dyer created a stone floor which was also a map of Britain but which, at the start of the storm, had two wedges removed so that it fell apart to leave jagged, awkward boulders across which the rest of the action was played, making the break-up on the kingdom brilliantly manifest.

The final example I want to add to this array is Grigori Kozintsev's film (1970). Where Gielgud at the Old Vic in 1940 had snatched the map from his chamberlain, crumpled it and hurled it to the ground,[40] Yuri Yarvets's anger is even more extreme. This Lear's rage is vented on the map which he pulls up, twists and turns, starts to tear, throws, kicks and otherwise man-handles. As the map starts to be destroyed the effect of the rage on the kingdom is anticipated (as it will be soon when the peasants outside pros-trate themselves at the sight of the king on the battlements, unable to hear his invective against Cordelia). But Kent, often in productions associated with the map from the start (as at the Old Vic in 1946[41] or in Jonathan Miller's 1982 BBC Shakespeare version), here kneels to plead for Cordelia but first straightening the distorted map at his feet, trying, as it were, to repair the tear in the kingdom that the rejection of Cordelia has created.

There are other possibilities and Marvin Rosenberg records some of them: Reinhardt's Lear whose throne had a dome above it with a painted map on it; Orson Welles who marked 'divisions on a map large enough for a man to walk through – and when he was angered, he walked through it'.[42] The map, if visible, need not represent Britain at all: a Shakespeare Performance group at UCLA used a map of California, an image that, I was told by a student,

> worked because California really is a three-part state, southern with the 'L.A.' lifestyle, central with a large agricultural-based culture and large stretches of rural land and the northern Californian/San Franciscans, with their own dis-tinct lifestyles, who swear that they would love to dissassociate themselves from L.A.[43]

A Hungarian production in 1993, directed by János Ács in the Új Színház (New Theatre) in Budapest, showed Lear playing with a heap of real soil on a table, drawing different shapes, forms and patterns, though the audience could not really see what those patterns were, making the materiality of the land of Britain brilliantly apparent.[44]

The map as sign of the kingdom functions as a chorography of Britain; it is the King of Britain who disunites the kingdom. The productions, in dif-ferent ways, explore the symbolic potency of the event. But the nature of the map itself still perplexes me. Brecht recurrently saw the map as the central prop, the crucial part of the scene's *gestus*. In *The Messingkauf Dialogues*, the Dramaturg's concern to 'show the feudal conditions' is taken up by the Actor:

> In that case you might as well take his division of his kingdom seriously and have an actual map torn up in the first scene. Lear could hand the pieces to his daughters . . . He could take the third piece, the one meant for Cordelia and

tear that across once again to distribute to the others. That would be a particularly good way of making the audience stop and think.[45]

In the 'Short Description of a New Technique of Acting' Brecht again saw the tearing of the map as a means of making

> the act of division . . . alienated. Not only does it draw our attention to his kingdom, but by treating the kingdom so plainly as his own private property he throws some light on the basis of the feudal idea of the family.[46]

But Brecht's most acute perception of all links the map differently, connecting to the audience and to the nature of the emotional charge that the performance without A-effects (i.e. Brecht's alienation effects) created:

> The spectators at the Globe theatre, who three centuries ago saw King Lear give away his kingdom, pitied honest Cordelia, who didn't get one of the pieces, not the thousands of people who were thus given away.[47]

It is with the relationship of the map to the people that I want to close.

As John Gillies has noted, the images created by Lear's limited description of Goneril's share are 'entirely consistent with the rich pictorial ornamentation of Saxton's maps of England'.[48] Saxton's mappings, the results of Thomas Seckford's aim of a national survey, show hills and rivers and the names of towns but the human spaces are distributed disconnectedly across the landscape. Copies of the maps owned by Lord Burghley list in their margins the names of leading families and where they lived; the map of Northamptonshire includes the names of justices. But Burghley is making up for Saxton's lack of such information. Human geography in Saxton's representational world shows communities, the natural traces of aristocratic ownership (he shows the parks but not the country houses to which they belonged), occasional bridges, a few mineral deposits and a very few antiquities.

When John Norden created the fragments of his chorography, *Speculum Britanniae*, (only two volumes were published by 1598), even though his format was half the size of Saxton's, he recorded more villages and parks (i.e. spaces of privately owned land), added many roads to Saxton's landscape so that the towns and villages become connected across the landscape, as well as marking some battlefield sites, the divisions of hundreds within the county (the next level down of administrative unit, rarely marked by Saxton) and, on some, a plan of the county town as an inset. He differentiated 'houses of the Queen's' from 'houses of nobility', noted chapels-of-ease – he was the only cartographer to mark this ecclesiastical category – and, for Cornwall, to indicate the mineral deposits that his text urged King James to exploit.[49] Norden's maps appear within a context of substantial documentation listing roads and gentry, churches, battles and beacons, the material evidence of human presences and human history. He also provided a grid system to enable readers to locate names on the map that were referred to in his chorographical descriptions, 'without which helpe a place unknown would be long to find in the Mappe',[50] something of which Norden was so proud that he included mention of it on the title-page of the first volume, 'wth direction spedelie to finde anie place desired in the mappe', a sign of the map's engagement with human use, the act of searching and locating.[51]

Norden's movement to the recording of human geography, or in effect making the chorography a reflection of a human landscape, accelerated with John Speed's *Theatre of the Empire of Great Britaine* in 1611. Speed's maps place much more as insets and marginalia: coats of arms of leading local families of the county, lengthy historical and topographical notes, much more elaborate town plans (over seventy in all), even views of antiquities (Stonehenge on the Wiltshire map, Verulamium on the one for Hertfordshire, inscriptions on Roman monuments for Northumberland), a feature that stretches the human history the map records. The geography of Speed's chorography is dominated by human history: an illustration of the battle of Ludlow on the map of Herefordshire with the three suns joined in the sky, the battle of Bosworth featured on Leicestershire with an account of what happened to Richard's corpse afterwards. As Michael Neill suggests, 'Speed discovers in the land itself a kind of historical "plot" whose story can be deciphered in all those visible characters of the past – the memorials or "monuments" . . . that antiquaries like John Weever were busy recording and preserving.'[52] The maps also include plenty of material on the back, including lists of hundreds and historical data, not quite what Serjeant Raven and yeoman Dogson in *The Puritan* wanted but still important. By 1618, in Barten Holyday's *Technogamia*, written for and performed at Christchurch, Oxford, a character can complain that the priorities of cartographers were wrong and superficial:

> 'tis a maine fault of your common Geographers, that now-a-dayes doe rather garnish the margine of a Map, then materially describe it; and onely draw a companie of lines through it; as if they had rid ouer the Countrie to take notice onely of the high-wayes; which yet a Carriers Horse knowes better then they.[53]

Against this mapping of the human world in maps, the landscape of Lear's world, the space of the map and the space that the map represents, is pretty much unpeopled. As Francis Barker eloquently stated,

> If the land is a place of fulsomeness and abundance, it is at the same moment one of ideal emptiness, a depopulated landscape. No one lives or works in the countryside of Lear's map.[54]

It is as empty as the map that so disappointed Serjeant Puttock, a world where we cannot 'see men peepe out of doore in' it. It is also a mapped world in which, again like Puttock, one cannot find one's own place and a world which, like the *mappae mundi* with their T-in-O form, represent the world as three regions, not Europe, Asia and Africa but now Cornwall, Albany and an England that had been intended for the Queen of France. It is a world traversed and travelled in the shifting instabilities that mark out the play's progress from the known and central to the dangerously marginal.

But the regions into which this country is now divided refuse in *King Lear* to maintain their boundaries, to keep to their space. Lear's remapped world is one of disturbing and disoriented fluidity of place. The names people carry (Kent, Gloucester, Albany, Cornwall) mean that the places they embody are relocated into what we might hear as the wrong place: Cornwall and Albany are in Gloucester, but Gloucester is probably not in Gloucester anyway, Gloucester and Kent go to Dover. As Flahiff suggests, '[t]here is a kind of mad pliancy about geographical reference in *King Lear*'.[55]

In this wilderness of wandering beggars and kings, an unstable geography of the placed and the displaced, there is little space for what Brecht called 'the thousands of people who were thus given away'. But if the map of 1.1 is visible there may be one such space of note. Maps encourage us to locate ourselves. As I look at the weather map on American television, I usually locate South Bend, not New York or Chicago, in England I look for Cambridge, not Bristol or London. At a performance of *King Lear* at the Globe or at the King's palace at Whitehall, a visible map will encourage the audience to find London, to find the place of performance. What happens when England is redivided, when the map of Lear's Britain is divided in two, not three, when the 'third more opulent than your sisters' (1.1.86), the tract of the country nearest to both France and Burgundy, the heart of England, the space of the *cor* in Latin that begins *Cordelia*,[56] that expanse which must include London itself, is split apart? Perhaps the new division runs straight through the capital, bisecting the city itself so that, as one crossed back from the Globe to the city after a performance of *King Lear*, one might be moving from Cornwall's territory to Albany's, passing through a border control in the middle of London Bridge. The population of London had been 'given away' by James's accession. The map had changed. The people's history had been rewritten in the new geography of the King of Great Britain, the king who now did rule 'this sceptred isle'[57] as neither Richard II nor Elizabeth I could ever have done, making true Shakespeare's geographical blunder. But while Speed's maps were a literal celebration of the new king's world, it may be that it is *King Lear* that should most properly have been called *The Theatre of the Empire of Great Britaine*.

Notes

1 All quotations from Shakespeare are from *The Complete Works*, eds Stanley Wells, Gary Taylor *et al.* (Oxford: The Clarendon Press, 1986).

2 On the rise of chorography see Richard Helgerson, *Forms of Nationhood The Elizabethan Writing of England* (Chicago: University of Chicago Press, 1992), esp. 105–47. For its application to the study of Shakespeare's English histories, though not his British ones, see especially Michael Neill, ' "The Exact Map or Discovery of Human Affairs": Shakespeare and the Plotting of History', in *Putting History to the Question* (New York: Columbia University Press, 2000), 372–97, and Phyllis Rackin, *Stages of History* (London: Routledge, 1990), especially her now well-known comment that '[t]he movement from *Richard II* to *Henry V* resembles the movement in Renaissance historiography from chronicle to chorography, from the history of royal dynasty to the maps and geographical descriptions that assembled a picture of national identity from the component parts of the land' (137). On mapping and Shakespeare see also especially John Gillies, *Shakespeare and the Geography of Difference* (Cambridge: Cambridge University Press, 1994); Bruce Avery, 'Gelded Continents and Plenteous Rivers: Cartography as Rhetoric in Shakespeare', in John Gillies and Virginia Mason Vaughan (eds) *Playing the Globe: Genre and Geography in English Renaissance Drama* (Madison: Fairleigh Dickinson Press, 1998), 46–62; Garrett A. Sullivan, Jr, *The Drama of Landscape* (Stanford: Stanford University Press, 1998), 92–158. See also Jess Edwards, 'How to Read an Early Modern Map: Between the Particular and the General, the Material and the Abstract, Words and Mathematics', *Early Modern Literary Studies*, 91 (May 2003): 6.1–58, http://purl.oclc.org/emls/09-1/edwamaps.html.

3 Thomas Middleton, *Anything for a Quiet Life* (1662), sig. F1r.

4 Christopher Marlowe, *The Complete Works*, vol. 5, eds David Fuller and Edward J. Esche (Oxford: Clarendon Press, 1998), 5.3.127 and 151.

5 *The Puritan* (1607), sig. E4r.

6 See Ingmar Bergman, *The Magic Lantern* (London: Penguin Books, 1988), pp. 258–9. My thanks to Russell Jackson for pointing out this passage.

7 In 1590 it appeared as an addition to Lydgate's *The Serpent of Devision* (STC 17029).

8 See Christopher Morash, *A History of Irish Theatre, 1601–2000* (Cambridge: Cambridge University Press, 2001), 2–3. My thanks to Kevin de Ornellas for pointing out this reference.

9 Scott McMillin and Sally-Beth MacLean, *The Queen's Men and their Plays* (Cambridge: Cambridge University Press, 1998).

10 The problem is, of course, to differentiate *Leir* from *Lear*, something no speaker seems able to do.

11 *Ibid.* 92.

12 Sir W. W. Greg, 'Three Manuscript Notes by Sir George Buc', *The Library* 4th ser., 12 (1932), 307–21.

13 Katherine Duncan-Jones, *Ungentle Shakespeare* (London: The Arden Shakespeare, 2001), 42.

14 Brian Jay Corrigan (ed.) *The Misfortunes of Arthur: A Critical, Old-Spelling Edition* (New York: Garland Publishing, Inc., 1992), 73.
15 *The Lamentable Tragedy of Locrine: A Critical Edition*, ed. Jane Lytton Gooch (New York: Garland Publishing, Inc., 1981), 1.2.150,189, 200, 204–7.
16 See *Holinshed's Chronicles of England, Scotland and Ireland*, 6 vols (London, 1807), 1, 443–4.
17 See Macd. P. Jackson, 'Shakespeare's *Richard II* and the Anonymous *Thomas of Woodstock*', *Medieval and Renaissance Drama in England* 14 (2002), 17–65.
18 A. P. Rossiter (ed.) *Woodstock: A Moral History* (London: Chatto and Windus, 1946), 4.1.182–4.
19 See John Gillies, 'The Scene of Cartography in *King Lear*', in Andrew Gordon and Bernhard Klein (eds) *Literature, Mapping and the Politics of Space in Early Modern Britain* (Cambridge: Cambridge University Press, 2001), 109–37, esp. pp. 120–1. Klein has some brief comments on the play in Bernhard Klein, *Maps and the Writing of Space in Early Modern England and Ireland* (Basingstoke: Palgrave, 2001).
20 John Goss, *The Mapmaker's Art* (Skokie, Ill.: Rand McNally, 1993), 161. On Saxton see especially Sarah Tyacke and John Huddy, *Christopher Saxton and Tudor Map-making* (London: The British Library, 1980). For other work on Tudor maps see also Sarah Tyacke (ed.) *English Map-making 1500–1650* (London: The British Library, 1983); P. D. A. Harvey, *Maps in Tudor England* (London: The Public Record Office and The British Library, 1993); and, for a longer vista, Catherine Delano-Smith and Roger J. P. Kain, *English Maps: A History* (London: The British Library, 1999).
21 See R. A. Skelton, *County Atlases of the British Isles 1579–1850: A Bibliography* (Folkestone: Wm Dawson and Sons, 1978), 26.
22 See Richard Knowles, 'How Shakespeare Knew *King Leir*', *Shakespeare Survey* 55 (Cambridge: Cambridge University Press, 2002), 12–35.
23 *The History of King Leir 1605*, ed. W. W. Greg (Oxford: Oxford University Press for the Malone Society, 1907), ll. 52–6.
24 Thomas Dekker, *The Dramatic Works*, ed. Fredson Bowers, 4 vols (Cambridge: Cambridge University Press, 1953–61), 2.260.
25 Ben Jonson, *Works*, ed. C. H. Herford and P. and E. Simpson, 11 vols (Oxford: The Clarendon Press, 1925–52), 7.84 (my translation).
26 David M. Bergeron (ed.) *Pageants and Entertainments of Anthony Munday: A Critical Edition* (New York: Garland Publishing, Inc., 1985), 6.
27 *Ibid.*, 4.
28 Richard Dutton, '*King Lear, The Triumphs of Reunited Britannia* and "The Matter of Britain"', *Literature and History*, 12 (1986), 139–51.
29 Bergeron, *Pageants*, 4.
30 Dutton, *King Lear*, 142.
31 Bergeron, *Pageants*, 4.
32 Dutton, *King Lear*, 143.
33 Marie Axton suggests that James was present at Munday's pageant but there is no evidence that he was; see *The Queen's Two Bodies* (London: Royal Historical Society, 1977), 136.

34 See, for instance, Leah Marcus, *Local Reading and its Discontents* (Berkeley: University of California Press, 1988), 148–59.

35 Andrew Gurr, 'Headgear as a Paralinguistic Signifier in *King Lear*', *Shakespeare Survey 55* (Cambridge: Cambridge University Press, 2002), 43–52, p. 45.

36 Title-page of Q 1608.

37 Kenneth Rothwell also considers them in his rather disappointing article, 'In Search of Nothing: Mapping *King Lear*', in Lynda E. Boose and Richard Burt (eds) *Shakespeare the Movie* (London: Routledge, 1997), 135–47.

38 J. S. Bratton (ed.) *King Lear: Plays in Performance* (Bristol: Bristol Classical Press, 1987), 65.

39 The Oxford edition reads 'crownet' but, since Olivier says 'coronet', I have retained his form.

40 See Terence Hawkes, 'Lear's Maps', in *Meaning by Shakespeare* (London: Routledge, 1992), 130–1.

41 Bratton, *King Lear,* 59.

42 Marvin Rosenberg, *The Masks of King Lear* (Berkeley: University of California Press, 1972), 53.

43 E-mail information from Brian Willis, to whom my thanks.

44 E-mail information from Géza Kállay, to whom my thanks.

45 Bertolt Brecht, *The Messingkauf Dialogues* (London: Eyre Methuen, 1965), 63.

46 Bertolt Brecht, *Brecht on Theatre*, ed. John Willett (London: Methuen, 1964), 143.

47 Quoted by Margot Heinemann, 'How Brecht Read Shakespeare', in Jonathan Dollimore and Alan Sinfield (eds) *Political Shakespeare* (Manchester: Manchester University Press, 1985), 202–30 (p. 216).

48 Gillies, *Shakespeare and the Geography of Difference*, 46.

49 See Delano-Smith and Kain, *English Maps: A History*, 73–4.

50 John Norden, *Speculi Britan[n]iae Pars* (1598), sig. ¶3a. See also his discussion of the details of his chorographical method in John Norden, *Nordens Preparatiue to his Speculum Britanniæ* (1596).

51 John Norden, *Speculum Britanniae* (1593), title-page.

52 Neill, ' "The Exact Map', 383.

53 Barten Holyday, *Technogamia* (Oxford, 1619), sig. I2r.

54 Francis Barker, *The Culture of Violence* (Manchester: Manchester University Press, 1993), 3–4.

55 F. T. Flahiff, 'Lear's Map', *Cahiers Elisabéthains*, 30 (1986), 17–33, p. 19.

56 See Gillies, 'The Scene of Cartography', 121.

57 *Richard II*, 2.1.40.

Afterword   *Graham Holderness*

Mots d'escalier: Clio, Eurydice, Orpheus

> The painting was like none of his others. It was just of me, of my head and
> shoulders, with no tables or curtains, no windows or powderbrushes to soften
> and distract. He had painted me with my eyes wide, the light falling across my
> face but the left side of me in shadow . . . the background was black, making
> me appear very much alone, although I was clearly looking at someone. I
> seemed to be waiting for something I did not think would ever happen.
>
> (Chevalier, *Girl*, 202–3)[1]

One of the tutelary spirits of *Shakespeare's Histories and Counter-histories*
is Clio, muse of history, daughter of Zeus and Mnemosyne: begotten by
power and wisdom upon memory.

Crowned with a conqueror's laurel-wreaths (her name means 'glory'),
Clio's attributes of book and trumpet delineated her functions of record and
proclamation. In one hand the book, document and archive, repository of
the past's disappearing traces; in the other the trumpet, annunciation and
performance, representation of the past in narrative and discourse. With the
volume of documentation and the instrument of fame, Clio acted as custodian of the past and in 'grand / And louder tone'[2] sang its stories to the
present and to the future.

But as Stuart Hampton-Reeves has shown in his 'Staring at Clio'
(Chapter 1 above), Clio was an ambivalent figure even in the sixteenth and
seventeenth centuries, when the historical plays that form the subject of this
volume were first written and performed. Clio was still what she had been
to the ancients, *magistra vitae*, 'The Mistresse of mans life, grave Historie'.[3]
She was the author of history's grand narrative. She not only kept the record
but set the record straight, duly apportioning praise and blame and thereby
ensuring permanent survival for the worthiest and most notable of human
actions and achievements. By distributing 'good, or evill Fame' and sustaining reputation, she was able to 'vindicate' the world's memory 'to
Eternitie'.

But Clio could also be seen as a tragic or elegiac figure, celebrating an aggrandised past and lamenting a diminished present. Clio can appear less of a proclaimer and more of a mourner, reviving the past only to lament and regret its passing: to embalm its pitiful remains and weep inconsolably over the body of entombed majesty. In his *Teares of the Muses*[4] Spenser imagined Clio's destiny foundering on the mundane rocks of the everyday, as the present fails to emulate the past, revealing no capability of ever becoming historical. Clio's page is blank, her trumpet dumb: 'I nothing noble have to sing.' With this prescient anticipation of what we have come to know as 'the end of history', Spenser approaches that point of realisation where a classical muse in antique costume must have begun to seem increasingly irrelevant to the incipient experience of modernity. Much later Clio was to evolve into a wholly demystified figure, the 'poor old woman, devoid of eternity' who for Charles Péguy summed up the modern age's disenchantment with history.[5]

Other early modern writers on history shared this haunting fear of historical oblivion. If history is a celebration of the deeds of great men, what about the rest of us?

> Now because the actions of meane and base personages tend in very few cases to any great good example; for who passeth to follow the steps and manner of life of a craftes man, shepheard or sailer, though he were his father or dearest frend? yea how almost is it possible that such maner of men should be of any vertue other then their profession requireth? therefore was nothing committed to historie but matters of great and excellent persons and things.[6]

In *Julius Caesar* Cassius represents Caesar as arrogating to his own personal aggrandisement the entire history of Rome. Those eliminated from history thus become subjected to *unhistoricity*, as unmarked and unremembered as Puttenham's craftsmen and shepherds:

> . . . he doth bestride the narrow world
> Like a Colossus, and we petty men
> Walk under his huge legs, and peep about
> To find ourselves dishonourable graves
>
> (1.2.135–8)

Both the successful life, and the tragic death, of such a hero reduce the surviving world to a flat desert of mediocrity, Walter Benjamin's 'homogenous, empty time'.[7] Shakespeare's Cleopatra (whose 'glorious' name shares an etymology with Clio) describes life after Antony in exactly such terms:

> . . . Young boys and girls
> Are level now with men. The odds is gone,
> And there is nothing left remarkable
> Beneath the visiting moon
>
> (4.15.65–8)

Although this transition from plenitude to vacancy is always represented chronologically, as historical cause and effect, it is in fact the operation of present memory that produces these waste landscapes of contemporary despair by generating contrasting visions of lost historical greatness. This process of converting history into nostalgia is self-reflexively disclosed in *Antony and Cleopatra*, when Cleopatra 'dreams' to the Roman ambassador Dolabella a legendary Antony on a gigantic scale:

> CLEOPATRA   His legs bestrid the ocean; his reared arm
> Crested the world . . .
> Think you there was or might be such a man
> As this I dreamt of?
> DOLABELLA   Gentle madam, no.
> CLEOPATRA   You lie, up to the hearing of the gods:
> But if there be nor ever were one such
> It's past the size of dreaming. Nature wants stuff
> To vie strange forms with fancy, yet t'imagine
> An Antony were nature's piece, 'gainst fancy,
> Condemning shadows quite
>
> (5.2.82–3; 93–9)

Here the process of remembering is explicitly defined as 'dreaming' or 'imagining' the hero in an exercise of nostalgic fantasy. If the historic Antony could be thought of as coterminous with Cleopatra's dream of him, he would have been a work of art too perfect for art to produce, a masterpiece of nature. Such a conception is however unimaginable, 'past the size of dreaming', therefore a mere 'fancy' or 'shadow'.

But Cleopatra, here the muse of counter-history, affirms that history is composed wholly of shadows; that historiography is the work of 'fancy'; and that dreaming is the only realisation of memory. Further, she also knows that she herself has no existence: that the 'I' with which she speaks is also an insubstantial 'shadow', realised only by that 'meane and base' actor who will in some theatre of the future scurrilously 'boy [her] greatness'; by those 'quick comedians' who 'Extemporally will stage' her as 'some squeaking Cleopatra' (5.2.215–19). This speaking Cleopatra has no existence, 'nor ever were one such'; s/he speaks only by virtue of an unhistorical, low-life comedian who re-enacts her tragic history a second time (Marx's phrase) as farce.[8]

History

In so far as Clio presided over 'history', her narrative was a kind of providential romance in which good deeds were celebrated and evil actions condemned and in which all individuals and societies met their just deserts. Translator John Brende summed up the wisdom of history, 'the most excellent kind of knowledge', in terms of a political ethics, where human conduct could be seen determining the fates of commonwealths:

> by reading of histories . . . men may see the groundes and beginnings of Common-wealths, the causes of theyr encrease, of theyr prosperous mainte-nance and good preseruation: and againe by what means they decreased, decayed and came to ruine. There the vertues and vices of men do appeare, how by theyr good doings they florished and by their evill acts they decayed.[9]

But the 'history' discussed in the preceding pages is often indistinguishable from tragedy, elegy, *Trauerspiel*. Here history is mourning, bereavement, loss; a 'hauntology' populated by spectres, revenants, ghosts; an unappeas-able hunger for presence continually wounded by an inconsolable aware-ness of absence. The contributors to this volume variously search for the elusive subject of history concealed within the narratives that render it an object; seek the origins of historical consciousness in the lost cause rather than the official record; and challenge dominant paradigms by redefining historiography as fiction, memory, narrative, urban legend and tall tale.

These reinterpretations will strike many as audacious appropriations, bold subjugations of the past to contemporary concerns: a godlike refash-ioning of Shakespeare's histories in our own postmodern image. But as the essays collected here abundantly testify, all these possibilities co-existed in the early modern period with the officially sanctioned dominant ideology of history as moral education and political wisdom.

> *Historia vero testis temporum, lux veritatis, vita memoriae, magistra vitae, nuntia vetustatis, qua voce alia, nisi oratoris, immortaliti commendatur?*

> (As history, which bears witness to the passing of the ages, sheds light upon reality, gives life to recollection and guidance to human existence and brings tidings of ancient days, whose voice, but the orator's, can entrust her to immor-tality?)[10]

History in Cicero's famous formulae is very different from the commonsense perception of history as fact, Aristotle's 'what has happened'. History here is above all a present consciousness that carries messages from a distant past, and witnesses its passing. But its chief value lies in the 'light' and 'guidance', truth and instruction, it derives from the past and applies to the present; and its power to confer 'immortality' on transient and mutable human actions. And of course it is by definition a kind of speaking or writing, discourse and narrative, entrusted especially to the orator. Cicero might well have agreed with Bryan Reynolds and Fredric Jameson that although 'history is *not* a text', being 'fundamentally non-narrative and nonrepresentational', 'history is inaccessible to us except in textual form'.[11]

Early modern historical thinking and historiographical practice followed Cicero and other ancients in a preoccupation with both truth and
instruction. Aristotle distinguished between history ('what has happened')
and poetry ('the kinds of things that might happen');[12] and Thucydides
doubted the veracity of Homer's historical evidence ('It is questionable
whether we can have complete confidence in Homer's figures').[13] This was
'truth' as modern historians would understand it: truth to historical record
and historical recollection; the avoidance of false and forged versions of the
past. Historians should, according to Thomas Blundevill, 'declare the
thynges in suche order, as they were done' (Blundevill, *True Order*, A.iv);
or in Roger Ascham's words, 'write nothyng false' and 'be bold to say any
truth'.[14]

But 'truth' as value-free objectivity was not at this point clearly separable
from 'truth' as moral instruction. The 'truthfulness' of history could be
thought of either as accuracy or fidelity to record; or as the revealed truth of
providential wisdom. 'Truth' was inseparable from 'instruction'. History's
positivist aspiration to provide 'an orderly register of notable things said,
done or happened in time past . . .' was easily subordinated to larger moral
and didactic missions: to 'serve for the instruction of them to come';[15] to
serve 'as a warnyng and monycion unto princes and governours thereby to
rule and order themselfe: and a comen wele';[16] and to 'teache the subjects
obedience to their King'.[17] As Thomas Beard put it:

> historie is accounted a verie necessarie and profitable thing, for that in recall-
> ing to mind the truth of things past, which otherwise would be buried in
> silence, it setteth before us such effects (as warnings and admonitions touch-
> ing good and evill) and layeth vertue and vice so naked before our eyes, with
> the punishments or rewards inflicted or bestowed upon the followers of each
> of them, that it may rightly be called an easie and profitable apprentiseship or
> schoole for everie man to learne to get wisedome at another mans cost.[18]

In these terms history is composed of 'examples', which are both exemplify-
ing instances, and instructive models for current and future government and
conduct: 'a certaine rule or instruction, which by examples past, teacheth us
to judge of things present, and to foresee things to come' (Amiot, 'Amiot to
the readers', xiv);[19] a memory of the past that 'maketh most to a sound and
perfect worldly wisedome, examining and comparing the times past with the
present and, by them both considering the time to come' (Puttenham,
English Poesie, 40–1). Humanist writers agreed that history was the best
ethical education, producing, as Puttenham phrased it, 'a stedfast resolution
what is the best course to be taken in all his actions and advices in this world'
(41); and leaving those who have studied it, in Sir Thomas Elyot's words,
'instructed to apprehend the thing which to the publicke weale, or to our

own persones, may be commodious; and to exchue that thing, which either in the begynnyng or in the conclusion, appeareth noisome and vicious'.[20]

In all these formulations, truth and instruction are indistinguishable. A detached contemplation of the past makes possible an informed approach to the political and moral problems of the present and the future. But elsewhere in early modern writing, especially in the writing of the theatre, we find a consciousness of the more disconcerting results sometimes generated when past and present intersect, when history recuperates the past and the buried dead rise into the light of common day. Many of this book's contributors allude and return to the now famous passage from Thomas Nashe's *Pierce Pennilese his Supplication to the Divell*,[21] which graphically depicts the theatrical resurrection of the hero Sir John Talbot, entombed for centuries, his 'valiant actes' buried in defaced monuments and decomposing books. The contemporary stage not only recalls a heroic legend but literally resurrects the hero from 'worm-eaten' oblivion to 'represent his person' in the 'open presence' of the public theatre. The language of 'revival' and 'presence' implies that the spirit of the past is literally in such exhibitions 'raysed from the Grave' and by the quasi-magical potency of the stage (not the neglected and 'worm-eaten' literary record) incarnated into the 'open presence' of public knowledge and contemporary perception.

At the same time, Nashe contextualises this claim to embody 'presence' with a contrary language of 'representation' that focuses rather on the stage, on the 'Tragedian', on the spectators and on the process of performance. The theatre enacts history in the concrete, bringing the dead to life, only by the power of the actor and the pleasure of the audience. Where the language of 'presence' metaphorically elides the distinctions between present and past, living and dead: the language of 'representation' acknowledges that this curious 'presence' is made possible only by absolute absence. The dead appear to live again, only in the *coup d'oeil* of theatrical artifice. Critics such as David Scott Kastan and Phyllis Rackin[22] have focused on the resurrection of the hero in this passage, but played down his repeated demise. Talbot is brought back, but only to bleed afresh; not to live, but to die, again; or, as some sixteenth-century tragedian, playing Brutus, anachronistically imagined his historical counterpart to have prophetically foreseen, to 'bleed in sport' (*Julius Caesar*, 3.1.115) where his historical original bled in earnest. As Stephen Greenblatt argues, present historical truth must contain the awareness of permanent loss:

> It is paradoxical, of course, to seek the living will of the dead in fictions, in places where there was no live bodily being to begin with. But those who love literature tend to find more intensity in simulations – in the formal, self conscious miming of life – than in any of the other textual traces left by the dead, for simulations are undertaken in full awareness of the absence of the life they

contrive to represent and hence they may skilfully anticipate and compensate for the vanishing of the actual life that has empowered them.[23]

In historical representation the dead, revivified, must die again. History can temporarily evade 'the Grave of Oblivion' only by immediately re-consigning the dead back again to the obscurity (and security) of the past. The condition of temporary presence is perpetual absence; or as T. S. Eliot put it, life and death are coterminous and interdependent: 'that which is only living / Can only die'.[24] In the midst of life, we are in death.

Clio

Clio is the subject of Johannes Vermeer's famous painting *The Artist in His Studio*, which appears on the cover of this book. In the picture an artist (who at least from behind resembles Vermeer) is painting the muse, furnished with laurel Crown, book and trumpet, posed in a studio against a large map of the Netherlands. The painter, professionally dressed and working at an easel with his back to the viewer, is beginning his canvas with Clio's laurel leaves. The curtain is looped back like a theatrical curtain to disclose the scene and the subject is illuminated by a 'light that breaks dramatically into the painting from a source outside it'.[25] Bathed in this radiance of eternity, Clio is Cicero's *lux veritatis*, history as the light of truth. Superimposed on to the map, she commemorates and celebrates a national history, the process which saw a unified and independent Holland emerge from the fragmented provinces of the Spanish Netherlands. In Lawrence Gowing's words, 'The model in the studio is Clio . . . Painting thus approaches Parnassus to take place with the ancient muses'.[26]

But as Stuart Hampton-Reeves has already indicated, I am here describing only one level in a multilayered painting. The portrait of Clio is one detail in a full and complex scene and as a painting is utterly different from Vermeer's own canvas within which it is contained. The art of Vermeer's painting is to reveal the artistry and artifice of the allegorical construction, to show how Clio is made: not begotten by divinity on remembrance, but built up from layers of pigment on a canvas. This composition will ultimately form a representational image of a live model, wearing the clothes and carrying the book and trumpet that only characterise her as Clio. In this dimension the curtain is pinned back to reveal a glimpse into an artist's studio; the muse is a model, a pretty but ordinary girl typical of Vermeer's domestic subjects, her symbolic attributes theatrical props; and the artist is both Vermeer and not Vermeer. The painting's double vision (we are looking at a painter looking at his subject) facilitates a self-reflexive metafiction that lays bare the device of its composition. Vermeer's picture dwells tenderly on all the domestic objects – chair, table, curtain – that the painter inside the painting will need to eliminate in order to secure Clio's abstract and eternal historicity. In this perspective we see the painter 'in the process of trans-forming his model into an allegorical figure of Fame or History' (Snow, *Study*, 98). Here the light that 'falls from the unseen window'[27] is the common light of an ordinary day in Delft around 1665.

The trappings of Renaissance neoclassicism worn by the model in *The Artist in his Studio* date the context of the painting, even as they focus on the aspiration of the age to absorb history into eternity. To transform an ordinary woman into an immortal muse is an ahistoricising initiative, abstracting the spirit of history from specific times and places so it can view unimpeded the whole of time, the entirety of space. But to show the context of this transformation is ironically to return the living woman to a specific time and place, Vermeer's Delft studio in 1665, the working space of an artist whose aesthetic preferences were not at ease with the taste of the times. Here we witness an early modern shift from neoclassical abstraction to the con-temporary and concrete, the world of material reality seen through the lens of a *camera obscura*, illuminated by Vermeer's extraordinary capacity for revealing the sublimity of the ordinary, the loveliness of the everyday.

The Artist in his Studio is both history and counter-history; time con-quered by eternity and time fixed in an eternal contemporaneity. The picture is both self-reflexive and realistic, both open and closed; self-absorbed and self-conscious; seeking truth in the immediate and showing truth to be elusive and displaced; seeing the artistry of reality and the reality of art. Edward Snow summarises some of the interpretative strategies the painting seems to invite:

> Whether we view [*The Artist in His Studio*] as open to its audience (in self-disclosure) or turned meditatively inward (in self-reflection), as penetrating through appearances to the heart of reality (and discovering there the ongoing act of representation) or as stepping back in order to restore painting to the ordinary world (and in the process identifying the world as the scene of art), it gives the impression of being a final, cumulative gesture. (Snow, *Study*, 96–7)

Pearl

The Artist in his Studio can be contrasted with another celebrated Vermeer painting, usually known as *Head of a Young Girl*. Here we see a further shift towards modernity, as the contemporary is restored to a new relationship with the permanent. The portrait is just a head against a black background, with no context to orientate or position it in time and space. The subject's clothing is improvised, invented; vaguely oriental, exotic; but more like dressing-up clothes than theatrical costume. Again, the dress does not specify or locate. The face is that of a peasant girl rather than a lady: yet she wears a rich jewel in her ear. She is still, yet mobile, as she turns towards the viewer; she is composed, yet shaken as by some extraordinary emotion; she is long dead, but as living an image as any in the whole history of painting. She seems absolutely present, of the here and now; yet about to regress into an unfathomable darkness; 'more distant than stars and nearer than the eye'.[28] The painting gives us, in Edward Snow's words, 'an image that looks back at us from the other side of a metaphysical divide':

> Against the impersonality and timelessness we associate with Vermeer's work, it insists on our involvement in something that is happening, now, in an instantaneous present . . . an immediate relation that takes place across an unquantifiable *abyss* of distance. (Snow, *Study*, 8)

Head of a Young Girl contrasts with *The Artist in His Studio* by its absence of contextual detail and self-referential artifice. The subject is displaced from her own time and we have no idea how she got to look like this. Arthur K. Wheelock[29] describes this feature of the painting as 'timelessness'. The subject 'belongs to no specific time or place' (Wheelock, *Vermeer*, 166); she 'cannot be placed in any specific context'. Unlike the girl in *The Artist in His Studio*, 'she holds no attributes that might, for example, identify her as a muse or sibyl'. This marked 'absence of a historic or iconographic framework' renders the painting capable of an absolute contemporary impact, a disturbing 'immediacy', wherever and whenever it is viewed (167–8).

Wheelock attributes to the painting an immanence and inviolability unaffected by time. Edward Snow on the other hand argues that in *Head of a Young Girl* Vermeer succeeded in breaking down conventional distinctions between art and reality, subjective and objective, seeing and feeling, so the viewer is disarmed, forced (reluctantly perhaps) to receive the full shock of that uninhibited, challenging appeal.

> to look at it is to be implicated in a relationship so urgent that to take an instinctive step backward into aesthetic appreciation would seem in this case a defensive measure, an act of betrayal and bad faith. It is me at whom she gazes, with real, unguarded human emotions and with an erotic intensity that demands something just as real and human in return. The relationship may be only with an image, yet it invokes all that art is supposed to keep at bay.
>
> Faced with an expression that seems always to have already elicited our response, we can scarcely separate what is visible on the canvas from what happens inside us as we look at it. Indeed, it seems the essence of the image to subvert the distance between seeing and feeling, to deny the whole vocabulary of 'objective' and 'subjective'. (Snow, *Study*, 3)

Tracey Chevalier's novel *Girl with a Pearl Earring* (1999) invents, very much in the spirit of Vermeer's own art, a counter-history for the *Head of a Young*

Girl.[30] The historical grand narrative of this painting, the story Clio herself would proclaim, is the story of a great artist's supreme masterpiece, the triumph of an art in its time neglected but subsequently recognised as epoch-making in its modernity. But Chevalier uses the painting as a pretext for adumbrating the imagined story of the girl who provided its subject. In the novel she is Griet, a serving-girl taken into the Vermeer household. Griet becomes the object of Vermeer's painting, but also its subject: objectively represented, but subjectively engaged in the process of painting and in an increasingly intimate relationship with the artist. She comes to self-consciousness as she enters the environment of painting. As she cleans Vermeer's studio she sees herself in a mirror, becoming aware of herself as objectively existent, as a subject that could form part of a painting (Chevalier, *Girl*, 34). She wants to enter the world of art and to know the painter (38). She compares people with their images in Vermeer's canvases: a woman who has sat for him is not as beautiful as her painted image; yet she seems by association more beautiful, perhaps because Griet now sees her through a 'memory' of her image in the painting (45). 'She was not as beautiful as when the light struck her in the painting. Yet she was beautiful, if only because I was remembering her so' (45). Griet's famously 'wide eyes' are an object of fascination for men in the novel. But they are also wide open subjectively, learning to see as a painter sees. Vermeer shows her his scene through the lens of the *camera obscura*, so she is able to understand how reality is transformed into representation: after which, she 'could not stop looking at things' (108). She becomes so closely engaged in the process of painting that she can suggest a change to the *mis-en-scene* of a portrait which Vermeer silently accepts (144).

But she remains, of course, an object: to Vermeer a potential subject; to his patron Van Ruijven a potential mistress. Vermeer's colleague Van Leeuwenhoek (a historical character who was known to have owned a *camera obscura*) warns her of the dangers of 'losing herself': '"take care to remain yourself"' (197). At one level this is a prudent warning against the dangers for a serving-girl of being morally 'ruined' and losing respectability. Vermeer, he tells her '"Sees the world only as he wants it to be, not as it is . . . He thinks only of himself and his work, not of you"' (197). Van Leeuwenhoek's advice however goes deeper than this and concerns the very existential condition of a subject who is also an object, subjected to others. '"The women in his paintings – he traps them in his world. You can get lost there"' (Chevalier, *Girl*, 197). When Vermeer finally embarks on his painting of Greit which is to become *Head of a Young Girl*, she happily accepts the role of object for the painter's gaze ('his eyes only on me', 201). But to complete the work Vermeer needs her active collaboration. The image is finished, but something else is needed to complete it as a picture.

She recognises this immediately, seeing that the painting needs a 'point of brightness' of the kind she has seen used to 'catch the eye in other paintings' (203). It takes him longer to reach the same conclusion: the painting needs the pearl earring. Her gaze is estranged because doubled back on to her own reflection, but instinctively forensic and diagnostic:

> I had not looked at the painting long – it was too strange seeing myself – but I had known immediately that it needed the pearl earring. Without it there were only my eyes, my mouth, the band of my chemise, the dark space behind my ear, all separate. The earring would bring them together, It would complete the painting. (Chevalier, *Girl*, 206)

To supply this lack it is necessary for the earrings to be borrowed from Vermeer's wife Catherina and, as Griet sees clearly, this will assuredly precipitate a domestic crisis and her ejection from the household. But she accepts the risk, the inevitability of disaster, the agony of piercing her own ears, in order to participate in the composition of her masterpiece. Like the merchant in Matthew 13: 45–6, she surrenders everything she has, to acquire the pearl of great price.

She herself never sees the finished painting. After Vermeer's death she is summoned by Catherina to learn that he had asked to see the painting before he died and left her the earrings in his will. She does not want to possess jewels that would disrupt her contented marriage to the butcher's son. But the Vermeer family's butcher's bill remains unpaid: the amount, says her husband Pieter, that she cost him to acquire. So she pawns the earrings for a sum that disburses the bill and leaves over the sum of 5 guilders. These she will hide and never spend. She has settled the debt her husband incurred in taking her ('I would not have cost him anything . . . a maid came free', 248). With the surplus of 5 guilders she has hidden her treasure, and bought the 'bright field'[31] that contains it.

Counter-history

I want to pay homage to the *Head of a Young Girl* as the other tutelary spirit of *Shakespeare's Histories and Counter-histories*, companion and counterpart to Clio: patroness of all the counter-histories these contributors are individually and collectively seeking.

Girl with a Pearl Earring is not the story of the painter, but the story of the painted: history seen not from the perspective of its agents and prime movers but from that of its instruments and ancillary characters. Vermeer may have died in debt and gained full recognition only centuries later. But we know him now as a moving force of artistic development, one of the heroes of our culture. Griet is never at the centre of any world she occupies: she is

always on the margins, the outsider looking in, unable to reconcile her subjective awareness with her objective existence. Her aesthetic instincts (she
colour-codes vegetables when peeling) estrange her even within her own
family, a condition of alienation exacerbated by her removal to the Vermeer
household. There of course she is explicitly marginalised as a servant, alter-
nately contemned and feared. Her privileged access to Vermeer's studio draws
her into an alternative world of art and beauty and she gains a position within
it: as helper, assistant, co-viewer, collaborator and finally subject. But her
destiny is to encounter this world without ever being acknowledged within
it; to know its beauty, yet not to possess it; to approach as closely as possible
to the object of her desire, only to find herself used and finally discarded.

In the painting and in the novel we have Griet's life as narrated by history,
and Griet's life as experienced by herself: history and counter-history, representation and reality (though our access to the real is only, as Michel de
Certeau explains, through fiction): 'Historians can only write by combining
within their practice the "other" that moves and misleads them and the real
that they can represent only through fiction.'[32] This story is not then what
happened, but what might have happened; what indeed, in order fully to
explain our response to the painting, *should* and *must* have happened. The
story is what Bacon called a 'Feigned Historie', a poetic fiction designed to
'give some shadow of satisfaction to the minde of Man in those points,
wherein the Nature of things doth denie it, the world being in proportion
inferior to the Soule'.[33] Griet's story is a story of loss and bereavement, her
whole history one of mourning for the love that never happened (for Griet
to be able to tell the story Vermeer must implicitly be dead, so the novel is
effectively an elegy); for the artistry practised upon her, but which she never
possesses or commands; for the pearl, deliberately thrown away, though
richer than all her tribe. The novel shows how Griet is eternally absent from
her own reality, alienated into an alternative universe of textures and surfaces, shapes and colours, where she encounters herself as an object, recog-
nisable but 'strange' (Chevalier, *Girl*, 206), her gaze 'An intimate mirroring
that is also a painful, disturbing estrangement' (Snow, *Study*, 3).

She lives alongside her present in much the way that De Certeau describes
the historical consciousness:

> The historians . . . reflect on the power that they lack. Their analysis is there-
> fore deployed 'next to' the present time, in a staging of the past which is anal-
> ogous to that which, drawn also through a relation to the present, the
> prospectivist produces in terms of the future. (De Certeau, *Reader*, 29)

According to De Certeau these activities are contingent or even identical. We
may be dreaming of the future, or imagining the past. We may be 'staging
the past' without ever being of it, so the performance runs in parallel to the

present; or trying to extrapolate the present into a foreseeable future. In each case, we are similarly preoccupied with the power that eludes us.

Orpheus

> Writing replaces the traditional representations that gave authority to the present with a representative labor that places both absence and production in the same area. In its most elementary form, writing is equivalent to constructing a sentence by going over an apparently blank surface, a page. But isn't historiography also an activity that recommences from the point of a new time, which is separated from the ancients and which takes charge of the construction of a rationality within this new time? (De Certeau, *Reader*, 27)

De Certeau's daring assertion here is that historical writing begins with a blank page just as surely as does the writing of fiction or poetry or drama. On the other hand the page is only 'apparently blank', since even for the most innovative new writing the author is to some degree copying the lineaments of language, tradition, convention and source that lie more or less obscured beneath it. For the historian this model would normally be understood as 'tracing' through a transparent medium the outlines of the documents, objects, records on which the blank sheet rests. But as De Certeau says, the blank sheet is starting again in 'new time'. History produces from absence and produces absence. Historical writing is working always 'through the intermediary of documents that the historian has been able to see on the sands from which a presence has been washed away and through a murmur that lets us hear – but from afar – the unknown immensity that seduces and menaces our knowledge' (24).

A blank page is both internal and external: a state of mind, *tabula rasa*, and a physical medium for writing on. It is a virtual space, which is neither in the mind nor outside it: a space of mediation in which whatever is written, however deep and private its source, is echoed back transformed. As soon as the historian has constructed that sentence, which alludes to the presence of history by absenting it from the scene of writing, the sentence becomes legible, therefore subject to innumerable potentialities of interpretation that move further and further away from the historical trace that has been 'washed away' and nearer only to that 'unknown immensity' into which all historical traces and all writing must eventually fall. The emptiness of a blank page is already virtually and potentially full, since it is as Timothy Clark[34] puts it 'the place of intersection of the writer's intentionality with the multiple possibilities of reading' (Clark, *Inspiration*, 29). The blank page is a point that links what is about to be said, with what has already been said and is already speaking to future interpretation, even if only the writer's. It is 'a chiasmatic structure in which the scene of composition is already a prolepsis of reception' (23). Writing may concern the past, but it is always by its very nature coming-to-be, future-oriented: it is full of promise, though it never quite exists.

What Blanchot[35] said of literature holds true also for historical writing: that it has no universal value, unchanged across time, but is rather 'radically ahistorical, as the bearer of a movement of transcendence that holds the text open as the question of its own nature' (Clark, *Inspiration*, 241). Both literary and historical writing are preoccupied with the search for their own nature and origin. Blanchot uses the myth of Orpheus and Eurydice to explore the relationship between the writer and the work, especially that moment in the work's coming-to-be that annuls the writer, allowing the work to realise itself for the first time as a singular and impersonal affirmation. By means of his art Orpheus draws Eurydice out of the underworld. But he cannot resist that backward look to see exactly how she is coming along. At that moment he loses her and she relapses into her own darkness.

> *carpitur adclivis per muta silentia trames,*
> *arduus, obscurus, caligine densus opaca,*
> *nec procul afuerunt telluris margine summae:*
> *hic, ne deficeret, metuens avidusque videndi*
> *flexit amans oculos, et protinus illa relapsa est,*
> *bracchiaque intendens prendique et prendere certans*
> *nil nisi cedentes infelix arripit auras.*[36]

> (Up they went, through the silent places, the path steep, dark, shadowy with thick mist, approaching the threshold of the upper world. Afraid she might fail him, eager to see her, he turned back his longing eyes. In an instant she dropped back. Stretching out his arms to hold her and be held, the unhappy man grasped nothing but the receding air.)

Even as he draws the work up from its dark origins, the writer has to read it; and as he reads it he loses both the work and his contact with its source.[37]

Orpheus is classically a model for the historian, one especially apt today given our preoccupation with history as a waking of the dead.

> Like Orpheus the historian must descend into the nether world to bring the dead back to life. How far will they follow his allurements and evocations? They are lost to him when, re-emerging into the sunlight of the present, he turns for fear of losing them. But does he not for the first time take possession of them at this very moment, the moment when they forever depart, vanishing in a history of his own making?[38]

In ancient literature this link between exploring the past and visiting the underworld was commonplace. Odysseus has to dig a grave-like plot to summon the spirits of the dead, including the seer Tiresias, who reveals the future to him;[39] Aeneas enters the underworld and is presented by the ghost of his father Anchises with an extrapolation of his own destiny that merges into the history of Virgil's own civilisation.[40] Shakespeare himself was handling exactly such material when writing of Macbeth's meeting with the weyward sisters (who in their previous appearance had agreed to reconvene at 'the pit of Acheron', 3.5.15), a meeting in which Scotland's future history is revealed to him (4.1).

But in every case the object of the historian's search proves intransigent, resistant to possession, eluding the grasp. As in Homer:

> As my mother spoke, there came to me out of the confusion in my heart the one desire, to embrace her spirit, dead though she was. Thrice, in my eagerness to clasp her to me, I started forward with my hand outstretched. Thrice, like a shadow or a dream, she slipped through my arms and left me harrowed by an even sharper pain. (Homer, *Odyssey*, 176)

Or Virgil:

> Three times he tried to cast his arms about his father's neck; but three times the clasp was vain and the wraith escaped his hands, like airy winds or the melting of a dream. (Virgil, *Aeneid*, 168)

Or Macbeth, perplexed by the witches' inexplicable vanishing:

> Whither are they vanish'd? . . . Into the air . . . (1.3.80–1).

History's effort to grasp and possess a stable and enduring knowledge of the past proves elusive and self-dispersing.[41]

Orpheus however is no simple hero but the offspring of a king and a muse, therefore affiliated to both history and to poetry. Like the historian he descends to the underworld hoping to restore the vanished past to life; and like the historian he returns empty-handed, having lost the object of his quest, Eurydice, at precisely the moment he seemed to have successfully repossessed her. In Rainer Maria Rilke's poem *Orpheus, Eurydike, Hermes* (1904) Orpheus the poet can charm the world of the dead into his power:

> . . . *eine Welt aus Klage ward, in der*
> *alles noch einmal da war . . .*[42]
>
> (. . . a whole mourning world arose
> and everything was again present . . .)

Orpheus' fatal error, suggests Martin L. Davies,[43] is that 'at the crucial moment he subordinates his poetic vision, which transcends time and history, to historical reflection'.

> *seine Hände hingen*
> *schwer und verschlossen aus dem Fall der Falten*
> *und wussten nicht mehr von der leichten Leier . . .*

(543)

(His hands hung heavily and clenched
From among the falling folds
Unconscious of the delicate lyre . . .)

Once he turns to look back ('*Er hat sich umgewendet*') his spells of poetry
and mourning are broken, and he loses everything he came for:

> Orpheus loses Eurydice because he transgresses his undertaking not to look
> back. It is as if he had momentarily doubted the power of song and detached
> himself from the desperate grief which had inspired it. In thus forsaking his
> poetic vocation which ensured his immunity from death and time, Orpheus
> succumbed to a purely mortal temptation for knowledge, that is, to ascertain
> and verify . . . the Orpheus myth, therefore, permits Rilke to expose the *hubris*
> of historical consciousness and reveal the cruel paradox of history. (Davies,
> 'Orpheus or Clio?', 198)

It is just because it has to look back, cannot but look back, that history
cannot retrieve the past; since looking back is to acknowledge death, lay the
dead to rest, separate the past irrevocably from the present. Looking back
destroys the whole historiographical enterprise, leaving its work always
undone, still to be done:

> . . . *Ware das Zuruckschaun*
> *Nicht die Zerstezung dieses ganzen Werkes,*
> *Das erst vollbracht wird* . . .

(543)

> (. . . If it weren't that such a backward glance
> Must be the instant undoing of all this,
> All that had to be completed first . . .)

Imp

As indicated earlier, such mythical horizons were also paradigmatic to the
early modern understanding of history. One of the commendatory poems
affixed to the 1623 Folio edition of *Mr William Shakespeare's Comedies,
Histories and Tragedies*, under the superscription 'I.M.S.' (see note 2), celebrates Shakespeare's achievement in the three major dramatic 'kinds', but
concedes a definite preferential emphasis to History:

> The buskined muse, the comic queen, the grand
> And louder tone of Clio . . .

(ll. 44–5)

The historical dramatist's mind is a glass or mirror that can bring an image
of the past into immediate visibility:

> A mind reflecting ages past, whose clear
> And equal surface can make things appear
> Distant a thousand years, and represent
> Them in their lively colours' just extent.
>
> (1–4)

The mirror of Shakespeare's mind makes available, to present vision, images of a remote past, causes things that are 'distant a thousand years' to *appear*. But it also uses a contemporary performative medium to simulate a past reality, making present things *appear to be* distant a thousand years. It represents and re-presents; familiarises and estranges. Shakespeare's imagination could make things from a thousand years ago *appear*; but he could do so only by making his stage and his actors take on the convincing *appearance* of a thousand-year-old reality.

The poem thus grasps immediately the two-way process of historical reconstruction. The past has to be made to be remade, its reconstruction being also its initial construction. And the past is simultaneously destroyed, deferred by the very language used to remake it. To access the past the writer's imagination has to defeat time and descend to the underworld:

> To outrun hasty time, retrieve the fates,
> Roll back the heavens, blow ope the iron gates
> Of death and Lethe, where confused lie
> Great heaps of ruinous mortality
>
> (ll. 5–8)

The past is occupied by a humanity indiscriminately mingled in universal decay. The historical dramatist can make sense of that past and out of a homogenised ruin isolate and identify the historically significant character:

> In that deep dusky dungeon to discern
> A royal ghost from churls
>
> (ll. 9–10)

Once the memorable character has been recognised, however, historical reconstruction involves more than merely drawing it forth from the 'ruinous' chaos of historical oblivion to the light of common day. The poet's emphasis falls more strongly here on the artistic skills needed to create a contemporary presence out of the disembodied spirits of history:

> . . . by art to learn
> The physiognomy of shades and give
> Them sudden birth
>
> (ll. 10–12)

Historical figures are in this conception not so much re-born, as born for the first time, and newly equipped with a physiognomy bestowed by 'art'. The poet then defines historical drama in precisely the language we have seen deployed by Nashe (and by Shakespeare himself):

To raise our ancient sovereigns from their hearse

(l. 19)

But the raised spirit is firmly subjected to the power of the conjuring writer, who can:

Make kings his subjects

(l. 20, my italics)

However sovereign their historical status, the 'subjects' of the plays are also in some sense 'subject' to the dramatist who creates them. Proud majesty changes places with the subjected. History becomes counter-history.

The dramatic imagination is celebrated here as a potent force, as a power that can invoke the dead, recuperate a vanished past, reconstruct a lost history. But in addition the poem also emphasises magic, playfulness and the social and political radicalism of the dramatist's art:

. . . the plebian imp from lofty throne
Creates and rules a world

(ll. 13–14)

The implicit republicanism of these sentiments is contextually focused by their sharing a page with John Milton's poetic tribute, 'An Epitaph on the Admirable Dramatic Poet, William Shakespeare', which forcefully asserts the moral superiority of the popular dramatist's reputation over that of his royal and historic 'subjects': 'kings for such a tomb would wish to die'.[44]

Despite its base origins on the common and popular stage, historical drama is none the less the power that *makes* history: engenders and directs, shapes and governs, 'creates' and 'rules' a retrospective but unprecedented historical 'world'.

Eurydice

I began with, and will end with, Vermeer's *Head of a Young Girl* (or *Girl with a Pearl Earring*). She is history, a landmark achievement in the development of European painting, woman born of early modern man's genius and ingenuity. She is also counter-history, history as subject rather than object, the victim rather than the victor. She is an icon of the historical subject as suffering, dispossession, martyrdom. She belongs to what Péguy called 'organic time', not the 'linear' and 'homogenous' time of history, but 'the time of reality' which houses real human events and all the 'innumerable different varieties of distress' (132). And she is Eurydice, drawing our desire into the underworld, conducting us to the land of the dead with her promises of fulfilment, reawakening, truth.

> Her eyes accuse yet have compassion, offer consolation yet give irresistible expression to the very desires of which the heart despairs. Their brilliant white reaches out to us in an attempt to hold onto the present instant, even as their heavy lids and limpid pupils reluctantly, voluptuously accept the inevitability of the void into which she already recedes. (Snow, *Study*, 4)

We glimpse her and she is gone, down into darkness, yet still inaccessibly there, just out of reach. In Kracauer's phrase, we 'take possession' of the dead at that moment when 'they forever depart, vanishing in a history of [our] own making' (Kracauer, *History*, 79).

The peculiarly intense rapprochement of presence and absence, offering and withholding, accompaniment and withdrawal that we find in this painting brings us close to what John Joughin has called the 'aesthetic' of history, the power of a merely virtual presence to lacerate and replenish with completion and longing, fulfilment and unappeasable dissatisfaction. The root of this power lies in the fact that history confronts us with the knowledge of death, ultimately of our own death. The past is the realm of the dead and 'far from dispelling the shadowy spectre of death, history only invokes it' (Davies, 'Orpheus or Clio?', 193). There was no history in Paradise: history arises from the knowledge of death. Or, as Foucault explains, Western man found science in 'the opening created by his own elimination'.[45]

Head of a Young Girl exemplifies this strange exchange of life for death:

> The image with which it confronts us is disorientatingly immediate, inward, presubjective – she seems to exist inside the eyes as well as at the end of their gaze. Yet the result is to make us only that much more self-conscious of our solitary presence over here, concentrated in an exchange of emotional energy with an image that looks back at us from the other side of a metaphysical divide. Does the desire maintained across this threshold seek to draw her out of the canvas, or to follow her over into the realm into which she recedes? If it is our life that would make her real, it is her vibrancy of being (as image, as art) that we lack and long for. (Snow, *Study*, 8–9)

And Snow concludes that the young girl is herself Eurydice:

> *Head of a Young Girl* might for all the world be the image etched on the retina of Orpheus when he looked back to make sure Eurydice was still there behind him. (Snow, *Study*, 21)

History then, in De Certeau's words, is a labour of death:

> Historiography tends to prove that the site of its production can encompass the past: it is an odd procedure that posits death, a breakage everywhere

reiterated in discourse and that yet denies loss by appropriating to the present the privilege of recapitulating the past as a form of knowledge. A labor of death and a labor against death. (De Certeau, *Reader*, 27)

But also a labour against death, a labour of life. The sweet song of Orpheus has powers beyond the 'grand / And louder tone' of Clio. Historian and poet, Orpheus transcends death: according to Rilke, dust can't stop his mouth ('*Nie versagt ihm die Stimme am Staube*'), though from the gods the shadow inevitably falls ('*daß von den Göttern ein Schatten fällt*'). Praiser and blesser, Orpheus is the messenger who stays and carries his gifts, his offerings, his bowls of fruit, across the thresholds of the dead:

Er ist einer der bleibenden Boten,
der noch weit in die Türen der Toten
Schalen mit rühmlichen Früchten hält.[46]

Notes

1 Tracey Chevalier, *Girl with a Pearl Earring* (London: Harper Collins, 1999).

2 'I.M.S.', 'On Worthy Master Shakespeare and his Poems' (1632), in Stanley Wells and Gary Taylor (eds) *William Shakespeare: The Complete Works* (Oxford: Oxford University Press, 1987), xli.

3 Poem attributed to Ben Jonson, frontispiece to Sir Walter Raleigh, *The History of the World In Five Books* (London: Walter Bvrre, 1614).

4 Edmund Spenser, 'Teares of the Muses', 1, 108.

5 Charles Péguy, 'Clio: Dialogue de l'histoire at de l'âme païenne', *Oeuvres en Prose 1909–1914*, ed. Marcel Péguy (Paris: Gallimard, 1969), 96.

6 George Puttenham, *The Arte of English Poesie* (1589), in G. Gregory Smith (ed.) *Elizabethan Critical Essays* (Oxford: Clarendon Press, 1904), 43.

7 Walter Benjamin, 'On the Concept of History', trans. Harry Zohn, in *Walter Benjamin: Selected Writings, Volume 4, 1938–1940*, eds Howard Eiland and Michael W. Jennings (Cambridge, Mass.: Harvard University Press, 2003), 395.

8 Karl Marx, *Selected Writings in Sociology and Social Philosophy*, ed. T. Bottomore (Harmondsworth: Pelican, 1963), 10.

9 John Brende, 'To the Right high and mightie Prince, Iohn Duke of Northumberland, Earle Marshall of England', in *The His[t]orie of Quintus Curtius, conteining the Actes of the great Alexander*, translated out of Latine, into English, by *Iohn Brende* (London: Thomas Creede, 1602), n.p.

10 Cicero, *De oratore*, trans. E. W. Sutton (London: Heinemann, 1962), 1, Book II, 224.

11 Bryan Reynolds, *Becoming Criminal: Transversal Performance and Cultural Dissidence in Early Modern England* (Baltimore: Johns Hopkins University Press, 2002), 3–4. He quotes from Fredric Jameson, *The Political Unconsious: Narrative as a Socially Symbolic Act* (Ithaca: Cornell University Press, 1981), 82.

12 Aristotle, *Classical Literary Criticism*, trans. T. S. Dorsch (London: Penguin, 1965), 43.

13 Thucydides, *The Peloponnesian War*, trans. Rex Warner (London: Penguin, 1954), 18.

14 Thomas Blundevill, *The True Order and Methode of Wryting and Reading Hystories* (London: Willyam Seres, 1574); Roger Ascham, second prefatory letter, 'R. Ascham, to Iohn Astely' in 'A Report and Discourse of the Affaires and State of Germany', in Roger Ascham, *English Works*, ed. William Aldis Wright (Cambridge: Cambridge University Press, 1970), 126–7.

15 James Amiot, 'Amiot to the Readers', in *The Lives Of The Noble Grecians And Romanes, Compared Together By That Grave Learned Philosopher And Historio-Grapher, Plutarke Of Chaeronea, translated by Thomas North* (1579; Oxford: Blackwell, 1928), xiv.

16 Alexander Barclay, 'The preface of Alexander Barclay preest unto the right hye and mighty prince: Thomas duke of Northfolke', in *The famous cronycle of the warre which the romayns had against Jugurth usurper of the kyngdome of Numidy. Whiche cronycle is compyled in latyn by the renowmed romayn Salust. And translated into englysshe by syr Alexander Barclay preest* (London: n.d. [1520]) a.v.

17 Thomas Heywood, *An Apology for Actors* (1612; facsimile, New York and London: Garland Publishing, 1973), III, F3r–v.

18 Thomas Beard, 'The Preface', *The Theatre of Gods Ivdgements* (1597, London: 1612), A.iv–v.

19 Compare Thomas Hobbes: 'the principal and proper Work of History being to instruct and enable Men by the knowledge of Actions Past, to bear themselves prudently in the Present and providently towards the Future'. 'To the Readers', in *The History of the Grecian War in Eight Books, written by Thucydides*, trans. Thomas Hobbes (3rd edition, London: D. Brown, 1723), n.p.

20 Sir Thomas Elyot, *The Boke Named the Governour* (1531, London: J. M. Dent, 1907), 280.

21 Thomas Nashe, *Pierce Pennilesse His Svpplication to the Divell* (1592; facsimile edition, Menston: Scolar Press, 1969), 26.

22 See David Scott Kastan, *Shakespeare and the Shapes of Time* (Hanover, NH: New England University Press, 1982), 19; and Phyllis Rackin, *Stages of History: Shakespeare's English Chronicles* (London: Routledge, 1990), 113–16.

23 Stephen Greenblatt, *Shakespearean Negotiations: The Circulation of Social Energy in Renaissance England* (Oxford: Clarendon Press, 1988), 1.

24 T. S. Eliot, 'Burnt Norton', *Collected Poems 1909–1962* (London: Faber and Faber, 1963), 194.

25 Edward A. Snow, *A Study of Vermeer* (Berkeley, Los Angeles and London: University of California Press, 1979), 99. This painting is the subject of another Vermeer-related modern novel, *Girl in Hyacinth Blue* by Susan Vreeland (London: Penguin, 2000), which traces the impact of the painting on the numerous lives it touches.

26 Lawrence Gowing, *Vermeer* (New York: Harper and Row, 1952), 139.

27 Christopher Wright, *Vermeer* (London: Oresko Books, 1976), 14.

28 T. S. Eliot, 'Marina', *Collected Poems 1909–1962* (London: Faber and Faber, 1963), 115.

29 Arthur K. Wheelock, Jnr. (ed.) *Johannes Vermeer* (New Haven and London: Yale University Press, 1995).

30 See Ludwig Goldschieder (ed.) *Johannes Vermeer: The Paintings: Complete Edition* (London: Phaidon Press, 1958, 2nd edition 1967), Plate 54.

31 R. S. Thomas, 'The Bright Field', *Collected Poems 1945–1990* (1993; London: Phoenix, 1996), 302.

32 Michel de Certeau in *The Certeau Reader*, ed. Graham Ward (Oxford: Blackwell, 2000), 35.

33 Francis Bacon, *The Advancement of Learning* (1605; London: J. M. Dent, 1973), 82.

34 Timothy Clark, *The Theory of Inspiration* (Manchester: Manchester University Press, 1997), 29.

35 See Maurice Blanchot, *The Space of Literature* (1955), trans. Ann Smock (Lincoln: University of Nebraska Press, 1982).

36 Ovid, *Metamorphoses*, ed. G. P. Goold (Cambridge, Mass.: Harvard University Press, 2nd edition, 1984), II, Book X, ll. 53–9.

37 Similarly Edward Snow quotes Paul Klee on the moment where a painting acquires a face and shocks the artist by looking back at him (Snow, *Study*, 2).

38 Siegfried Kracauer, *History: The Last Things Before the Last* (New York, 1969), 79.

39 Homer, *The Odyssey*, trans. E. V. Rieu (Harmondsworth: Penguin, 1946), 171–88.

40 Virgil, *The Aeneid*, trans. W. F. Jackson Knight (Harmondsworth: Penguin, 1956), 147–74.

41 For a wonderful modern recuperation of this ancient motif see Philip Pullman, *The Amber Spyglass* (London: Scholastic, 2001).

42 Rainer Maria Rilke, *Sämtliche Werke*, eds Ruth Sieber-Rilke and Ernst Zinn (Frankfurt am Main: Insel-Verlag, 1955), vol. 1, 544.

43 Martin L. Davies, 'Orpheus or Clio? Reflections on the Use of History', *Journal of European Studies*, (1987), 197.

44 John Milton, 'An Epitaph on the Admirable Dramatic Poet, William Shakespeare', in Stanley Wells and Gary Taylor (eds) *William Shakespeare: The Complete Works*, xli.

45 Michel Foucault, *The Birth of the Clinic: An Archaeology of Medical Perception*, trans. A. M. Sheridan-Smith (London: Tavistock, 1973), 197.

46 Rainer Maria Rilke, 'VII', *Die Sonnete an Orpheus* (1922), in *Sämtliche Werke*, vol. 1, 735. 'He is one of the immortal messengers / Who deep inside the dead's doors / Raises his bowls of glorious fruit.'

Index

Note: literary and artistic works can be found under author's or artist's names

Anonymous
  Jack Straw 135–6
  King Leir 207–8
  Locrine 202–4
  Misfortunes of Arthur, The 203
  Puritan, The 200–1
  'Song of Ladye Bessye, The' 92–4
  Tract on the Succession, A 76
  Woodstock 136–47, 204–6
Ashcroft, Peggy 186–8
Axton, Marie 161

Bacon, Francis
  Of Deformity 101
Baldo, Jonathan 44
Balen, Hendrick van
  Banquet of the Gods, The 1
Barton, Anne 44–5, 147
Bell, Fiona 187, 192–6
Benjamin, Walter 23–4, 35, 39–45
Berger Jr, Harry 68
Bernstein, Jay 25
Berry, Cicely 211–12
Bhabha, Homi 24
Billington, Sandra 143
Blackwood, Adam
  Martyre de la Royne d'Ecosse 69, 77, 79
Blanchot, Maurice 232
Boyd, Michael
  Henry VI Cycle (2000) 187, 192–4, 195–6
Branagh, Kenneth 211
Brecht, Bertolt 212–13
Brodsky, Joseph 2

Brook, Peter
  King Lear (1971) 211
Buc, Sir George
  History of Richard III 93
Budra, Paul 68

Camden, William
  Annales of England 74
Caygill, Howard 42
Certeau, Michel de 49, 230–1, 237–8
Chevalier, Tracey
  Girl with a Pearl Earring 227–30
Cohen, Derek 76
Cornwell, Charlotte 192–5
Cunningham, William
  Cosmographical Glasse, The 199

Dekker, Thomas
  Magnificent Entertainment, The 208
Derrida, Jacques 15, 18, 28
Downie, Penny 187–8

Elizabeth I
  'The Doubt of Future Foes' 72–3
Elliot, Michael
  King Lear (1983) 210
Engel, William 36
Erne, Lukas 35

Ford, John
  Perkin Warbeck 94–9
Ford, Julia 192–5
Fox, Adam 51, 55, 63

Gainsford, Thomas
  Perkin Warbeck 97–8
Gascoigne, George
  Jocasta 152–4
Grady, Hugh 27
Greenblatt, Stephen 15–16, 224
Greene, Robert
  Groats-worth of Witte, A 182–4
Grove, Matthew
  'Pelops and Hippodamia' 3

Hall, Peter and Barton, John
  The Wars of the Roses (1963) 186–8,
    192–5
Hands, Terry
  Henry VI Cycle (1977) 186–8, 192–5
Heinemann, Margaret 137
Helgerson, Richard 140
Holderness, Graham 17, 21
Holyday, Barton
  Technogamia 214
Honigmann, E. A. J. 91–2
Howard, Jean 169
Hunter, G. K. 144

'I.M.S.'
  Commendatory poem, *First Folio*
    234–6

Johnson, Richard
  'Musarum Plangores' 3, 4

Kozintsev, Grigori
  King Lear (1970) 212

Lacan, Jacques 24
Lacoue-Labarthe, Philippe 24

Marlowe, Christopher
  Edward II 89
  Jew of Malta, The 86–9
  1 and 2 Tamburlaine 200
Middleton, Thomas
  Anything for a Quiet Life 199–200
Mirren, Helen 186–8
Mirror for Magistrates, A 140–2, 152–7,
  161–2
Mitchell, Katie
  Henry VI: The Battle for the Throne
    (1994) 186, 189

Mullaney, Steven 146
Munday, Anthony
  Triumphs of Re-United Britannia, The
    208–9
Murphy, Andrew 34

Nashe, Thomas
  Pierce Penniless 4, 17, 38–9, 103–4, 110,
    170–1, 224
Nixon, Anthony
  'Hymen's Holiday' 3
Noble, Adrian
  The Plantagenets (1988) 187–8, 192–3,
    195
  King Lear (1994) 211
Nora, Pierre 59–60
Norden, John
  Speculum Britanniae 213–14

Parker, Patricia 57
Patterson, Annabel 35, 37
Pechter, Edward 38
Peele, George
  'Anglorum Feriae' 3
  'Polyhymnia' 105
Pickering, Thomas
  Horestes 156, 161–2
Preston, Thomas
  Cambises 158–61
Puttenham, George
  Arte of English Poesie, The 146

Rackin, Phyllis 169
Reynolds, Brian 4–5, 222
Rilke, Rainer Maria
  Orpheus, Eurydike, Hermes 233–4,
    238
Rogers, Thomas
  'Celestial Elegies' 3

Sackville, Thomas and Norton, Thomas
  Gorboduc 152–6, 202
Seneca 154
Shakespeare, William
  Antony and Cleopatra 4–5, 220–1
  Hamlet 21–3, 114
  1 Henry IV 8, 171, 176, 179
  2 Henry IV 49–65
  Henry V 32–45, 124, 179–80
  1 Henry VI 173–4, 190–2

3 Henry VI 6–7, 174, 183–5
Julius Caesar 220
King John 116–20, 175–7
King Lear 126–8, 201–2, 209–10, 215
Richard II 15, 17–22, 25–9, 67–80,
    123–4, 135, 178
Richard III 89, 94, 102–13, 120–3, 129,
    172, 177
'Sonnet 107' 125
Venus and Adonis 109–10, 112
Sidney, Sir Philip
    Defence of Poesy 7
Skura, Meredith Ann 144
Smithe, John
    Instructions 171
Southwell, Robert 69, 75, 78
    'Decease Release' 75
    'Time Goes by Turnes' 76
Speed, John
    Theatre of the Empire of Great Britaine
    214
Spenser, Edmund
    'Teares of the Muses' 3, 220
Stanley, Thomas
    'The Stanley Poem' 90–1, 96–7

Stella, Jacques de
    Minerva Visiting the Muses 1
Stuart, Mary 68–80
    'Diamond Speaks, The' 70
    love sonnets 71–2
Sueur, Eustache le
    Clio, Euterpe and Thalia 1
Suzman, Janet 192–5

Thomas, Keith 54
Tipton, Alzada J 140

Vermeer, Johannes
    Allegory of Painting, The (also known
        as *The Artist in His* Studio) 2, 225–6
    Head of a Young Girl 226–9, 236–7

Walpole, Henry 77–8
Warner, William
    Albion's England 97
Weever, John
    Epigrams 106
Weimann, Robert 41
Williams, Roger
    Brief Discourses of War 121